ALSO BY DALE McCORMICK

Against the Grain:
    A Carpentry Manual for Women

DALE McCORMICK

HOUSEMENDING

Home Repair for the Rest of Us

E. P. DUTTON   NEW YORK

This book was supported in part by Cornerstones Energy Group.

Published in the United States by E. P. Dutton,
a division of NAL Penguin Inc.,
2 Park Avenue, New York, N.Y. 10016.

Published simultaneously in Canada by Fitzhenry and Whiteside, Limited, Toronto.

Library of Congress Cataloging-in-Publication Data
McCormick, Dale.
Housemending: home repair for the rest of us.

Includes index.
1. Dwellings—Maintenance and repair—Amateurs'
manuals. I. Title.
TH4817.3.M35   1987   643′.7   86-24191

0-525-48258-X (paper)
BOMC offers recordings and compact discs, cassettes
and records. For information and catalog write to
BOMR, Camp Hill, PA 17012.
DESIGNED BY EARL TIDWELL

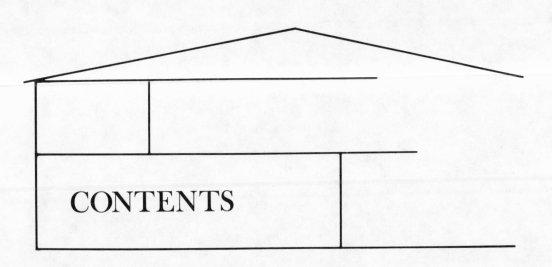

CONTENTS

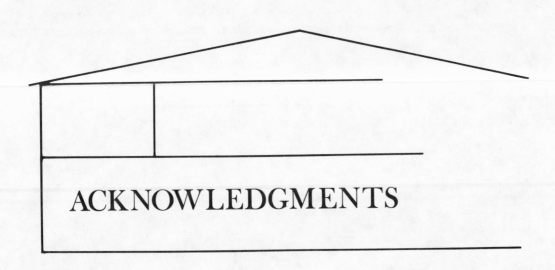

ACKNOWLEDGMENTS

Many people have added their expertise to *Housemending*. Master electrician Joan Pinkvoss gave invaluable comments as did master plumber Ginny Blair and master painter Adele Evans. Peter Hollander provided many suggestions from the home handyman's point of view. Lynette Breton, who is an established cabinet-maker, reviewed the chapter on furniture and cabinets. Christine Torraca kindly offered to read the manuscript as a layperson and pick out the words she didn't understand. They are all in the glossary.

Anne McCormick's initial guidance around literary New York got the project off the ground, and led to my association with Jennifer Josephy and Carole DeSanti. They have been supportive and astute editors.

I appreciate the help of my friends and family, especially Ken McCormick and Betsy Sweet.

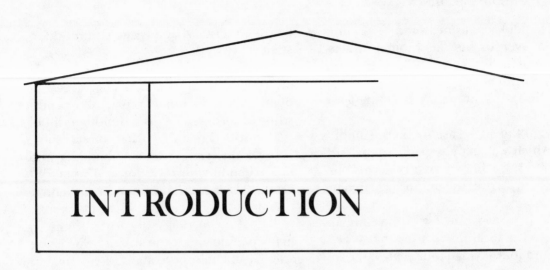

INTRODUCTION

There were no jobs for teachers in 1971. The colleges had produced too many. I had just graduated from the University of Iowa with teaching credentials that I was not finding useful. One day, as I sat contemplating my economic future, an old friend dropped a clipping from a newspaper into my lap. It announced that the local carpenter's union would be accepting apprenticeship applications the following week.

I did not grow up wanting to be a carpenter. I did, however, grow up with tools. In the second and third grades, the school I attended offered shop classes for both girls and boys. I do not have in my memory a time when I could not use tools, and, in fact, I can measure the stages of my life by what I was building. While in grade school I built forts and jails. A few years later I built puppets, sets, and benches for the neighborhood puppet show. I was in 4-H in high school, so I built pens, creeps, and sheds for my sheep. Although I have always had confidence with tools, it took the women's movement to suggest to me that women could be carpenters.

I applied to be an apprentice the day after I read that newspaper article. Actually, I asked a male friend to go down to the union hall and deliver my application. When I finally did appear in person at the union hall, the business agent did a double take that lasted for five minutes.

"This is for your husband, is that right?"

"No, it's for me."

"It's for your brother, then?"

"No, really, my name is Dale."

1

He looked at me for a long time, walked over to his file cabinet, walked back, and finally said, "Who sent you? The government?"

"Nobody sent me. I want to be a carpenter."

I got the highest score on the union's test, which was mainly math, spatial reasoning, and a few carpentry terms. Because of my score, the union accorded me an interview.

As it turned out, I was the only apprentice the local union took that year. I became a journeyman four years later and was the first woman to complete the union carpentry apprenticeship in this country.

Girls traditionally have not been taught mechanical skills while growing up. This leaves most women illiterate in the lingo of the trades and without the basic mechanical knowledge to fix ordinary household problems. I knew this from my own experience. Through my teaching, I realized that there are many men in the same situation. Feeling powerless to deal with simple problems is no fun. Many repairpeople won't do small jobs. If you can do it yourself, you save money and make sure it gets done. I've found that there is also a sense of empowerment that eddies into other parts of your life when you have mastered a few repairs.

The training I received during my apprenticeship moved me to write my first book, *Against the Grain: A Carpentry Manual for Women.* The textbooks that the union was using at that time were Greek to me. They used carpentry terms without defining them. As I sat poring over the meaning of terms, I swore I would someday write a book that defined all technical words in terms that anyone could understand.

Housemending is a continuation of that effort. The idea for *Housemending* grew out of my class on home repair at Cornerstones. Cornerstones is a building school in Brunswick, Maine, that offers short courses on energy-efficient building and how to build your own house. I've taught classes for men and women in carpentry, plumbing, electricity for the last six years. It's exciting to demystify what seems to many people an arcane subject. Since you and I can't talk personally, I've tried to anticipate your questions in this book. I will guide you step by step through repair procedures and define all terms along the way.

I've paid particular attention to the illustrations because I rely heavily upon demonstrations when I teach. I show basic things such as how to hold tools, interrelationships of parts, and the order in which repairs should be done. There is a lot of information in each illustration. Please refer to them frequently while reading the text.

In 1977 I went into business for myself and started my own general contracting company. We specialize in small additions, sunspaces, and energy-efficient building. Over the years I've learned when to try something myself and when to call in an expert. Tips on working with plumbers, electricians, lumberyards, and hardware stores are included throughout the book.

Most houses aren't designed for handicapped people. We continue to build houses that aren't wheelchair accessible inside or out. It is left up to individuals to adapt the house to their needs. This book will cover a few common repairs and accommodations that handicapped people often do.

In 1983 I built my own house. My friends and many Cornerstones students helped. I trusted my house to people who were learning, because I believe that if you explain a procedure well enough, anyone can do anything. My house was a practicum for many people. I did all the electrical and plumbing work myself because I wanted to learn more about it. It took a lot of reading and asking questions of friendly plumbers and electricians, but in the end I did an excellent job. Everyone needs someone they can ask questions of. I hope *Housemending* answers many of yours.

1

GETTING STARTED

McCormick's Law #2

While I was an apprentice, I was constantly confronted with tasks that were over my head. I had two choices: give up in frustration or accept that the vast body of mechanical knowledge might take time to master. Since I'm prone to lofty thinking, I developed a rule for myself that I call McCormick's Law #2.

McCormick's Law states that whenever anyone tries to do something mechanical for the first time, she or he will have no luck, and almost everything that can go wrong will go wrong. In order to survive and grow from the experience you must plan for the frustration. Allow twice as much time as you think the job will take. If you provide for this in your planning, you will not get frustrated.

When I first developed McCormick's Law, I thought it applied only to women. After teaching mixed classes in carpentry, I realized that some men also have had no experience with tools or repair. I know how humiliating it can be to ask a question when you don't know the lingo. I know how frustrating repairs can be if you don't have the right tools or know-how. I don't want that to happen to you. That's why I wrote *Housemending*.

Patience is a virtue I never had before I became a carpenter. If you get frustrated by a problem and allow yourself to become so angry that you swear or yell or even cry, you will never solve the problem. Problems aren't solved in that state of mind. You must be calm. I call this the "carpenter alpha state."

For example, let's suppose there's a

nail in a board you want to pull out. You get out your hammer, hook the claw around the nail, and give a yank. Nothing. You reposition your body and really pull. Still nothing. Now you're getting frustrated because this simple task is not yielding to your powers. You decide to really give that nail one final yank. When it only squeaks a little, you throw down your hammer in frustration and say, "I'm so weak, I'm so stupid, I can't even pull out a little nail."

Or, let's say, you are going to screw a plant hanger to a board or post. You begin by driving the screw in and the first couple of turns are easy. Then they become harder and harder until the screw barely turns at all. The tip of the screwdriver begins to slip out of the slot in the screw and you begin to panic. Finally you realize that you won't be able to get the screw in so you had better back it out. As you begin to turn the screwdriver counterclockwise, and the tip slips out of the slot, you scream, "Why can't I do something as easy as screwing in a screw?"

The problem in each case is not a defect in your moral character. The problem is a tangible, physical aspect of the work that you haven't considered. You won't solve the problem with a self-deprecating state of mind. As soon as you start thinking that you're incompetent, you've lost the battle. The problem isn't in yourself; it's in the work. You've got to calmly step back and analyze the problem. Obviously, there is something that is keeping the nail from coming out easily. Maybe it is clinched (bent over) on the other side of the board, or maybe it is one of those nails that are coated with a substance that makes them go in easily but makes them hell to pull out. This is a physical fact; it isn't due to anything lacking in your personality. The answer is to increase your strength so that you are equal to the nail's resistance. You must maximize your leverage. Either get a crowbar with a long handle or lengthen the handle of your hammer by slipping a piece of pipe over it.

In the case of the screw, it is a little-known fact that screws need pilot holes drilled for them. They aren't like nails that spread the wood fibers as they are driven in. A small column of wood must be taken out so the screw can be inserted. This is a trick of the trade that you would only know if (1) you read it in a book; or (2) you picked it up from hanging around people who were screwing in screws.

Before delving into the realm of house repair, it would behoove you to meditate for a moment on the fact that learning takes time. It is impossible to learn everything there is to know about a new area right away. I have been a carpenter/contractor for fifteen years, and I know in my heart that I will be learning about mechanical things my whole life.

Empowerment

One of the exciting things about teaching housebuilding and repair is observing how people of different occupations take to it. I especially like to have lawyers in my classes because they're such fun to watch. The constant use of math and spatial reasoning, which they don't have in their daily practice of law, makes their brows knit with concentration. They aren't prepared for carpentry to be such an intellectual challenge. I remember one day near the beginning of my housebuilding class for women, I asked Rhonda, a constitutional rights lawyer, to use a chalk line to mark a line on a form so we would know to what level to pour the concrete. (The form is the wooden structure that holds the concrete in a particular shape until it hardens.) When I checked back, I found three lines—two red and one blue —an inch apart. I asked Rhonda which line was the right one, and she said, "Any one of them, they're all pretty close together." I was horrified and responded, "Rhonda, when you argue a case before the Supreme Court, does it matter if you bring it under the First Amendment or the Third?"

When we decide to fix a dripping faucet or repair a lamp, we stretch ourselves by moving out of our chosen niche. We become more powerful. As you begin to do things around the house, gradually you will encounter all the materials that make up our physical world and you will come to understand the principles that govern them. Each bit of knowledge is connected to every other. Learning how to change your oil helps you when you change the washer on the faucet to stop its drip. You're building a base. The oil-pan plug, which you unscrew to drain the oil, has some type of plastic washer under the head. When the drain plug is screwed tight against the pan, this washer keeps the oil from leaking out. The same principle is at work within a faucet. After a while you will make these connections.

Learning about the way things work is like building a pyramid: the first pieces of knowledge take the longest to position and don't look like much. It doesn't appear at first that there will be any relationship between the first course and the ones above. Laying each subsequent course is progressively easier with the pattern of the blocks and the shape of the whole beginning to emerge. As you become familiar with different materials such as wood, metal, glass, and glue, you feel more connected to the physical world. Mastering household emergencies makes us feel effective, and this effectiveness causes a ripple effect into other parts of our lives.

Dealing with Hardware Stores and Lumberyards

One place where this new feeling of power will be evident is at hardware stores. Right now you don't recognize half the items in the store. By the time you finish this book, when you walk up and down the aisles, items that were mysterious before will have names and purposes. You will be able to say "Oh, this is the fastener section," or "There are all the plumbing fittings with the solder and flux over here." The hardware store will cease to be an intimidating place and become the place where they have everything.

Still there are a few things to remember about hardware stores and lumberyards. First, most people who look like they know what they're doing at a hardware store don't know exactly what they want either. They have to ask. Second, there is at least one salesperson in every store who knows just about everything there is to know about mechanical things. Your job is to pick him or her out and make friends. Then every time you need help figuring out how to fix a thing or don't understand how something works, you can wait patiently until your friend is free and then ask.

Third, if by some twist of fate, you find yourself in a strange hardware store where no one seems friendly, you need to remember to assert yourself. Just sidle up to the counter, taking up as much physical space as you can, and as you ask for what you need, drop as many technical words as you can. This may take a little research if you're totally in the dark, but any technical term having the least relationship to the subject will do. Let's say you have a structural problem. After you ask for what you think you need, quickly say something like, "The joists in the other part of the house are sound. There's no structural damage." Or if it's a plumbing question, mention that you had searched through the valve stems and cartridges in your plumbing-parts box but couldn't find what you needed. This technique works for me. It makes salespeople take you seriously and listen to your questions.

Everyone Needs an Expert

No matter how good you get at mechanical things, you still need someone to consult when you don't have the least notion of what's wrong. This may be a hardware-store person, a friendly tradesperson, industrial arts teacher, or the handyperson down at the garage. It doesn't matter who that person is, but you need to begin to cultivate such relationships. You'll find as you get to know people like these that they in turn have people they consult.

How can you tell who will be good advisors? First, they probably won't act like they know everything. They won't

brag or build themselves up, because they don't have to. Second, you'll rarely see them angry at their work. Someone who understands mechanical things also knows that it's not their fault when they don't work. Third, they'll be able to explain things to you easily and clearly, because their knowledge of mechanical things is well organized in their minds.

Basic Household Tool Kit

Most people have a tool drawer or toolbox. It doesn't matter where you keep the household tools as long as you have some. If you live with someone who owns lots of tools because of his or her job or in a house where there are tools in the garage or shop, it's still important to have your own small set of tools just for the house. Otherwise you will find either that the tools are being used when you need them or that there are strict stipulations on their use. Besides, you don't need a fancy set of expensive tools to do repairs around the house. You just need a basic few and a selection of nails, screws, and odds and ends. Believe me, the odds and ends will just collect in your toolbox; you won't have to buy them. A toolbox is like a magnet for stray nails.

Here is a list of tools for a basic tool kit. These tools and many others are illustrated in the next chapter, where their use is explained.

1. Hammer. A 16-ounce, curved-claw hammer is best.

2. Screwdrivers. It's a good idea to have two screwdrivers: a standard slotted and a #2 Phillips.

3. Saw. An 8- or 10-point handsaw makes a good all-purpose saw.

4. Pliers. Any kind of pliers will do. Lineman's pliers are especially good because they also have the capability to cut wire.

5. Tape measure. A 12- or 16-foot tape is long enough for most jobs. Get one that is at least ¾ inch wide, so it won't bend easily.

6. Level. An 18- or 24-inch level is a good size for around the house.

7. Utility knife. A knife with a retract-able blade is safest and doesn't get dull as quickly.

8. Circuit tester. A circuit tester is essential for electrical repairs. It tests whether the current is on or off.

9. Stud finder. This useful gadget locates the studs behind a wall.

10. Pipe wrench. A 14-inch pipe wrench is useful in plumbing repairs.

11. Apron. Lumberyards give canvas nail aprons away free. They hold your tools, leaving your hands empty.

2

TOOLS AND HOW TO USE THEM

Having the right tool for the job is a key to a successful repair. If the appropriate tool isn't available or you don't know what it is, the job can take twice as long. The next best thing to having the right tool for the job is knowing how to use it. The correct way to use the tools in the basic toolbox, as well as a few power tools, is explained in the following pages.

Hammering

The best hammer to have is a 16-ounce curved-claw hammer. Any heavy object will do for pounding nails. I hesitate to admit it, but I've used pliers and even a rock to put in nails to hang pictures on the wall. For pulling out nails, a curved-claw hammer offers more leverage than a straight claw, and requires less

strength. Hammers come in three sizes: 13-ounce, 16-ounce, and 20-ounce. The 13-ounce is a finish hammer and can be too light for some jobs; the 16-ounce is an all-purpose hammer; and the 20-ounce is for driving 16d nails all day when you are framing a house.

If you are going to buy a hammer, try this trick when you are in a hardware store. Turn the hammer upside down to see if it balances at about a 45-degree angle (Fig. 2-1). This test works only for curved-claw hammers with handles of wood, fiberglass, or hollow metal. It's basically a test to see where the weight is in the hammer. Hammers with their weight in the head are easier to wield. If the weight is more in the head, the hammer will stand more vertically. If it's more in the handle, the hammer will be hard to balance. The hammers with solid metal handles are so heavy in the handle that they topple right over.

To be able to hammer effortlessly, you must have a powerful stroke; and to hit the nail almost every time, you need some technique. The secret is keeping your arm relaxed. A lot of power is lost in stiff-arm hammering.

Hold the hammer in a relaxed grip as shown in Fig. 2-2. Raise your whole arm until the upper arm is parallel to the ground. Start the downward stroke with a little effort, but then let gravity do the work while you guide the hammer to the nail. When the hammer head is about 6 to 8 inches above the nail, snap your wrist for extra power. It's important that your arm be relaxed, or the wrist snap won't amount to anything.

The hammer face should be parallel to the nail head upon impact. If it isn't, the nail will bend. So if the nail keeps bending, it's not because it is made of in-

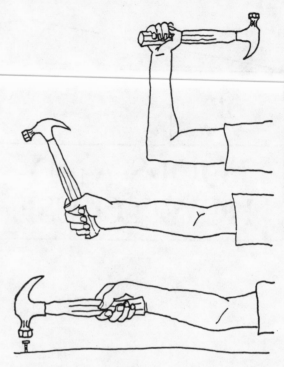

FIG. 2-2. HAMMERING

ferior steel or because you are hopeless. It's because you're not hitting the nail squarely. Skinny nails like finish and box nails tend to bend easily. Smaller nails, like 4d to 10d, don't require as big an arm stroke. For these, raise the hammer head to the level of your shoulder. The wrist snap is even more important here since you aren't raising your arm as high and gravity isn't working for you as much.

NAILING TIPS

As Fig. 2-3 shows, there are two ways of putting in nails. Face-nailing is when the nail is fairly perpendicular to the face of the top board. Toenailing is angling the nail through both pieces. It is a harder technique to learn because the first board has a tendency to slide horizontally with the force of each hammer blow until the

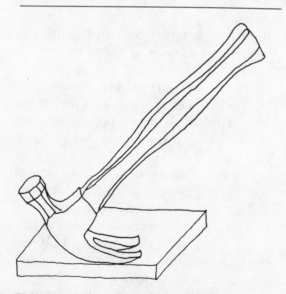

FIG. 2-1. A WELL-BALANCED HAMMER

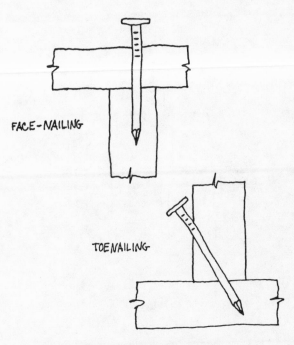

FACE-NAILING

TOENAILING

FIG. 2-3. TWO METHODS OF PUTTING
IN NAILS

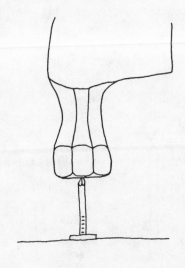

FIG. 2-4. BLUNTING A NAIL

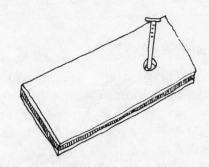

FIG. 2-5. A HOMEMADE NAILING GUARD

nail penetrates the other piece of wood. A foot or knee placed against it helps keep it from moving. Toenailing is useful in repair and retrofit, because there is often not enough space around a board to face-nail it.

If the wood splits, blunt the nail point. A sharply pointed nail spreads the wood fibers as it is driven and sometimes causes the wood to split, especially near the edge. A blunted nail cuts the fibers instead. Turn the nail upside down with its head on something solid like concrete and hit it squarely with your hammer (Fig. 2-4). If the wood still splits, you should drill a pilot hole for the nail a little smaller than the nail shank (see "Pilot Holes," pages 12–13).

If you are afraid of missing the nail

and leaving hammer marks (some people call them smiles) in wood that needs to be kept pristine, make a nailing guard (Fig. 2-5). Drill or cut a small hole through any thin material like ⅛- to ¼-inch plywood, masonite, heavy cardboard, or a cedar shingle. Start the nail into the wood by giving it a firm tap. Place the nail guard around the nail and proceed with carefree hammering. When the nail is flush with the guard, remove the guard and finish driving the nail carefully.

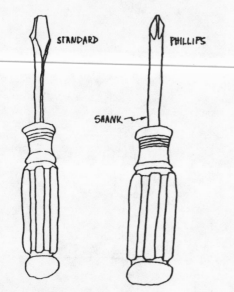

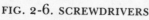

FIG. 2-6. SCREWDRIVERS

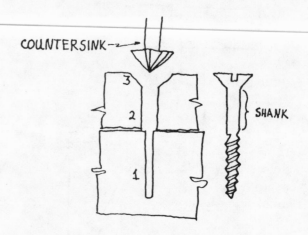

FIG. 2-7. A PILOT HOLE FOR A SCREW

Screwdrivers

You should have at least two screwdrivers in the toolbox: a standard and a Phillips (Fig. 2-6). You may have other junk screwdrivers that you use for chisels or putty knives when no one is looking, but be sure to have two good ones. While I was working in heavy construction, I got in the habit of carrying a very large standard screwdriver in my apron. It wasn't always practical to carry a crowbar, chisel, or putty knife around, so instead I used my "magic screwdriver." That's what I still call it. It tickles me to hear someone I'm working with ask to borrow my "magic screwdriver." It is a good all-purpose tool, but a lousy screwdriver. Using a screwdriver as a chisel to gouge out wood or as a small crowbar to increase your leverage tends to round the tip, so that it will slip out of screw slots.

The tip on the standard screwdriver should be flat on top with nice square edges. This helps the tip stay in the slot of the screw. The best Phillips screwdriver to have is a #2, a middle size. A #1 Phillips is for small screws, like those that fasten a door bottom or carpet-hold-down strip. A #3 is for large screws like door-hinge screws. The number notation is written either on the handle or on the shank.

PILOT HOLES

Most screws except little skinny ones (number 6 screws) need pilot holes drilled for them. Pilot holes are ordinarily drilled with three different bits, as shown in Fig. 2-7.

First, drill a small hole for the threaded part of the screw. To decide what size bit should be used, hold the bit in question in front of the screw against the light. If the threads just show behind the bit, it's the right size (Fig. 2-8). Second, drill a larger hole for the shank of the screw with a bit that is the same size or bigger than the shank. Finally, using a countersink bit, drill out the conical hole for the head of the screw.

There is also a special tapered bit called a counterbore that drills this odd-shaped hole all at once (Fig. 2-9). Counterbores cost around ten dollars each and a different one is needed for each diameter screw, so they are used mostly by cabinetmakers who use the same-size screw repeatedly.

If all this sounds like a lot of trouble, it is. That is why I love drywall screws. They are self-tapping screws and do not need pilot holes. This kind of screw has specially designed threads and a point like a drill bit. These act to draw the screw into

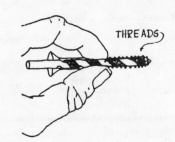

FIG. 2-8. SELECTING A BIT FOR A PILOT HOLE

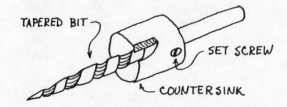

FIG. 2-9. COUNTERBORE

FIG. 2-10. LOOSENING A SCREW

the wood without a pilot hole. It is best to drive these screws with an electric variable-speed drill equipped with a screwdriver bit. Drywall screws can be used on just about any project that requires screws. They make fastening easy.

LOOSENING STUBBORN SCREWS

If a screw just won't budge, insert a small screwdriver into one side of the slot. Don't hold the screwdriver perpendicular to the head as you normally would. Hold it at a 45-degree angle and at one end of the slot so that the tip of the blade is actually against one of the slot's vertical sides. Tap the handle of the screwdriver with a hammer so that the screw will turn in a counterclockwise direction (Fig. 2-10). The force of the blow may loosen the screw.

If the screw is in metal, penetrating oil may do the trick. Penetrating oil seeps down around the threads and loosens the rust bond. It is available at hardware stores in regular and spray cans. Tapping the head of the screw sharply with a hammer sometimes helps the oil work in deeper.

Drills

A push drill is an excellent tool for starting screws and drilling small holes (Fig. 2-11). It looks a little like a screwdriver and is held the same way. It comes with a set of special bits that are usually carried in a compartment in the handle. The bits are notched and snap into the chuck. The chuck is the mechanism that grips the bit. To insert a bit, pull the spring-loaded chuck back toward the handle (in some models, away from the handle), slip in a bit, and let the chuck snap back. Usually, the bit must be rotated until a click is heard. That means it is seated in the chuck.

A push drill is operated much like a ratchet screwdriver. Hold the handle as you would a screwdriver. Place the bit against the wood and move your hand up and down, keeping the bit in contact with the wood. As you push your hand down, the bit drills into the wood (Fig. 2-12).

An electric drill is the least-expensive power tool you can buy. A drill with one forward speed can be purchased for ten to

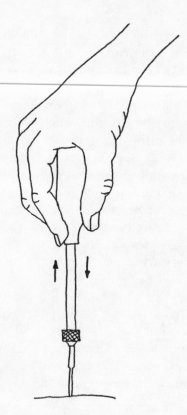

FIG. 2-12. USING A PUSH DRILL

twenty dollars. However, if you are going to invest in a drill, I recommend a ⅜-inch, variable-speed drill with forward and reverse (Fig. 2-13). The ⅜ inch refers to the chuck, which will accept bits that are up to ⅜ inch in diameter. Variable-speed drills allow you to vary the rotation speed of the bit by changing the amount of pressure on the trigger. This is useful when using the drill as a screwdriver. Most drills are double insulated. The motor is surrounded by a material that won't conduct electricity, so if a wire comes loose inside the drill, you won't get a shock.

The bits are locked into the chuck with a chuck key. The tip of the chuck key is inserted into one of the three holes

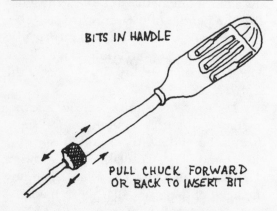

BITS IN HANDLE

PULL CHUCK FORWARD OR BACK TO INSERT BIT

FIG. 2-11. PUSH DRILL

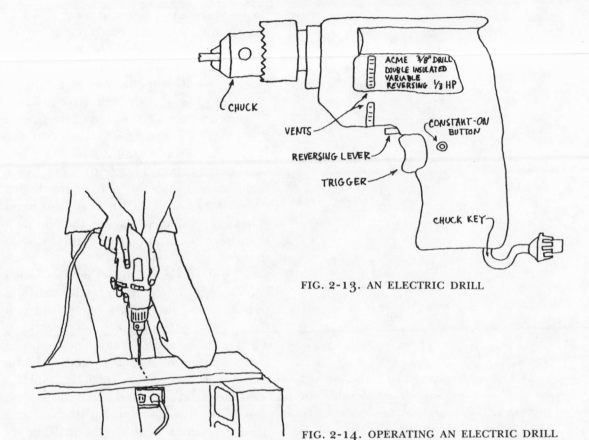

FIG. 2-13. AN ELECTRIC DRILL

FIG. 2-14. OPERATING AN ELECTRIC DRILL

located around the chuck. When it is rotated clockwise, the slots in the key mesh with the slots around the chuck and the jaws of the chuck close around the bit. To remove a bit, turn the chuck key counterclockwise.

When drilling, hold the drill in your strong hand (Fig. 2-14). I like to put my first finger along the housing and operate the trigger with my middle finger. This grip affords more control to those of us with small hands. Hold the drill perpendicular to the wood. When the bit begins to rotate, there is a tendency for the drill bit to slip off the mark. To prevent this, make a small indentation on the mark with a nail or nail set. Push the drill into the wood with even pressure. When you have reached the appropriate depth, pull the drill straight up, keeping your finger on the trigger. The rotation of the bit removes shavings from the hole and makes removing the bit easier. After the drill is clear of the wood, release the trigger.

The depth of the hole depends on the length of the screw. The hole should be as long as the screw. Sometimes I wrap a piece of tape around the bit to indicate how deep to drill the hole.

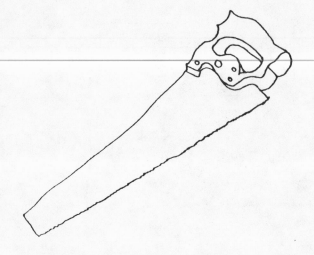

FIG. 2-15. A HANDSAW

Saws

HANDSAW

An 8- or 10-point crosscut saw is a good all-around saw (Fig. 2-15). The number of points indicates how many teeth per inch on the blade of the saw. A 6-point saw is for rough work. A 12-point saw is for fine interior work. A crosscut saw is for cutting across the grain—across the width of the board. A rip saw cuts parallel with the grain. All the handsaws you'll find at the hardware store will be crosscut saws. The hand rip saw has been replaced with the electric circular saw. When you pick one out, sight down the blade from the handle to make sure the blade is straight with no bends or kinks. If you notice a bend, go ahead and try to straighten it out with your hands by bending the blade the other way. If you can unkink it, it's all right to buy it. Saws that are bought new from the store will not necessarily be sharp. You will probably

have to take it to a saw sharpener. Look in the Yellow Pages or keep your eye out for little saw-sharpening shops as you drive or walk around town. They usually have a saw hung out near the road as a sign.

Hold the saw in your strong hand. Place it on the wood on the waste side of the line you wish to cut on. The waste side is the side of the line away from the piece you want to keep (Fig. 2-16). Your other hand should grip the part of the board you wish to keep. The thumb of this hand is held about 2 inches above the board so that there is no danger of cutting it with the saw.

To start the cut, draw the saw toward you several times, guiding it with the thumb of the nonsawing hand until you have a ¼- to ½-inch kerf in the board. The kerf is the groove a saw blade cuts out for itself. When the cut is started, slide the nonsawing hand approximately 8 inches away from the cut and then continue with long, even strokes, holding the saw at a 45-degree angle with the board (Fig. 2-17). Don't push the saw into the wood too forcefully. If the saw is sharp, the teeth will cut the wood. All you need to do is

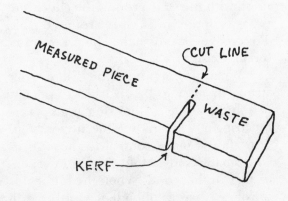

FIG. 2-16. WASTE SIDE OF LINE

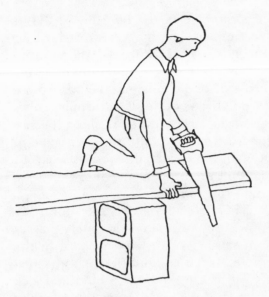

FIG. 2-17. SAWING

move your arm up and down, applying steady pressure.

If the saw is not cutting smoothly, but is catching and taking a lot of strength to move, there is one of three things wrong.

1. The saw may be dull.

2. Something may be binding the saw blade. Binding means there is too much friction against the blade and the sides of the kerf are probably pinching it. Make sure that the waste side of the board is hanging freely in the air.

3. The saw can also be binding if the finish end of the board is moving around. Grip it more tightly. Put your knee on it if you have to. I always do.

CIRCULAR SAW

A circular saw is a hand-held power saw (Fig. 2-18). The saw table rides on the wood and can pivot around the blade for bevel cuts. It has a spring-loaded guard

that rises as you saw and snaps back to cover the blade when the cut has been made. The depth of the cut is determined by how far the blade extends below the table. The depth-adjustment screw is at the base of the handle on models such as that pictured in Fig. 2-18. In drop-foot models the depth-adjustment knob is in front above the bevel-adjustment scale (Fig. 2-19).

To saw off a piece of board with a circular saw, hold it in your strong hand

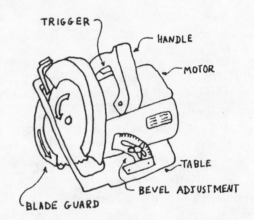

FIG. 2-18. CIRCULAR SAW

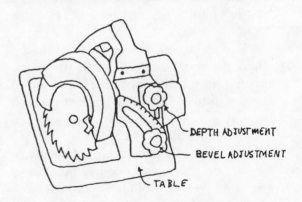

FIG. 2-19. DROP-FOOT SAW

FIG. 2-20. USING A CIRCULAR SAW

and rest the front of the table on the board (Fig. 2-20). The saw is powered when the trigger is squeezed. Sometimes a safety button must be simultaneously pushed to start the blade. Hold the saw so that the blade is approximately perpendicular to the board to be cut. Making sure that the blade is not touching the board, squeeze the trigger and start the blade turning. If the blade is touching the board when the blade begins to turn, the initial torque of the blade would rip a large gouge out of the wood. This also causes a needless load on the motor.

Some people have trouble judging where to begin the cut. With the blade turning, move the saw along the edge of the board until the blade is lined up with the cut line. Bend over so that you can see the exact place where the blade contacts the line. Cutting along a line is not a guessing game; you need to be able to see what you're doing. A circular saw blade cuts a kerf that can be ⅛ inch wide. For accurate cuts this kerf should be on

the waste side of the line (Fig. 2-21) or else the piece you have measured will be ⅛ inch too short. Now push the saw into the wood and move it smoothly along the waste side of the line until the waste piece of wood drops off. Follow-through is important in sawing. Keep pushing the saw along the cut line until the back edge of the blade has cleared the wood. Take your finger off the trigger only after the waste piece drops off.

There are a few safety rules for using a power saw. Always wear safety glasses when sawing. Never saw a board in the middle when it is supported at both ends; this will cause the saw to bind and kick back. The correct way to saw is to have the waste piece entirely unsupported. Never change the blade when the saw is plugged in. Know where your fingers are all the time. Don't work with power tools when you are tired or angry. Treat power tools as if they are wild animals that can eat your fingers. They deserve that kind of respect.

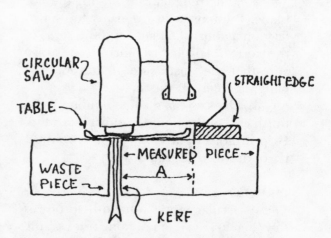

FIG. 2-21. THE KERF SHOULD BE ON THE WASTE SIDE OF THE LINE

To change the blade, first unplug the saw. Some saws have a button or lever that, when pushed, locks the blade in place. If the saw is not so equipped, re-tract the guard and push the teeth of the blade into a scrap piece of wood so that the blade won't turn. Remove the blade by loosening the nut that holds it on with a wrench. The sharp blade should be put on with the teeth pointing toward the front of the saw. Usually each blade and the guard will have arrows indicating the direction of rotation. Make sure the arrow on the blade is pointing in the same direc-tion as the one on the guard. When the new blade is in place, replace the nut and tighten it.

Tape Measure

If you have been getting along by using a 3-foot tape, yardstick, or a dress-maker's tape, it's time to break down and buy a new one. It's important to have a tape that you can work with one hand, so that the other is free to mark the measure-ment. A 12- or 16-foot steel tape that is ¾ inch wide and is equipped with a locking mechanism is good for household use (Fig. 2-22).

MEASURING

Measuring is often hard for adults. We all learned it in the third grade, but unless we pursued a career that required us to use measuring tools, we have forgot-ten how to do it. It is easy to relearn, but beware of frustrating thoughts like "My nine-year-old daughter could do this bet-ter than I."

Open your tape measure so that at least 16 inches are showing or look at Fig.

FIG. 2-22. TAPE MEASURE

2-23. There's a lot of information on this tape. First, notice that after the 1-foot mark, there are numbers at the top and bottom of the tape. The fine print near the 1-inch mark tells you what this is. The top of the tape is marked in feet and inches (read 1 foot, 3 inches) and the bot-tom of the tape is marked in cumulative inches (read 15 inches). There are also special marks at 1 foot and at 16 inches. These bold arrows make the tape easier to use. They are used in laying out, which is the process of marking the locations of studs on the bottom plate of a wall while you're building it. At a glance you can see the 16-inch on center marks, because each one is bold. Also notice that for the first foot the bottom of the tape is marked in thirty-seconds of an inch. This is for very

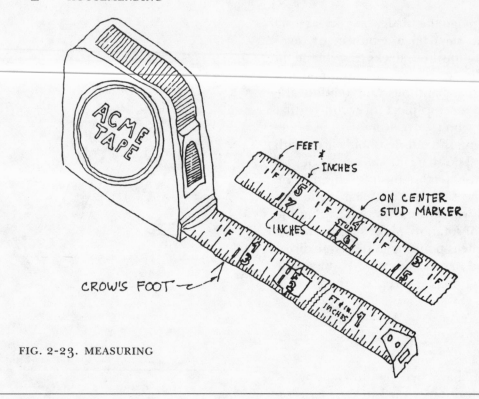

FIG. 2-23. MEASURING

fine measurements, such as those used in cabinetmaking.

The crow's foot is the correct way to mark when measuring. It is the most accurate mark. Start with your pencil right next to the tape and boldly and assertively strike two lines away from the tape in a **V** shape. I say assertively, because the two lines in the crow's foot should be ½ inch long and dark enough to be seen. Don't draw this mark. Don't go over and over it. Don't start with your pencil ½ inch away from the tape and draw your lines toward the mark on the tape you are indicating. The purpose here is not to be neat; it is to be accurate.

The crow's foot in Fig. 2-23 indicates a measurement. It can be read either of two ways, depending on which side of the tape you are reading from. Reading from the top of the tape you would say, "1 foot, 1³⁄₁₆ inches." Reading from the bottom of the tape it would be, "13³⁄₁₆ inches." They mean the same thing. The first is expressed in feet and inches, the latter only in inches.

People usually find reading the sixteenths the hardest part of measuring. There is an old joke about two carpenters who are working together. One is measuring and telling the other how long to cut the boards. The measurer looks at his tape and says, "Cut it two-foot-three and five of them little marks." "Them little marks" are sixteenths, and the funniest part about this joke is that I've heard carpenters do this. So don't feel bad if you can't figure out the little marks right off.

Feet and inches are like foreign languages, and it takes practice before you can think in these measurements without translating in your head. While you are waiting for that day, use the road signs on the tape. For instance, in reading the measurement indicated by the crow's foot, notice the parts of the measurement in descending order: feet, inches, fractions of an inch. First, notice that the mark indicates at least 1 foot. Second, notice that it indicates at least 1 inch. Last, notice that it points to $\frac{3}{16}$ of an inch. A helpful road sign is the $\frac{1}{4}$-inch mark. The crow's foot is pointing to $\frac{1}{16}$ less than $\frac{1}{4}$ inch. Since $\frac{1}{4}$ inch equals $\frac{4}{16}$, one of the little marks less than $\frac{1}{4}$ is $\frac{3}{16}$. You can use this same reasoning to determine the other difficult measurements: one little mark less than an inch is $\frac{15}{16}$, one mark more than $\frac{3}{4}$ is $\frac{13}{16}$, one mark more than $\frac{1}{2}$ is $\frac{9}{16}$, and so on.

Pliers

Every toolbox ought to have a pair of pliers. Any old kind of pliers will do. If you have to buy a pair, then I suggest you get lineman's pliers or Channellocks. Lineman's pliers not only have the ability to grip and hold things but also to cut wire (Fig. 2-24). Channellocks are great for gripping because they adjust to handle pipes or nuts up to 1½ inches in diameter (Fig. 2-25). They are good for plumbing work but do not have the wire-cutter capability. The name Channellock is a brand name that, like Kleenex, has come to have generic meaning. The generic name for this tool is waterpump pliers.

Grip pliers as shown in Fig. 2-26. One handle is held firmly at the apex of

WIRE CUTTER

FIG. 2-24. LINEMAN'S PLIERS

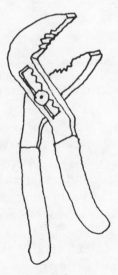

FIG. 2-25. CHANNELLOCKS

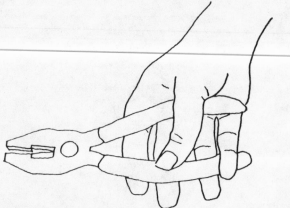

FIG. 2-26. GRIPPING PLIERS

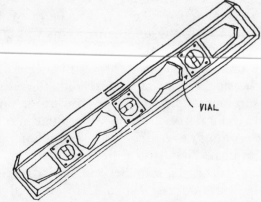

FIG. 2-27. LEVEL

the joint between thumb and forefinger. The first three fingers wrap around the other handle and squeeze. The little finger slips to the inside of the lower handle and pushes the handle out to make the jaws open. If you are cutting heavy wire and need the strength of all four fingers, the little finger moves out to help the other three.

Level

An 18- or 24-inch level is a good size for around the house. There are two types: those with the vials puttied in and those with the vials screwed in like the one shown in Fig. 2-27. The former is more expensive and usually of better quality—that is, it stays level longer. If a vial breaks, you can find replacement screw-in vials in the hardware store, whereas the puttied level must be sent back to the factory.

Picking out a level that is accurate at the store can be frustrating. In this age where nothing is certain anymore one

would hope, in the words of one level company, that at least "levels always tell the truth." But no. Most of the levels you place on a counter or shelf at the store will not agree with each other. When you get two that do, buy either one, for both are accurate.

A level can do two things. It can tell you when something is level (parallel to bodies of water and the horizon) and when something is plumb (perpendicular to the horizon or exactly vertical). A level is only as accurate as you make it. When you are holding the level horizontally look at the middle vial (Fig. 2-28). When the bubble is *exactly* in the middle of the two lines, then the level is level. To eliminate as much perceptual error as possible, always have your eye level with the vial. Any line you draw along the long edge is a level line. If the bubble is to the right of center, the surface on which the level rests is not level (Fig. 2-29); the left side of the level is low. If the bubble is to the left of center, the right side of the level is low.

If the level is being held vertically so

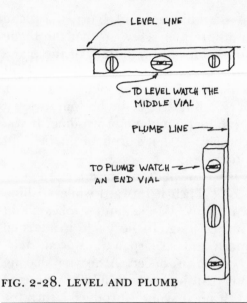

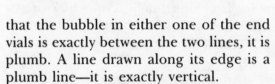

FIG. 2-28. LEVEL AND PLUMB

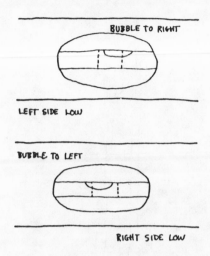

FIG. 2-29. HOW TO READ A LEVEL

that the bubble in either one of the end vials is exactly between the two lines, it is plumb. A line drawn along its edge is a plumb line—it is exactly vertical.

The use of a level is best explained by example. If you need to level an appliance, such as a stove, place the level along the front edge of the kitchen stove. If the bubble is exactly between the two lines of the middle vial, then the front of the stove is level. If the bubble is off to one side, raise one end of the level and watch to see if this brings the bubble between the lines. If raising one end makes the bubble go farther off to the side, then raise the other end of the level. When the bubble is exactly between the lines, look to see how much space there is between the bottom edge of the level and the top of the stove. This is the approximate distance that that corner of the stove must be raised to make the front level. Level one side of the stove next by placing the level along the top of that side. Finally, level

the back. Before you begin, it's a good idea to determine which corner of the stove is the lowest and begin there.

Utility Knife

Some kind of knife is a must; it has thousands of uses. A utility knife with a retractable blade is best (Fig. 2-30). There is a compartment for extra blades in most knives. Unscrew the large central screw that holds the two halves of the knife together to reveal it.

FIG. 2-30. UTILITY KNIFE

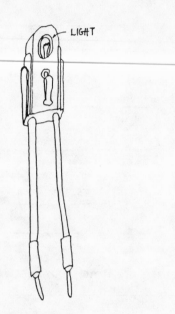

FIG. 2-31. CIRCUIT TESTER

Circuit Tester

This tool will be one of the cheapest in your toolbox, and it may save you from getting a shock when doing electrical repairs. A circuit tester tests whether there is electricity flowing through a particular circuit, outlet, lamp, et cetera (Fig. 2-31). To operate it, place one of the tails against one bared wire and the other tail against the other. If the light glows, the circuit is "hot." The circuit tester's prongs are made thin enough to be inserted into the slots of an outlet to see if the current is on. Figs. 5-24, 5-25, and 5-28 show some specific uses for this tool.

Plane

The handiest plane to have is a block plane (Fig. 2-32). It is a small plane that is used with one hand. Turn the plane iron adjustment screw so that the blade protrudes from the bottom of the plane about $\frac{1}{16}$ inch, but use your sense of touch instead of your sight. Run your fingers lightly across the bottom to see if you can feel the blade protruding. If you can barely feel it, it's probably in the right position.

Place the plane on the edge of a piece of wood. Push it forward while pushing down lightly. Use smooth strokes about 24 inches long. If the blade is adjusted properly and is sharp, a translucent shaving will be produced. A heavier shaving means that the blade should be retracted a bit. If no shaving is produced, turn the plane iron adjustment screw clockwise to push the blade farther through the plane bottom. Hold the plane as shown in Fig. 9-14.

Another type of plane is the surform (Fig. 2-33). It is a plane with a rasplike bottom. The short ones are held like a plane; the longer surform planes are held like a rasp. A rasp is a coarse file used in shaping wood (Fig. 2-34). Hold the han-

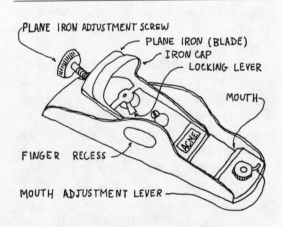

FIG. 2-32. THE PARTS OF A BLOCK PLANE

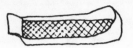

FIG. 2-33. A SURFORM PLANE

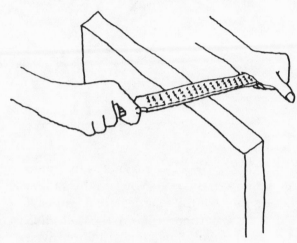

FIG. 2-34. USING A RASP OR FILE

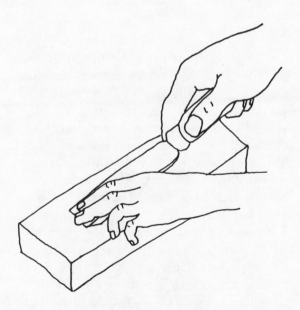

FIG. 2-35. SHARPENING A CHISEL

dle of the rasp or surform with one hand and the tip of it with the other. Hold these tools at a 30-degree angle with the wood. Rasps and surforms cut only on the forward stroke, so push the tool across the wood, lift it off the wood, bring it back to the original position, and stroke again.

Sharpening

Plane blades and chisels are sharpened by rubbing them across a special stone. The stone must be lubricated to facilitate sharpening. Stones that are lubricated with oil are called oilstones; those that can be wetted with water are called whetstones. A stone that is 8 inches × 2 inches is a good size.

Plane blades and chisels have a bevel at the tip. The bevel is placed against the stone to hone or sharpen the edge. Lubricate the stone and, holding the blade with the bevel flat against the stone, rub the blade across the stone in a figure-eight pattern (Fig. 2-35). Holding the bevel against the stone requires holding the blade at a constant angle while sharpening. I have trouble seeing this angle so I feel it. I place the tip of my first finger so that it is half on the stone and half on the blade. This way I can feel when the blade changes angle and correct it. There is one drawback. It rubs a little skin off the tip of my finger. When I sharpen especially dull blades, I have a red fingertip for a couple of days.

Sanding Block

Heavy rubber sanding blocks can be purchased at any hardware store or made at home. A sanding block can be made

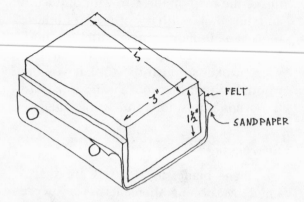

FIG. 2-36. SANDING BLOCK

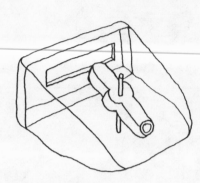

FIG. 2-37. STUD FINDER

from any block of wood by covering the bottom with a piece of felt and wrapping sandpaper around it. Cut a block 3 inches × 5 inches × 1½ inches out of a 2×4. (A 2×4 is actually not 2 inches, but 1½ inches thick.)

When a 12-inch-×-10-inch sheet of sandpaper is folded in sixths and torn on the folds, it yields six smaller pieces 4 inches × 5 inches. The extra inch of width allows the sandpaper to be fastened to the side of the block (Fig. 2-36).

Glue the felt onto the bottom and sides of the block with rubber cement. Now tack the pieces of sandpaper onto the block with thumbtacks. The felt prevents the sandpaper from scratching or marring the surface during delicate refinishing work. Hold a sanding block as shown in Fig. 9-11.

Stud Finder

This is definitely a useful gadget. It locates the positions of studs in a wall by using a magnet to detect the nails in the stud (Fig. 2-37). The magnet is mounted so that it can pivot. As you run the gadget along the wall the magnet will align itself so that it is perpendicular to the wall when it is over a nail. Since nails can be driven only into studs, wherever there is a nail, there is a stud.

Pipe Wrench

A pipe wrench may be the most expensive item in your toolbox, but for plumbing repairs it is a necessity. A plumbing wrench has jaws that are designed to open wide for pipes and teeth designed to grip and turn them (Fig. 2-38). A 14-inch pipe wrench is the best size for most work. There can be quite a variation in price and, as with other tools, you get what you pay for. Just be sure you buy a wrench whose jaws move smoothly when you turn the adjustment wheel.

Pipe wrenches are always used in pairs—one to turn the fitting and another to hold the pipe. Using two ensures that the pipe won't break from the stress ex-

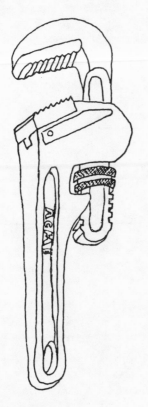

FIG. 2-38. PIPE WRENCH

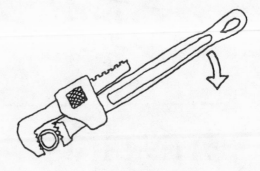

FIG. 2-40. DIRECTION OF BITE

erted by just one wrench. The wrenches are positioned as in Fig. 2-39. The jaws should be facing in opposite directions. The teeth of a pipe wrench are slanted so that they grip only while the wrench is being turned toward the jaws, as shown in Fig. 2-40.

Apron

The next time you go to a lumberyard, ask them for a nail apron (Fig. 2-41). They give them away free. You need an apron to hold your tools while you're working, so that both hands can be free. If you don't have one, you'll waste a lot of time hunting for where you put the tool you need.

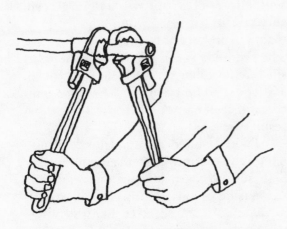

FIG. 2-39. HOW TO USE A PIPE WRENCH

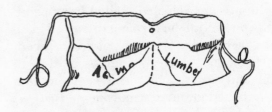

FIG. 2-41. NAIL APRON

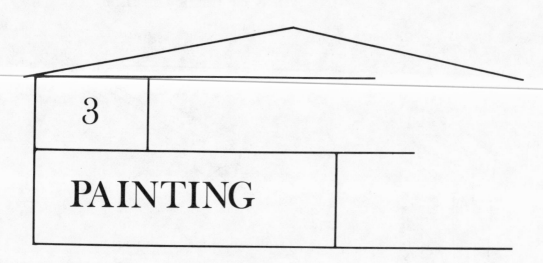

3

PAINTING

Types of Paint

There are so many different types of paint that choosing one can be confusing unless you know a few definitions and a little about what's in paint. All paints contain both a pigment and a vehicle. The pigment consists of coloring agents like white lead, titanium, or zinc. The vehicle is the liquid part of the paint that carries the color and can be either water or oil. Paint with a water vehicle is called latex paint, and paint with the pigment dissolved in oil is called oil-base. Alkyd paint is a recent hybrid. Its vehicle is composed of both oil and water, which are made to mix by the addition of emulsifiers. Brushes used with latex paint can be cleaned in water; those used with oil-base paint

must be cleaned in turpentine or thinners.

The main ingredient of paint is resin. Resins form the hard film that protects a surface. Resins can be either natural or synthetic. Shellac contains a natural resin secreted by insects; when that resin is mixed with alcohol, shellac is formed. The synthetic resins are acrylic, phenolic, silicone, urethane, vinyl acetate, alkyd, and epoxy. The resin is part of the vehicle, and each paint must have at least one resin.

Latex paint is an emulsion; oil-base paint is a solution. If you remember your high school chemistry, an emulsion is a suspension of particles in a liquid, like silt in river water. A solution like salt water undergoes no settling. Latex paint is a suspension of oily globules of pigment and resin in water. When the water evaporates, the globules form a hard skin. Oil-base paint dries by the evaporation of the solvent (turpentine or thinners) in the vehicle; a hard, glossy film is left behind.

CHOOSING THE RIGHT PAINT

The big question is when to use oil-base and when to use latex paint (Table 1). Either paint can be used for most jobs whether inside or out, but there are a few for which oil-base paint is better. If you are painting over old oil-base paint, then you must use oil paint. Recoating with a quick-drying latex paint can actually pull the oil-base paint off the wall. Any paint put on prior to 1950 is most likely oil-base, since latex wasn't invented until then.

Table 1.
TYPES OF PAINT

TYPE OF PAINT	USES	CLEANUP/ SOLVENTS	CONTAINS
Latex	Interior or exterior paint for wood, masonry, or metal. Least expensive paint.	Water	A suspension of synthetic resins (polyvinyl acetate, styrene butadiene, acrylics) in water.
Alkyd (oil-alkyd)	Interior or exterior paint for wood. A middle-priced hybrid of latex and oil-base paint.	Mineral spirits	A synthetic resin modified with oil that gives good adhesion, gloss, and color retention.
Oil-base	House or shelf paint. Used when a hard glossy surface is required. Resists stains by industrial fumes. Most expensive paint.	Turpentine or mineral spirits	A solution of pigment and resins in oil (linseed oil).
Varnish	A clear finish for wood that stays on the surface and seals wood.	Turpentine or mineral spirits	A solution of gums and resins in oil. It contains no pigment.
Shellac	A clear finish for wood that stays on the surface and seals the wood.	Alcohol	A solution of a resin secreted by insects in alcohol.
Pigmented shellac	Applied over water stains, knots, etc., before painting. Prevents the stain from bleeding through the paint.	Alcohol	A pigment (usually white) is added to shellac. B-I-N is a common brand.

Table 1. *(Continued)*

TYPE OF PAINT	USES	CLEANUP/ SOLVENTS	CONTAINS
Primer	A specially formulated paint that seals the surface (wood or drywall) and helps bind the topcoat of paint to it.	Latex— water; oil-base— mineral spirits or turpentine	A paint (either latex, alkyd, or oil-base) that contains special sealers and binders.
Stain (oil or latex)	A thin paint that allows the wood grain to show through.	Mineral spirits, turpentine, water	Oil stain—a solution of pigment, mineral spirits, resins, and linseed oil. Latex stain—a suspension of pigment and acrylic resin in water.
Enamel	A high-gloss paint for wood or metal.	Mineral spirits, turpentine	Traditionally a varnish that contains pigment. Now "enamel" is used to describe any glossy paint.
Polyurethane	A clear, hard finish for wood. Often used on floors.	Mineral spirits, turpentine	A solution of urethane resins in mineral spirits and oil.
Penetrating oils and stains	A finish for wood that soaks into the wood and seals against water.	Turpentine	A solution of petroleum distillates and preservatives to which pigment may be added.
Preservatives	A treatment against rot. Used on decks and any wood that will be within 18″ of the ground.	Cuprinol— soap and water; creosote— gas, thinner, or kerosene	Of the three brands, Penta, which contains pentachlorophenol, is the most carcinogenic. Cuprinol contains zinc naphthanate and is safer. Cuprinol stain contains BIS. Creosote is the brown liquid used on telephone poles.

Another job where oil-base paint is preferable is the shelves of kitchen cabinets. Latex paint dries faster than oil when it's on walls, but when the air flow is constricted, as it is inside a cabinet, oil-base paint dries just as fast. Oil-base paint also dries from the inside out, so that when it is dry to the touch, it is dry through and through. It is best for surfaces that will have things placed on them, because it dries to a hard enamel finish.

Both latex and oil-base paint come in flat, semigloss, and glossy finishes. Latex paint, which is naturally flat, can be made glossy by additives; and oil-base paint, which is naturally shiny, can be made to look flat with other additives. The rule of thumb is that semigloss and glossy paint are washable and flat paint is not. Recently, however, flat paints that can be scrubbed have been developed. A common convention is to paint the ceiling with flat paint, the walls with semigloss, and the trim with glossy paint.

If you are painting a surface that has never been painted, the first coat should be a primer. These paints have additional sealers and agents that help the paint adhere to the surface. If you are painting bare wood and you will use oil-base paint, choose a primer containing a lot of linseed oil. It will soak into the wood and help keep it healthy. Paints with a lot of oil in them take longer to dry, so plan accordingly.

Exterior paints have to endure a lot of abuse from atmospheric conditions. Some paints are called self-cleaning: over the years the outer layer slowly chalks off (turns to powder) and is washed away by the rain, thereby keeping the house looking clean. There are several problems with this kind of paint. First, it is difficult to repaint over chalking paint. Second, this type of paint should not be used on wood located above a masonry surface of brick or stone. Runoff from a rainstorm containing the chalked paint will streak the brick as it washes down the house.

Some areas of the country are susceptible to mildew. If you live in one, ask your paint dealer to add a mildew-resistant additive to your paint. Many paints already include this additive. Fume-resisting formulas are available for paints to be used on houses in areas where industrial fumes may stain paint.

If you have recently insulated your house, the next time you paint the interior you should choose a vapor-barrier paint for the exterior walls. This is a specially formulated paint that has a low permeability rating. That means that it lets very little water vapor through its skin and into the wall cavity (see pages 108–10). Not all companies make vapor-barrier paint.*

Preparing the Surface

NEW SURFACES

It's easiest to paint new surfaces because you don't have to deal with anyone else's mistakes or 100 years of dirt and cracking. For any virgin surface, be it drywall, wood, or plaster, some kind of primer is needed. All-purpose primers, as their name suggests, work on all surfaces.

*The best ones, according to Rodale's Product Testing, are Benjamin Moore's Alkyd Primer Sealer and Satin Impervo Low Lustre Enamel, Sears Best Oil Base Primer 5881, Glidden's Insul-Aid, B-I-N Primer Sealer, and Thermo-Paint from the Enterprise Company in Wheeling, Illinois, 60090.

The primer seals the surface and binds the paint to it. If the surface is porous, a sealer may be necessary. A sealer is a thinner version of primer, which is so thin it soaks into the pores of the surface instead of staying on the surface.

Drywall should be painted with alkyd or oil-base primer if you will be wallpapering over it. New plaster can be painted immediately with latex paint, because moisture released by the drying plaster can penetrate through it. If oil-base paint is the choice, you must wait ninety days until the plaster cures.

OLD SURFACES

All surfaces should be clean and free from glue, grease, and oil before painting. The preparation of the surface is the most time-consuming and least glorious part of painting. As with most tasks, if you spend a little extra time at the beginning, you will save time overall. In painting, preparation is everything. Wallpaper must be removed, paint scraped, and cracks filled. Paint does not hide surface blemishes. Anything that is on the wall before you paint will be there afterward; it will just look a little cleaner. All cracks must be filled (see "Repairing Holes in Walls and Ceilings," pages 102–108). The new texture paints will cover some cracks but won't hide differences in level around a patch, for example. A surface covered with texture paint is hard to clean, so it is best used on ceilings.

Old Interior Surfaces

Interior surfaces are usually covered with either wallpaper or old paint. Painting over wallpaper is only advisable when it is bonded firmly to the wall. Only latex paint should be used, and even then it sometimes causes the wallpaper to blister. Oil-base paint doesn't adhere to wallpaper. Some wallpapers have an embossed design that may be attractive when painted over. In most cases you will find that wallpaper was hung for a reason and that reason was to hide a cracked and bumpy plaster wall. Painting the wallpaper gives the wall a sheen that exposes all surface imperfections.

If there is any indication of peeling, it's safest to remove the wallpaper. There are many ways to do this. Steamers can be rented and they work very well. There are a number of chemical wallpaper removers that mix in water, but I've found that water by itself works about as well. Score the wallpaper with a knife in long strokes about 6 inches apart. With a rag or sponge dripping with water or remover solution, soak the wallpaper thoroughly. A scraper of either the hooked or knife variety will now scrape off one or two layers (Fig. 3-1). Repeat the scoring and soaking as you scrape off the remaining layers.

If the interior surface is painted, the trim around doors and windows will have the most layers of paint, and this seems to be where the paint tends to peel. Before repainting, all loose paint must be removed. One way is to scrape the places that are peeling, until no more paint is lifted by the scraper. This will yield patches that have been taken down a layer or two in the midst of the flat surface of the last coat. The trim will look something like a map of northern Minnesota, land of a thousand lakes. Feathering the edges of the patches by sanding them down will ameliorate this a little. The only way to

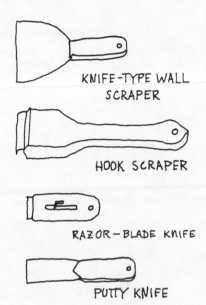

FIG. 3-1. PAINT SCRAPERS

---

avoid the patchy look is to either fill each lake in with Spackle, or remove all the paint.

If the paint is tightly bonded to the interior walls, you can paint over it. Semigloss or glossy paint must be deglossed before painting. Any standard deglosser, like Paso or any store brand, can be used. Merely wash the wall with it. This lets the new paint adhere to the surface.

Any water or mildew stains should be covered with a sealer like B-I-N. B-I-N is one of a number of shellac-based primers to which white pigment has been added. The sealer keeps any stain from bleeding through the new paint. Mildew should be washed with bleach before it is painted over (Fig. 3-2).

Old Exterior Surfaces

The rules for preparing the exterior surface of your house for painting are similar. Ideally the house should be hosed off before surface preparation begins. Wipe your hand over the paint. If the paint wipes off, it means the paint is chalking and the house should be washed with TSP and rinsed. TSP is a surface preparer that is available at paint and hardware stores. (It is not available in some states.) Soffits, the underside of the eaves, and the ceilings of an outdoor porch are areas that are not washed by the rain and dried by the sun. These protected areas of the house should be washed with brushes dipped in a mild detergent and water. Any paint that is not tightly bonded to the surface must be removed. A knife-type paint scraper with a stiff blade works well on blisters and peeling paint; the curved-blade scraper is good for obstinate areas.

Usually it is enough to remove only the peeling paint. However, if the house has many layers of paint, the addition of one more layer can cause paint failure. New paint shrinks when it cures, but old paint has lost its elasticity. The result is no

FIG. 3-2. MILDEW-CLEANING AGENTS

bond between the newest coat of paint and the rest, resulting in wrinkling and peeling. A thick paint buildup will eventually crack and alligator anyway. When the paint layer reaches this stage, it is time to remove all the paint.

Removing Paint

There are many ways to remove paint, whether it be interior or exterior. The healthiest way for you and the environment is to use heat. An electric heat plate certainly is the best way to remove paint from flat surfaces like clapboards or trim (Fig. 3-3). The device consists of a heating element within a reflective container that directs the heat toward the painted surface. Hold the heat plate by the wooden handle near the surface until the paint begins to blister. The paint will begin to give off wisps of smoke when it is getting to the optimum softness. Now move the heat plate along the surface slowly, while scraping the softened paint with the other hand. Be careful not to scorch the wood by leaving the plate in any one spot too long. Oil-base paint is flammable, so be careful not to heat it to the point that it catches fire.

A heat gun, which looks like a large hair dryer and blows air heated to 500 to 700 degrees Fahrenheit onto the paint to soften it, works best on detailed work like porch spindles or molded trim. After the paint is softened, it is scraped off with a scraper. Steel wool works well on curved areas.

Other stripping tools are either too dangerous or mar the wood. Flame-producing tools are too liable to cause a fire. Rotary sanding tools can all too easily cut into the surface. Chemical strippers can

FIG. 3-3. ELECTRIC HEAT PLATE

burn the skin and generate toxic fumes.

Old paint contains lead, and scraping it or heating it produces toxic dust and gases. A dust mask will protect you from the dust but not from the gases. For these you need a rubber mask. Both are sold in hardware stores; read the label carefully so you know the limits of each kind of mask.

Exterior Paint Problems

Before you repaint the house, the causes of the peeling must be found and corrected. Look the house over and note where peeling has occurred. Moisture is usually involved somewhere. If an entire wall of the house is peeling or peeling is found outside rooms that have a high moisture content like bathrooms, kitchens, or laundry rooms, the problem is moisture migrating from inside the house. The water vapor contained in the warm inside air travels through the wall and when it reaches the exterior paint, it pushes the paint off the wall to get out. Although most latex exterior paints are more permeable to vapor than oil-base or alkyd paints, a thick layer of any paint will act as a barrier to vapor.

To prevent water vapor from entering the wall cavity, paint the interior walls with a vapor-barrier paint and caulk inside around all penetrations through the wall, like vents, pipes, and wires. The old practice of installing small round exterior vents near the bottom and top of each stud cavity to vent the moisture does not work. Studies have shown that this practice reduces moisture levels only in the wall facing the prevailing wind, and then just slightly.

If the blistered areas are located at the bottom of the siding, the problem is probably water splashing onto the siding from the ground and traveling up the wall via capillary action. By this means, water can travel uphill in the tiny space between two pieces of siding. It's like the tiny capillary tube a nurse uses to capture some of your blood so it can be tested. The nurse pricks your finger and puts the end of a capillary tube in the drop of blood that forms. The blood moves up the tube by capillary action, not by suction.

Among the causes of peeling near the ground is siding that is touching or too close to the ground, the ground level sloping toward the house rather than away from it, bushes too near the siding to allow it to dry, and gutters and downspouts that drain too near the house. If you can't stand the looks of the siding, scrape the paint off and paint this area with a thin latex paint. This will do until you can correct the faulty drainage.

If the top courses of siding are peeling, there is probably water leaking down into the wall from the roof. The cause might be leaky gutters, rotted roof trim, damaged flashing, or ice dams in winter that are letting the water in. Any of these must be fixed before painting.

Paint can also peel when it is on masonry. I once knew a bricklayer who vowed that there was a special place in hell reserved for people who painted over brick. I doubt that the peeling paint is God's vengeance. It is the result either of moisture in the brick or the surface's being too crumbly to hold the paint. In the first instance, the solution is to keep water away from the brickwork. In the second, repoint and replaster the surface so that the paint can adhere to it.

Paint failure is rarely a fault of the paint. It is usually caused by poor surface preparation, poor application, or moisture problems. Let's consider the different kinds of paint failure and analyze the cause and cure (Fig. 3-4).

CHECKING AND CRACKING

CAUSE. Cracking is usually noticed first. It is found in paint that is old and has dried to a very hard and inflexible finish. Because wood constantly swells and shrinks with the seasons, when the paint no longer has the flexibility to move with it, hairline cracks appear.

CURE. If cracking is noticed while the cracks are still small, the surface can be wire brushed and repainted with a different brand of paint from the one that cracked. When the cracks have progressed down to bare wood, as is true for advanced cracking, or alligatoring, all the paint must be removed. Prime with an oil-alkyd primer and paint with either oil-base or latex paint.

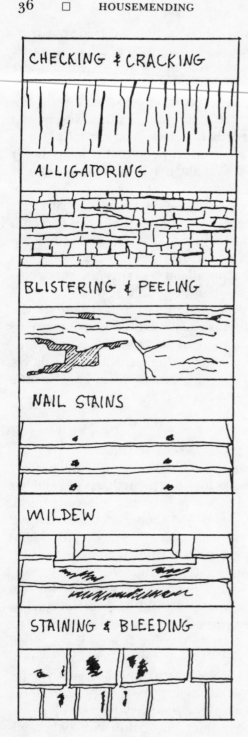

FIG. 3-4. PAINT PROBLEMS

ALLIGATORING

CAUSE. Alligatoring is an advanced state of cracking. It is caused by too many coats of paint, one coat applied too thickly, or a primer that was too glossy for the topcoat to bond to. A variation called wrinkling is caused when the topcoat is applied before the undercoat is completely dry.

CURE. Remove all paint down to the bare wood. Prime with an oil-alkyd primer and paint with either latex or oil-base topcoat.

BLISTERING AND PEELING

CAUSE. Blistering is the early stage of peeling. Cut open the blister. If there is bare wood under the blister, moisture probably caused it. If there is paint under it, improper surface preparation and weather conditions are the cause. Painting in direct hot sun can cause the top of the paint film to dry too quickly, leaving liquid solvent underneath to vaporize into a bubble. If the surface wasn't cleaned enough before painting, the paint won't stick to it and will peel. This often happens on soffits and other protected areas that aren't washed by the rain.

If the culprit is moisture, it can come from a number of sources: leaks from cracks in the siding or near trim; leaks through faulty flashing, gutters, or ice dams; moisture traveling from the living space through the wall; and shrubs and bushes that trap moisture in the siding by not letting it evaporate.

CURE. If the problem is moisture, the condition must be corrected before repainting. Cracks in the siding should be caulked, leaks stopped, and vegetation trimmed back. Moisture flowing through the wall can be stopped by painting the interior side of the exterior walls with vapor-barrier paint. If the relative humidity in your house is more than 30 percent, your wet life-style should be curbed. Cook with lids on pots, shorten showers, and don't vent driers into the house (see "Moisture Problems," pages 108–10).

When these underlying causes have been corrected, remove all blistered and peeling paint. Prime with an oil-alkyd primer and paint with either oil-base or latex paint.

NAIL STAINS

CAUSE. High moisture levels in the siding have caused the nailheads to rust and stain the paint.

CURE. Correct the underlying moisture problems as described above. There are then two ways of dealing with the nail-stain problem itself. One requires a lot more work than the other. First, try the easier way on a test patch and see if it works. Sand off the rust with steel wool or sandpaper, prime the nail heads with a sealer such as B-I-N, and let dry forty-five minutes before applying the topcoat. If rust still bleeds through the topcoat, you must repair the more difficult way, by setting every nail below the surface with a nail set (Figs. 3-5 and 3-6). Then prime each nail head with B-I-N and let dry. Fill the holes with putty and let dry before applying the topcoat.

MILDEW

CAUSE. Mildew, which appears as dark spots, is a fungus that grows in areas shaded from direct sunlight—for example, around eaves and porches. It is caused by moisture, warm temperatures,

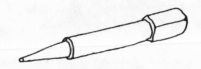

FIG. 3-5. NAIL SET

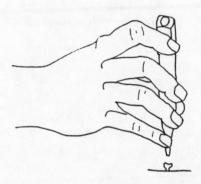

FIG. 3-6. USING A NAIL SET

and poor ventilation. To test to see if a dark spot is mildew, put a few drops of bleach on it. If it lightens, the spot is mildew, not dirt.

CURE. Wash the mildewed areas with a commercial mildew remover or scrub with a solution of 1 quart household bleach, ⅔ cup detergent, and ½ cup trisodium phosphate in 3 quarts of hot water. Rinse thoroughly with a garden hose and let dry. Use a mildew-resistant primer and then paint.

STAINING AND BLEEDING

CAUSE. Some woods, especially cedar and redwood, contain natural water-soluble coloring agents that bleed out through paint when moisture is present in the wood. Cedar shingles will bleed for a year after they are first painted. Try to wait this out.

CURE. Wash the stain off with water or, if needed, a solution of ½ water and ½ denatured alcohol. Rinse with a hose and allow to dry for two days. Cedar can be primed with any quality exterior paint, but prime redwood with an oil-base primer, as this seals most effectively. Finally, apply a compatible topcoat.

Getting Ready

First, calculate the area in square feet that you have to paint. For interior painting, multiply the height of each wall by its width to get the area. To figure the area of a room, measure the perimeter of the room and multiply this by the wall height. Don't subtract for windows and doors. To estimate the area of a house, measure its perimeter and multiply that by the height of the wall.

To calculate the number of gallons needed, divide the area to be painted by either 350 (for primer) or 450 (for top-coat). Primers usually cover 350 square feet and finish coats, 450 square feet. For example, consider the house in Fig. 3-7. The total perimeter of the house is 40 + 36 + 18 + 12 + 22 + 24 = 152 linear feet. If the wall height is 12 feet, the total wall area of the house is 1,824 square feet. To calculate the number of gallons required for one finish coat, divide the total area of the house, 1,824 square feet, by the number of square feet 1 gallon can cover, 450 square feet. The answer is 4.05 gallons. Four gallons should be enough. Don't forget to do a similar calculation to

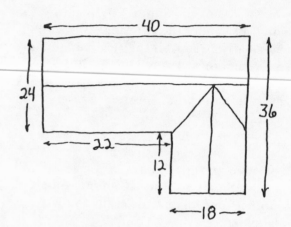

FIG. 3-7. ESTIMATING

estimate the amount of primer if one is needed.

BRUSHES AND ROLLERS

There are two basic types of hand painting tools: brushes and rollers. Each one is appropriate for different painting jobs.

A good paintbrush spreads paint evenly, leaves no brush marks or loose bristles in its wake, and is comfortable to use. With proper care, a good brush will last forever. Of course, a high-quality brush is not always the right tool for the job. A cheap brush should be used for epoxy-resin paints and fiberglassing, because these materials will never come out. I also like to use a throwaway brush when I'm using B-I-N to cover stains. B-I-N is a pigmented shellac that cleans up only with denatured alcohol, which I never seem to have on hand.

Brushes are made with either natural or synthetic bristles. A brush should be full-bodied with half the bristles full length and the rest of varying lengths.

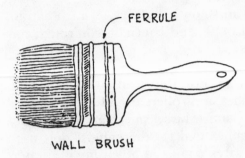

FERRULE

WALL BRUSH

BEVELED TRIM BRUSH

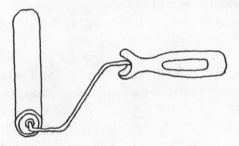

ROLLER

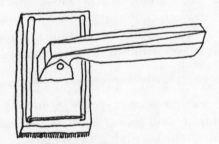

EXTERIOR BRUSH PAD

DISPOSABLE FOAM BRUSH

FIG. 3-8. BRUSHES AND ROLLERS

This allows the brush to hold a good deal of paint and release it gradually. If a brush has synthetic bristles, half should be flagged (split at the tip) and the other half should come to a taper. A good brush has a ferrule (the metal band that holds the bristles to the handle) of a noncorrosive metal and a handle of plastic or hardwood (Fig. 3-8).

Never use a natural-bristle brush with latex paint, because the bristles will swell and lose their ability to spread paint evenly.

Brushes come in different sizes. The size you choose should be based largely on what's comfortable for you. Wall brushes come in 3½-inch, 4-inch, and 5-inch widths and are designed to hold a lot of paint. They are used to paint flat surfaces like clapboards, shelves, walls, and ceilings. Brushes that are 6 inches wide are used for ceilings, but get very heavy.

Varnish brushes come in 2-inch, 2½-inch, and 3-inch widths. They are used to paint smaller flat surfaces like cabinets, moldings, and baseboards. The tips of the bristles are beveled to allow you to cut into corners easily.

Trim brushes come in three styles: flat, angled, and oval. Flat trim brushes are designed to paint the face of narrow interior trim, such as around doors and windows. The angled sash brush is excellent for painting the edge of trim when you don't want to slop over onto the already painted wall. Oval brushes are designed for round or irregular surfaces like porch spindles and furniture legs. The round design keeps the bristles from separating the way a flat brush would on irregular surfaces.

Some people like to paint with a pad.

These are excellent for applying oil stains or linseed oil to new wood.

Disposable brushes are made of foam or bristle. They are useful for substances that are hard to clean up, such as B-I-N, epoxy, or polyurethane.

To paint the outside of your house you should have three brushes: A 4-inch wall brush for the siding, a 3-inch trim brush, and a 1½-inch or 2-inch sash brush. To paint the inside of your house you should have a 9-inch roller and pan for the walls, a 3-inch trim brush, and a 1½-inch or 2-inch sash brush.

Rollers are used almost exclusively for painting interior wall surfaces. The standard-size roller is 9 inches wide, although they come wider for painting floors. The best kind of roller frame to buy is one with a hard plastic handle that will accept a wooden extension handle. The roller frame itself is made of wire in the shape of a bird cage and rolls easily. Small 2-inch rollers are made for painting trim, and a donut-shaped, foam roller is designed to paint corners. Most painters, however, use brushes for these two jobs.

Roller covers come in three different materials: lamb's wool, mohair, and synthetic fibers. A lamb's wool cover should only be used with oil-base paint; latex will ruin it. Mohair provides the smoothest finish when applying enamels, semigloss paint, varnishes, and shellacs. The most common covers are the synthetic ones that are designed for water-base paint. Use a roller with a ⅜-inch nap on smooth walls, ½-inch nap on sand-finished plaster, stucco, or drywall, and ¾-inch nap on rough-textured walls. For exterior staining, use a lamb's wool cover with a ½-inch nap on smooth surfaces, ¾-inch nap on semirough, and 1-inch nap on rough surfaces.

Rollers are seldom used for oil-base paint because the cleanup is so difficult. Brushes and rollers used for oil or alkyd paint must be cleaned in the thinner recommended for the paint. Tools used with latex paint can be cleaned in water. Hold the brush under a flow of warm water and, with a nylon-bristled scrub brush, brush the hardened bits of paint out of the brush. While holding the brush under the tap, squeeze the bristles until pigment flows out. Turn the brush over and squeeze the bristles again. Continue this until no pigment is squeezed out near the ferrule. Shake the brush dry and smooth the bristles in place. If the brush is to be stored for a long time, wrap the bristles in heavy paper.

The procedure for cleaning roller covers is similar. Hold the roller cover under warm water, wrap your fingers around the cylinder, and move them down the cover, squeezing pigment out as you go. The movement is similar to a baseball player rubbing the handle of a bat. Continue until no pigment can be squeezed out. Fluff out the nap and stand the roller cover on end to dry. Some pigmented water will collect at the bottom of the cover, so be sure it has been placed on newspapers or a washable surface.

Exterior Painting

Before beginning, it is important to mix the paint well. Even if it has been shaken up at the paint store, stir each can thoroughly, bringing the paddle up to the top as you stir. Then "box" the paint by pouring it from one container to another. This mixes the pigment into the liquid part of the paint.

Always paint from a can that is no more than half full. Dip the brush about 2 inches into the paint and tap off the excess first on one side of the can and then on the other. Don't drag the brush along the rim to remove paint because this can damage the bristles.

PRIMING AND CAULKING

If the house has never been painted before, all the bare wood must be primed. If you are repainting the house, spot priming the parts that you have scraped is adequate. Use an alkyd primer if you don't know what kind of paint is on the house. Alkyd primers adhere to both latex and oil-base paint.

Weathered wood will not hold paint and must be sanded and treated before it is primed. Weathered wood will draw all the binder out of paint, so treat the surface with a mixture of two parts linseed oil and one part turpentine or a wood preservative. The primer should be an oil-alkyd type that doesn't contain zinc oxide.

All knots should be sealed or they will bleed through the finish coat of paint. Prime all the knots with a pigmented shellac like B-I-N. Also caulk all cracks in the siding and around all door and window trim with a high-quality paintable caulk. Polyurethane caulk is the longest lasting.

In painting metal, preparation and priming are as important as they are in house painting. Metal objects on houses such as lamps and railings should be wire-brushed and scraped or sanded with #360 wet sandpaper to remove loose paint. Spot priming usually makes the

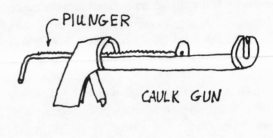

FIG. 3-9. CAULK GUN AND CARTRIDGE

finish coat look messy, so prime the whole object. A red-lead primer should be used if no bare metal is showing, because this primer penetrates down to the metal, driving out moisture and air. If bare metal is showing, use a zinc chromate primer to seal against moisture and air. Finally, apply two coats of any oil-base paint.

After the house has been primed is the perfect time to caulk (Fig. 3-9). All surfaces are clean so that the caulk will stick. It's important to caulk any place where it looks like water may penetrate the house. Just think like a drop of water and imagine rolling down the side of the house. Use a high-quality paintable caulk like polyurethane or butyl rubber. Silicone and butyl rubber are available in any hardware store, but polyurethane, which is the superior caulking material, must be special-ordered or obtained from a contractor supply store.

Caulking may be unfamiliar to you,

but it's really fun and easy once you catch onto it. Many products come in caulk tubes and a lot of them, like some glues and bathtub caulks, are much cheaper if you buy them in this form as opposed to smaller toothpastelike tubes. Caulking guns can be purchased at any lumber or hardware store for three to five dollars.

Insert the caulk tube into the caulk gun in the following way:

1. Pull the plunger all the way out of the gun.

2. Insert the caulk tube into the gun by putting the butt end of the caulk tube into the trigger end of the gun first and then pushing the tube tip through the slot at the front of the gun.

3. Push the plunger in as far as it will go and turn it so the teeth are pointed down.

4. With a knife (a utility knife is best) cut the tip off the tube at a 45-degree angle, so that there is a hole approximately ¼ inch in diameter.

5. Insert a 16d nail, slender stick, or piece of heavy wire into the hole in the tip and puncture the aluminum-foil seal at the base of the plastic tip.

Hold the gun by the handle and squeeze the trigger a couple of times until you see the caulk come into the tip. The caulk will continue to flow while you squeeze the trigger, because every squeeze pushes the plunger farther into the tube. If you want to stop the flow of caulk, simply turn the plunger so that the teeth are up. This reduces the pressure on the caulk inside the tube.

To caulk, hold the gun at a 45-degree angle to the crack you want to fill (Fig. 3-10). Squeeze the trigger and move the

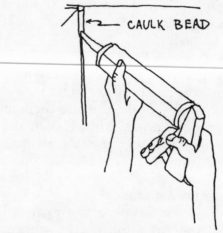

FIG. 3-10. CAULKING

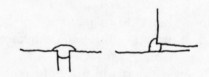

FIG. 3-11. A GOOD CAULK BEAD

caulk gun down the crack slowly enough so that caulk goes into the crack and makes a rounded bead over it. If you go too slowly, too much caulk will be squeezed out and the job will look sloppy. If you go too fast, not enough caulk will penetrate into the crack and some voids (holes in the caulk bead) may appear. It takes a little practice to get the hang of it. A key to neat caulking is a clean tip. I always carry a rag with me and wipe off the tip the minute globs of caulk start clinging to it.

Practice on the back of the house where no one will see. A good caulk bead is shown in Fig. 3-11. If the crack you are going to caulk is wider than ¼ inch, it should be filled with something, so that you don't squeeze tube after tube into its bottomless pit. Stuff it with either oakum, an oily stranded rope, or backing rod, a foam rope. Both are available at lumber and hardware stores.

APPLYING PAINT

There is an order to painting a house. Start at the top and work down, so that the top of your ladder is never resting on a recently painted surface. Paint the siding first, then the trim, and finally porches and decks. Remove the shutters, wooden screens, or storm windows before beginning. These can be painted in the garage or basement on a rainy day. Paint when the temperature is above 40 degrees Fahrenheit and the weather is clear and dry. If you are using oil-base paint, wait a couple of days after a rain before painting. When painting in hot weather, never paint in the direct sun. Move around the house, painting where the sun has just left.

When painting horizontal siding, paint the edges of five or so courses first. Make sure you cover them well, because gaps can be seen from the ground. Next, paint the faces out as far as you can reach on either side. Use long horizontal strokes. Lap paint onto the window and door trim. This makes painting the trim easier, because the joint between the siding and the trim will already be sealed with paint, making cutting in easier.

Don't waste time putting masking tape on the glass of windows to make painting the sash and muntins easier. It is much quicker to do as neat a job as possible and then scrape any excess paint off the glass with a single-edged razor blade (see Fig. 3-1). Anyway, it's important to get paint on the glass to seal water out. Paint should cover the glazing putty and just touch the glass.

How many coats of paint should you apply? It's a question of trade-offs. A two-coat job lasts longer, but is more expensive. Also paint buildup must be considered; too many paint layers causes problems with alligatoring and makes the house so tight that moisture can't escape. If it's not bare wood, spot priming and one finish coat over a clean, dry surface should be sufficient in most cases. Areas that see a lot of water, like windowsills and porches, should get two finish coats.

If you are painting the upper part of a two-story house, the top of the ladder should be resting on unpainted wood. The highest rung you should stand on is the third one from the top. Paint all you can reach from there.

You will need an extension ladder to paint a two-story house. Aluminum ones are lighter to use than wood, but be careful to keep them away from overhead electric wires, because they conduct electricity.

Large ladders aren't so difficult to raise if you follow these steps (Fig. 3-12). First, place the feet of the ladder against the foundation of the house so the ladder is lying on the ground perpendicular to the house wall. If bushes interfere, use a stake driven into the ground, a concrete block, or a friend's foot. Then, pick up the top of the ladder and lift it above your head so that one hand is on the top rung and the other is on the one below it. Now walk toward the house and, as you do move your hands down from rung to

FIG. 3-12. RAISING A LADDER

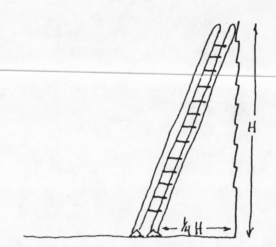

FIG. 3-13. CORRECT LADDER ANGLE

rung, pushing the ladder up. When it is raised and against the house, pull the bottom of the ladder out from the house until it is stable. Most extension ladders are equipped with a rope and pulley so that the ladder can be extended by pulling on the rope. To do this, pull the top of the ladder slightly away from the house as you pull the rope. This allows the extension to be raised without getting hung up on the butt ends of the clapboards.

The bottom of a ladder should be pushed into the dirt so that it won't slide out from under you. If the ladder rests on a smooth surface, it should be equipped with rubber feet. The safest angle for a ladder is when the bottom is one-quarter of the ladder height away from the house (Fig. 3-13). Never move a ladder when you are on it. This may sound like silly advice, but it's mighty tempting to slide the top of the ladder over a foot in order to reach that one last patch, instead of

coming all the way down. When moving the ladder over to the next section, move the bottom a couple of feet and then move the top back into vertical position. Repeat until you have scooted the ladder over to where you want it.

To move it any distance, get under the ladder with your side to the rungs and grasp the highest rung you can reach with one hand and the lowest you can comfortably reach with your strong hand (Fig. 3-14). Lift with your bottom hand and control the ladder with your upper hand, while you walk to the new position. The trick is to keep the ladder close to vertical.

When you lift awkwardly shaped objects like ladders or refrigerators, there is a point at which they are balanced. Maintaining this balance point makes the job easier. In the case of the ladder, it is when the ladder is exactly vertical and you can use all your strength to carry the weight of the ladder, instead of also having to keep

FIG. 3-14. MOVING A LADDER

the top from swinging back and forth, which takes much more strength than carrying it.

Interior Painting

Rooms are painted from top to bottom: ceilings, walls, trim, and finally doors and window sashes. Painting is easier if all fixtures like thermostats, lamps, and electrical outlet covers are removed or loosened. This way you can paint right up to them with a roller and not have to paint neatly around them with a brush.

First cut in around the perimeter of the ceiling with a brush. This means that you carefully paint a 2- to 3-inch strip around the ceiling perimeter. If the walls are going to be painted, it's not fatal if you get a little paint on them.

It's pretty easy to paint a ceiling using a roller and extension pole. The exten-

sion pole eliminates the need for ladders or scaffolding. Paint the ceiling in 2- to 3-foot-wide strips across the width (not the length) of the room. Fill the deep part of the roller pan with paint. Dip the roller into the paint and roll it against the sloped part of the pan to spread the paint evenly over the roller. Begin in one corner and roll a 2- to 3-foot strip against the wall. Start the next strip 2 to 3 feet away from the first strip, and work the paint toward the painted strip. As for technique, first roll the roller parallel to the width of the room. Then cross-roll to make sure the area is covered. Finish with strokes in one direction (not back and forth) parallel to the width of the room. Proceed across the room until the whole ceiling is painted.

Walls can also be painted with a 3-inch trim brush and roller. Again, begin by cutting in around the perimeter of the room against the ceiling and at the baseboard, around all window and door trim, and in all corners. Now, with a roller, paint the large sections of wall, beginning in one corner and working around the room. Paint in 1- to 2-foot strips from ceiling to baseboard. The first stroke of the roller should be upward. Follow it with a down stroke over the same area and then cross-roll to assure even coverage. Finish with up-and-down strokes. Begin the next strip on the unpainted surface and work toward the strip you just painted. Continue this around the room.

When painting the trim, paint the baseboards first, window and door trim second, the window sash and doors themselves third, and finally any shelves or built-in cabinets. Paint woodwork with a trim brush. Dip it into the paint so that one-third the length of the bristles is covered with paint. Slap the brush against the rim of the can first on one side and then on the other to remove excess paint. Brush in 1- to 2-foot strokes along the length of the trim piece. Hold the brush near the base of the handle and exert enough pressure so that the bristles curve a little. At the end of each stroke lift the brush, relaxing the pressure slightly. This feathers the strokes into the part previously painted and makes for a smoother job. Sometimes too much paint is applied and runs or drips occur. Keep a watchful eye, and brush them out as you paint. In painting, as in other tasks covered in this book, it is important to strike a balance between the small task that you are doing and the overall picture.

WINDOWS, DOORS, AND CABINETS

There is a particular order for painting these items. The trim around the windows and doors is painted first, along with the other woodwork, then the window sashes and doors themselves.

The sash is the movable part of the window. Some people purposely paint shut the upper sash of double-hung windows to keep out air infiltration in the winter. If that is your desire, painting your windows will be a little easier. If not, pull the top sash down and the bottom sash up, so that you are able to paint the meet-

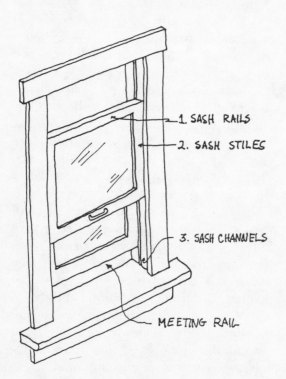

FIG. 3-15. PAINTING A WINDOW

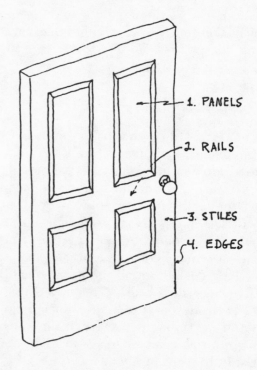

FIG. 3-16. PAINTING A DOOR

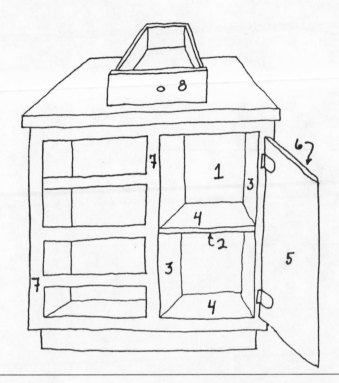

FIG. 3-17. PAINTING A CABINET

ing rail (Fig. 3-15). This is the part of each sash that touches the other in the middle of the window. A rail is a term for any horizontal piece in woodwork or cabinets; a stile is any vertical piece. Generally, rails are painted before stiles. Paint the sash rails first, the sash stiles second, and the channels last. Casement windows are ones that hinge on the side. They are painted in a similar order.

There are two kinds of doors: flush and panel. Panel doors are the older type and are made up of panels and cross-pieces. Paint the panels first by painting the perimeter and moving toward the center of each panel. Then paint the rails and next the stiles. The edges come last, and don't forget the top (Fig. 3-16).

Unlike panel doors, flush doors have a smooth surface. Work from the top down, painting in sections. Painting enamel or varnish on a door without leaving runs or brush marks is a challenge. Work quickly so that edges of adjacent sections blend with each other. Lay on paint with strokes parallel to the grain. Then cross-brush to assure coverage. Continue this across the door, and finally brush all the sections of one course together with long horizontal strokes. Proceed down the door in this fashion.

When painting a cabinet, move from the inside to the outside, painting the drawers last (Fig. 3-17). Paint in this order: the back wall of the inside of the cabinet, the underside of all shelves, the side walls, the top surface of shelves, the inside of doors, the outside of doors, the face of the cabinet, and the drawers.

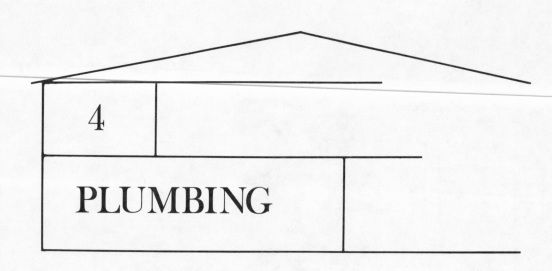

4

PLUMBING

Plumbing suffers from a bad reputation. Many homeowners think of plumbing repairs as dirty and complicated, but actually, painting is messier than plumbing. After you have made a plumbing repair, soap and water (not gasoline or turpentine) will get your hands clean. Besides, plumbing is fun. If you liked Tinkertoys or jigsaw puzzles as a child, you'll love plumbing. There are many similarities.

The Plumbing System

The plumbing in your house is like the circulatory system that moves blood through your body. The plumbing system has arterylike tubes, called supply pipes, which bring fresh water to the faucets. There are also veinlike tubes, called drainpipes, which take the wastes away. The wastes are divided into two categories: gray water that is drained from sinks and washers, and black water that is drained from toilets. If you live in the city, all waste water goes into the city sewer system. If you live in the country, waste water goes into a septic tank where it is held until bacteria break it down. From there it flows through a system of pipes with holes in them so that it can seep into a leach field. A leach field is a large gravel bed twelve inches deep, through which the effluent is filtered before it drains down into the soil. Septic tanks are not things that one buries in the ground and forgets; they must be pumped out every several years.

Fig. 4-1 shows where the supply pipes and drainpipes are located in a typical house. The hot-water pipes are represented by dotted lines, and the cold by dashes. These pipes are usually parallel to

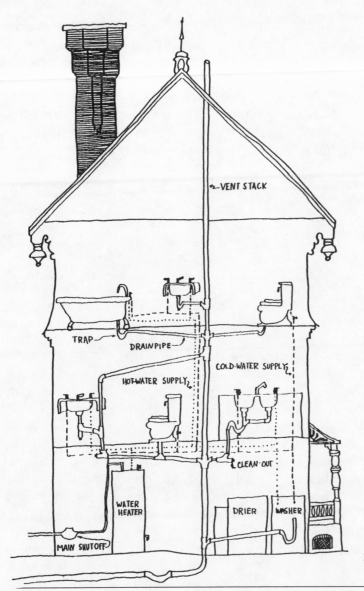

FIG. 4-1. THE PLUMBING SYSTEM

each other and are ½ inch in diameter. The drainpipes in a house range from 1½ inches in diameter near the fixture, to a 4-inch-diameter pipe near the foundation wall. Fixture is the word given to things like sinks, tubs, washers, and so on. Notice that all the drainpipes in Fig. 4-1 slant downward away from the fixture. The pitch (slant) on a drainpipe is ⅛ to ¼ inch per foot of pipe. This means that the pipe travels downward ¼ inch for every foot of its length. Keeping waste water flowing down and away from the house is very important to avoid clogged drains.

The vertical pipe into which all the drainpipes slant is the vent stack. Without it, the sinks and tubs wouldn't drain. We include vent stacks in houses for the same reason that we punch two holes opposite each other on large juice cans. Without the small one at the top, the juice could not be poured. Air must be able to flow into the system or drainage won't occur.

As you drive down the street, look at the roofs of the houses you pass. Notice the different protrusions. One is the plumbing vent stack. It extends above the roof about 18 inches and can be from 1½ to 3 inches in diameter. A house may have more than one if the kitchen and bathroom are so far apart that they can't use the same vent stack.

In the basement are a number of items related to the house's plumbing. If you get your water from the city supply, there will be a water meter and main shutoff (Fig. 4-2). By turning the knob clockwise, all the water in the house will be turned off. If you have your own well, there still should be a main shutoff just inside the foundation where the black plastic well pipe comes into the house. It's important to know where the main shutoff is in case of emergency. If the pipes freeze or burst in the basement, you will most likely need to turn all the water off. If there are no shutoff valves under each

sink, you will have to turn the main shutoff, thereby stopping the flow of water to *all* parts of the house, solely in order to change a washer on one dripping faucet upstairs. This can be very inconvenient. For this reason I have included in this chapter an explanation of how to install a shutoff valve beneath a sink.

A Plumbing Tool Kit for the House

In addition to the general tools mentioned in Chapter 1, it is a good idea to have some specialized plumbing tools around the house (Fig. 4-3).

1. Snake. A snake is a tool for unclogging drains. It consists of a length of flexible steel cable that can be pushed into and through pipes. After it is inserted, tighten the set screw and turn the handle. This will make the other end, which is down in the pipe, turn and break up the clog.

2. Plunger. The plunger is also called the "plumber's friend." No house should be without this simple tool. The one shown in Fig. 12-6 is a more expensive model equipped with a flexible rubber flap that can be flipped down for use on toilets. The simple plunger shown here is more useful.

3. Pipe wrench. The reason you need a pipe wrench is because it can open its mouth so wide. There are a lot of plumbing pipes and nuts that are more than 1½ inches in diameter. Crescent wrenches don't open this wide. Pipe wrenches also have pipe-gripping teeth that enable one to unscrew pipes from fittings. It's actually best to have two pipe wrenches, since they should be used in tandem—one to hold the pipe and the other to hold and turn the fitting or joint. Pipe wrenches are

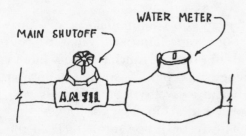

FIG. 4-2. MAIN WATER SHUTOFF

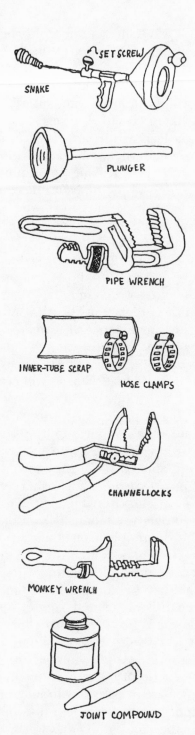

SNAKE

SET SCREW

PLUNGER

PIPE WRENCH

INNER-TUBE SCRAP

HOSE CLAMPS

CHANNELLOCKS

MONKEY WRENCH

JOINT COMPOUND

FIG. 4-3. HOUSEHOLD PLUMBING TOOL KIT

sized by how long they are. Your primary wrench should be 14 inches long. The second one can be 10 inches long.

4. Pipe-patching material. Commercial pipe-patching compounds are available. They look like black putty. Another alternative is a couple of hose clamps and a scrap of inner tube, as shown in Fig. 4-3.

5. Channellocks. Channellocks, also called waterpump pliers, are adjustable, offset pliers. They, too, can grip pipe and are good for turning large nuts. Unlike a pipe wrench, which has jaws designed to grip the pipe without any effort on your part, Channellocks require a good grip to loosen stubborn nuts.

6. Monkey wrench. A monkey wrench is a smooth-jawed tool (similar to a pipe wrench but with no teeth) used for turning nuts. A crescent wrench is also a toothless tool for turning nuts, but won't open its jaws as wide as the more versatile monkey wrench. These tools are used on chrome-plated nuts, which are visible. Using a wrench with teeth would scrape away the chrome.

7. Joint compound. Sometimes called "pipe dope," this material comes in cans or sticks and is applied to pipe threads before a fitting, such as a shower head, is screwed on. Joint compound prevents water from leaking out around the threads.

Leaks

EMERGENCIES

It's always an emergency when a pipe bursts, with water spurting everywhere.

First: Get the water flow stopped. Hurry to the main shutoff and turn it clockwise to turn off the water supply to the house (see Fig. 4-2). If the house does not have a shutoff valve just inside the basement wall, it will be outside in the ground in an accessible box.

If you are not connected to a water supply but have a well instead, there should be a main shutoff on the house side of the pump. The pump draws water from the well and has two pipes coming into it: one from the well and one to the house. The shutoff should be near the pump in the pipe supplying water to the house.

If there is no main shutoff in your house, then locate the shutoff valve nearest the pipe that has burst. To be useful, it must be between the pipe and the water main entrance into the house. Once the water has stopped spurting, you can put a temporary patch on the pipe and then turn the water back on.

Now is the time to reach into your tool kit and pull out the scrap of inner tube and two automotive clamps. A patch can be fashioned out of this material. Cut the piece of inner tube into one long, ½-inch-wide strip. Wrap the strip tightly around the pipe, starting above the hole and ending below it (Fig. 4-4). Clamp each end with the automotive clamps. This should hold for a while. If it doesn't, place a third clamp directly over the hole. Pipe-patching compound can work also. Place it over the hole and tighten a clamp

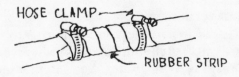

FIG. 4-4. REPAIRING A LEAK

over it. Eventually, you or a plumber will have to replace the burst section of pipe.

LEAKS AROUND FIXTURES

If the bottom of the sink cabinet is damp, there could be several causes: there's a leak in the drainpipe; water is getting in underneath the faucets or countertop; water is leaking in around the sprayer; the supply pipes are leaking; or the garbage disposal is worn out.

Tighten all the slip nuts on the drainpipes under the sink (see Fig. 4-27). If this does not stop the leak, unscrew the cleanout plug on the trap and give it another coat of joint compound. It comes in a thick paste that you brush onto the threads or in stick pencil form. Coat the threads and tighten the plug. Traps tend to corrode over time, which is why they leak. It is likely that the trap will crumble in your hands while you are replacing the plug. Do not panic. Take the parts to a hardware or plumbing-supply store and purchase a replacement trap and washers. Your old slip nuts will probably still be good. Make sure there is a washer for each slip nut, as shown in Fig. 4-27. Slip the new trap over the tailpiece from the sink and the drainpipe protruding from the wall or floor and tighten the slip nuts.

If a wetness persists under the sink, the leak may be coming from the crack between the sink rim and countertop (Fig. 4-5). Loosen the hold-down clips by inserting a screwdriver into the end of the treaded screw. Apply plumber's putty to the underside of the rim. You can move the sink an inch or two without breaking the supply pipes. Retighten the clips and remove the excess putty that squeezes out from under the rim.

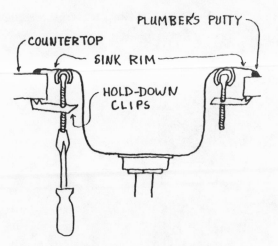

FIG. 4-5. LEAK UNDER SINK RIM

If water is getting under the faucet fixture, the two lock nuts that hold it to the countertop should be loosened, so that the fixture can be raised ¼ to ½ inch above the countertop. The supply pipes usually have this much play.

The method of holding a faucet fixture to a countertop is similar to that of holding a toilet valve stem to the tank (see Fig. 4-33). Two lock nuts screw on to the shank base of both the hot and cold faucets and hold the fixture to the countertop. These lock nuts must be loosened from underneath, using a basin wrench. Fig. 4-18 shows a basin wrench being used to loosen the coupling nut that holds the supply tube on to the shank base of the faucet fixture. The lock nut is located above the coupling nut, snug tight against the underside of the countertop. After the two lock nuts have been loosened and the fixture raised above the countertop, apply a ¼-inch-diameter snake of plumber's putty around the base of the faucet and retighten the lock nuts.

Faucets

Water in the supply pipes is under pressure and only the faucets prevent it from gushing out. A faucet enables you to control when the water flows. Fig. 4-6 shows the parts of a faucet. The cold-water handle is in the off position. When the handle is turned clockwise to shut off the flow, the stem is screwed down through the stem threads until the washer is tight against the faucet seat. The seal between the washer and the faucet seat prevents cold water from coming out. When the handle is turned counterclockwise, as the HOT handle has been in the illustration, the stem is unscrewed, thereby raising the washer off the faucet seat. Hot water can flow out of the spout. The packing, which is a rubber fitting around the stem, prevents the hot water from seeping up through the threads and out around the packing nut.

TROUBLESHOOTING FAUCET PROBLEMS

Always begin by checking the easy problems first. If the water flow is limited, unscrew the screen and aerator from the faucet spout and check for debris. Usually there is an accumulation of small rocks that is stopping the water flow.

A dripping faucet is caused by a bad washer or an uneven faucet seat. Try replacing the washer first, because it's easier. Before you start, turn off the water to the supply tube under whichever handle you are removing. If the faucet set has hot and cold running out of one spout, try to feel the temperature of the drips. It's a good bet that they will be coming from the hot-water side, because the heat to which the washer is subjected hastens its deterioration.

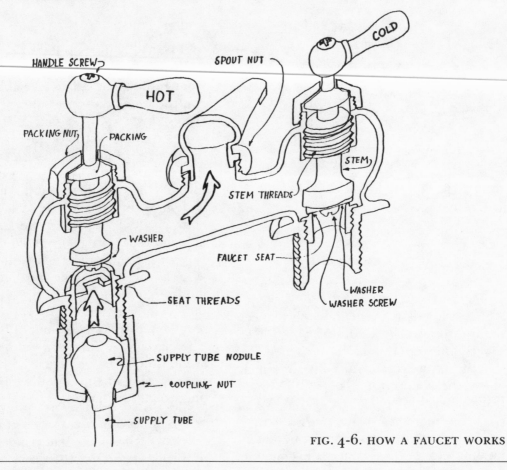

HANDLE SCREW
SPOUT NUT
COLD
HOT
PACKING NUT
PACKING
STEM
STEM THREADS
WASHER
FAUCET SEAT
SEAT THREADS
WASHER
WASHER SCREW
SUPPLY TUBE NODULE
COUPLING NUT
SUPPLY TUBE

FIG. 4-6. HOW A FAUCET WORKS

Unscrew the handle screw (Fig. 4-7). If there doesn't appear to be a screw on the top of the handle, don't panic. It's hidden under the plastic button that says HOT or COLD. Work the blade of a thin knife under the edge of the plastic button and pop it off. It's held on by friction; you don't have to unscrew it. Some old faucets have a porcelain button embossed with an H or a C in the middle of the handle. The button can be unscrewed. Anything that unscrews usually has some type of grip. It is usually a knurled metal band under the porcelain button.

Pull the handle straight up and off. If the faucet is old and corroded, you may need a handle puller. These can be purchased at any hardware store. With the handle removed, the lock nut becomes visible (Fig. 4-8). In modern faucet sets this holds the stem in place. In older models like the one in Fig. 4-6, the packing nut holds the stem in place. Whichever kind you have, unscrew it. A crescent wrench can be used on the lock nut, but you may need a monkey wrench for the packing nut, since they tend to be larger. In either case, use a wrench with no teeth or pad the teeth of a plumbing wrench with tape or cloth, if this is the only tool available.

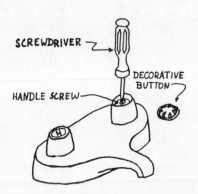

FIG. 4-7. DISASSEMBLING A FAUCET

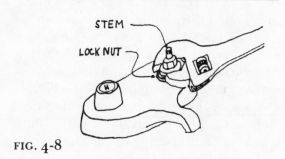

FIG. 4-8

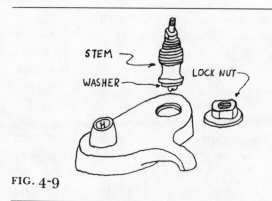

FIG. 4-9

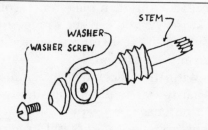

FIG. 4-10

Now the stem can be removed (Fig. 4-9). Slip the handle on again, just to make it easier to unscrew the stem. Turn the handle as if you were turning the water on and the stem will come out. Once the stem is out, inspect the washer. It will probably have grooves worn in it. Unscrew the screw in the center of the washer and remove it (Fig. 4-10). Replace it with one of the same diameter. If you have a package of assorted washers handy, the replacement will most likely be found there. If not, take the old washer to the hardware store and buy one like it. Also buy a package of assorted washers to keep in your toolbox for future leaks.

Carefully retrace your steps. First screw the stem back in. Next replace the lock or packing nut. Finally replace the handle. Before you screw the handle on, turn on the water to see if replacing the washer has stopped the drip. If it did, that was the problem. If it didn't, then either the other washer needs replacing or, more likely, the faucet seat of the faucet you've been working on should be replaced.

Many newer faucets have cartridges instead of traditional stems and washers (Fig. 4-11). Follow steps for the removal of the handle and lock nut washer (see Figs. 4-7–4-10). If you see a stop sticking up, the faucet is most likely of the cartridge type. Pull up on the cartridge. There is usually an O-ring in contact with the sides of the sleeve surrounding the cartridge, so firm pressure may be necessary. Sometimes there is a clip where the slots for the keys are. The keys are small bumps on the cartridge that must be fit into slots on the sleeve. This maintains

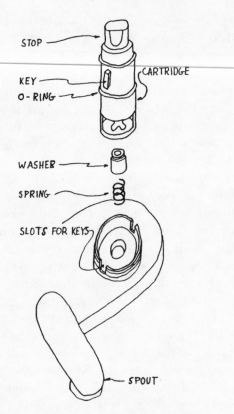

FIG. 4-11. REPLACING A CARTRIDGE

correct orientation of the cartridge during replacement. The clip must be slid off horizontally before the cartridge can be removed.

Unfortunately, there are several different types of cartridges. They vary depending upon the manufacturer. Inspect the removed cartridge. There may be a rubber diaphragm over the bottom that can be replaced. If not, look down into the sleeve from which the cartridge was removed. There may be a washer and spring hiding there. If so, fish them out with a small screwdriver. Replacements for either the washer and spring or the diaphragm can be purchased at any hard-

ware store. A replacement cartridge can also be purchased, and if replacing the worn parts doesn't stop the drip, the whole cartridge should be replaced. Take the cartridge along to the store to help identify which replacement kit is appropriate. If you know the manufacturer, tell the hardware-store clerk. Sometimes the manufacturer is noted on the HOT and COLD buttons.

Many cartridges have O-rings around the cylinder. They operate like packing (see Fig. 4-11) to keep water from leaking out around the handle. To remove an O-ring, squeeze it between your thumb and forefinger until a gap between the O-ring and the cartridge appears. This will allow you to grasp the ring and pull it off. New O-rings can be purchased at the hardware store also. Replace all these parts while you have the cartridge out in the open.

To replace a faucet seat, proceed through the steps of removing the stem (see Figs. 4-7–4-10). When the stem is out, insert your finger into the hole left by the stem and feel the rim of the faucet seat. You are looking for any burrs or depressions. If you find signs of this, remove the seat. This requires a special tool: the seat wrench (Fig. 4-12). It can be purchased at hardware stores or rented. Insert the end of the seat wrench into the hole in the faucet seat and turn the wrench counterclockwise. As you can see in Fig. 4-6, the outside of the seat is threaded and therefore can be unscrewed.

With the faucet seat in hand, go to the hardware or plumbing-supply store and purchase a replacement. Don't bother going to a wholesale plumbing-supply store because they will sell only to plumbers, no matter how much charm you can muster. Many hardware stores sell a tool called a seat dresser. It is basically a conical file attached to a 5-inch handle. Don't buy this. It is supposed to file down the irregularities on the seat, but it must be held absolutely vertical while being used, and this is almost impossible to do. You may smooth down the seat, but if it's lower in one place than in another, the faucet will still leak.

To reassemble the faucet, once again retrace your steps. The seat can be tricky to insert because it's hard to work down in the hole. Try putting some heavy grease or other sticky material like Crisco or toothpaste on the tip of the seat wrench to hold the seat on as you lower it into the hole. After all the parts are in place, turn

the water on again. There should be no drip.

When water appears to be leaking out around the base of the faucet or dribbling down from the packing nut, the cause is faulty packing. The leak happens when the faucet is on because there is water under pressure escaping around the stem. Usually the packing or packing washer stops the water from leaking out. If there is a leak, the packing must be old or faulty. For this repair it's not necessary to turn off the water below the faucet, but it's a good habit to get into. Either way, at least make sure that the faucet handle is in the off position.

Remove the handle as in Fig. 4-7 and remove the lock or packing nut as in Fig. 4-8. Remove the old packing and go to the hardware store to purchase a replacement. Packing comes in two forms: a conically shaped graphite washer, as in Fig. 4-13, or the self-forming graphite-im-

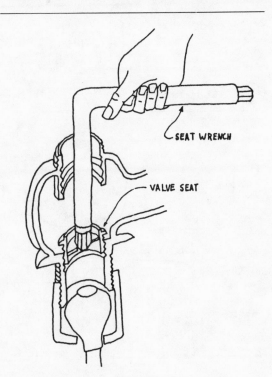

FIG. 4-12. REMOVING A VALVE SEAT

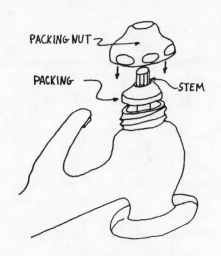

FIG. 4-13. FIXING A STEM LEAK—
REPLACING PACKING

pregnated ⅛-inch-diameter string, which is available in small packages at all hardware stores. Teflon string is also now available. The self-forming type can be used if you cannot find a packing washer to fit.

Slip the packing washer over the stem and retighten the packing nut. If you are using the graphite or Teflon string, wrap it around the stem until you have made a conical shape that is one-quarter larger in diameter than the inside dimension of the packing nut. When the packing nut is screwed on, it will compress the excess and squeeze tightly around the stem, thus stopping the leak. Tighten the packing nut firmly, but don't overtighten.

Installing a Shutoff Valve

If you have ever run down to the basement to turn off the water, you will understand the convenience of shutoff valves under each fixture. Installing them involves soldering copper pipe, but soldering isn't as difficult as it is reputed to be. This is the Tinkertoy part of plumbing.

Fig. 4-15 shows what happens to the supply pipe when it comes up through the floor of the sink cabinet. It goes straight up to the faucet. Usually the pipe comes into the sink cabinet as ½-inch-diameter pipe and then is reduced to ⅜-inch diameter in the final approach to the faucet. This ⅜-inch pipe is called a supply tube and comes in different lengths, depending on the need. Supply tubes are chrome-plated copper, so that they look good under your sink if there isn't a cabinet below to hide them, and are made of a soft copper alloy, so that they can be easily bent in case the faucets are not di-

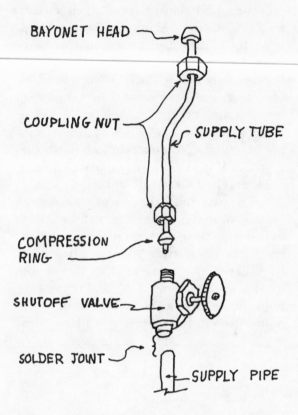

FIG. 4-14. INSTALLING A SHUTOFF VALVE

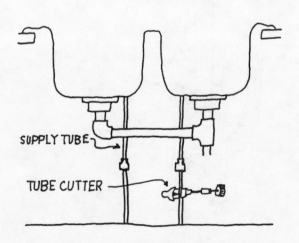

FIG. 4-15. CUTTING A PIPE

rectly above the spot where the ½-inch supply pipe comes through the wall or floor. Fig. 4-14 shows how the supply tube and shutoff valve connect with the ½-inch pipe from the basement. The shutoff valve pictured in the illustration has a solder fitting suitable for copper pipe. There are also threaded shutoff valves, which screw onto threaded galvanized pipes or onto a threaded adaptor of a plastic supply pipe.

TOOLS

Before beginning, assemble all the tools you will need: a propane torch, a roll of 50/50 solder (half tin, half lead), a can of flux, a flux brush, a fitting brush, a piece of emery cloth or a Scotch Brite pad, matches or a flint starter, a pipe cutter, and a heat shield, such as an old license plate or other piece of sheet metal for the torch, so that you don't burn down the house. All these tools are pictured in Figs. 4-16–4-20.

Other materials you will need include a ½-inch shutoff valve and a ⅜-inch supply tube appropriate for whatever fixture you're going to work on. The hardware store can help you with this; they have shorter ones for toilets and longer ones for under sinks.

CUTTING THE PIPE

The first thing you must do is turn off the water. You may not have to shut off the water to the whole house if you can find a shutoff valve on the supply pipe that leads to the part of the house in which you are working. Also remember that if you are going to cut into the hot-water pipe first, you must be careful to shut off that pipe and not the cold. The consequences of a mistake like this are worth a double check.

With the water shut off, take a deep breath and cut the ½-inch supply pipe (Fig. 4-15). Make a cut 2 to 3 inches above the floor of the cabinet. This will be the bottom of the shutoff valve. Open the jaws of the pipe cutter by turning the adjustment knob counterclockwise (Fig. 4-16). When the jaws have been opened enough to admit the copper pipe, tighten the adjustment knob until the pipe is touched in three places by the jaws: two rollers and the cutter wheel. Make the rollers snug up against the pipe so that the cutter is tight. Now rotate the pipe cutter around the pipe. The cutting wheel should put a score line around the pipe. Turn the adjustment knob one-quarter turn tighter and rotate the pipe cutter twice. Repeat this until the pipe is cut clear through. Turn the adjustment knob only one-quarter turn at a time.

Often the pipe is too close to the wall to allow a standard-size pipe cutter to ro-

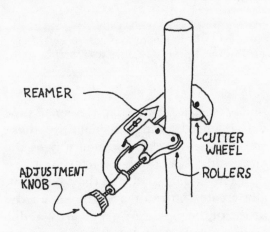

FIG. 4-16. A PIPE CUTTER

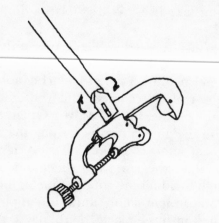

FIG. 4-17. REAMING A PIPE

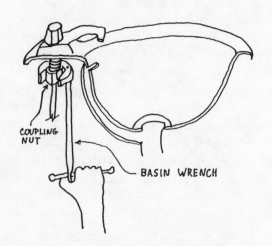

FIG. 4-18. USING A BASIN WRENCH

(Fig. 4-17). Push the reamer out into its working position and insert it in the pipe. A couple of rotations will peel off the lip and any burrs.

The pipe above the cut can now be removed. The coupling nut up under the faucet is the only thing holding it. This is a very difficult place to get into with a wrench or Channellocks. The right tool for the job is the basin wrench (Fig. 4-18). Get yourself comfortable under the sink. A light is very helpful if you are working inside a cabinet. Hook the basin wrench around the coupling nut. It is similar to a ratchet wrench in that it can turn a nut only one way. To turn the nut the other way, merely flip the spring-loaded jaws over to the other side of the vertical handle. From your viewpoint under the sink the jaws should be on the right side of the vertical handle, in order to tighten the nut, and on the left side in order to loosen.

SOLDERING

The next step is to solder the shutoff valve onto the ½-inch pipe that is sticking up from the floor of the cabinet. It is essential that no water be in the pipe near where you are soldering. The heated water will sizzle and spit, blowing small holes in the solder. This will cause the joint to leak. If water continues to run through the pipe, no matter how little, it must be diverted. An old plumber's trick is to wad up a piece of white bread and insert it into the pipe above the fitting you will be soldering. The bread will absorb the water flow. It will slowly dissolve and later can be washed out of the pipe.

First, take a look at the shutoff valve. There are two coupling ends protruding

tate around the entire pipe. A small pipe cutter, called an imp, is made for these situations. It works the same way as the larger one, but is only 2 inches long.

The cutting action of the wheel usually creates burrs or a slight lip on the inside of the pipe. Any irregularity of this kind can constrict water flow, so it is important to ream the pipe after you cut it from it. One is smaller than the other in diameter and is threaded with a small coupling nut screwed onto the threads. If you unscrew the coupling nut, a brass compression ring should fall out. These pieces fit together as shown in Fig. 4-14. This arrangement is a way of connecting a pipe and a fitting (the shutoff valve) and is called a compression fitting. The smaller coupling nut and brass compression ring (also called a ferrule) is slipped onto the supply tube. As the nut is screwed onto the threaded male end of the shutoff valve, the soft brass of the compression ring is pressed against the supply tube, thereby preventing any leaks.

The other protrusion is larger and has no threads. This is the female fitting that will go over the ½-inch pipe from the basement. The ½-inch pipe fits inside the shutoff valve. The joint will be held together by solder. It is called a sweated or soldered joint.

The type of shutoff pictured in Fig. 4-14 is the straight-line type. This is the right shutoff valve to buy if the ½-inch copper supply pipe is coming up through the floor. In some cases the supply pipe comes through the wall. For this situation you should buy a right-angle shutoff valve, where the compression-fitting end and the end to be soldered are at right angles to each other (see Fig. 4-21).

Soldering is really very simple. There are three steps: (1) Clean the pipe; (2) Apply flux to the pipe; and (3) Heat the pipe so that the solder melts into the joint.

Begin by cleaning both parts of the joint you are going to solder (Fig. 4-19). The right tools for this job are a ½-inch fitting brush and a piece of emery cloth or

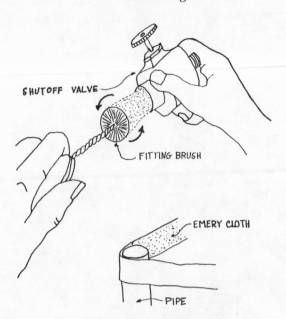

FIG. 4-19. BURNISHING THE FITTING AND PIPE

a Scotch Brite pad. Insert the fitting brush inside the female end of the shutoff valve and rotate it a couple of times. This cleans off all dirt and oxidation. Use the emery cloth to shine up the outside of the pipe. You need to clean only the very end of the pipe—¾ inch in—because the female end of the shutoff valve will fit over only ½ inch of the pipe's length.

The next step is to flux the pipe and fitting. Dip the flux brush into the flux and brush a thin, even coat around the end of the pipe and around the inside of the female end of the shutoff (Fig. 4-20). The flux functions to draw the solder into the joint. Slip the shutoff valve over the copper pipe.

Before you begin, place the old license plate or other sheet of metal between the wall and the joint to be sol-

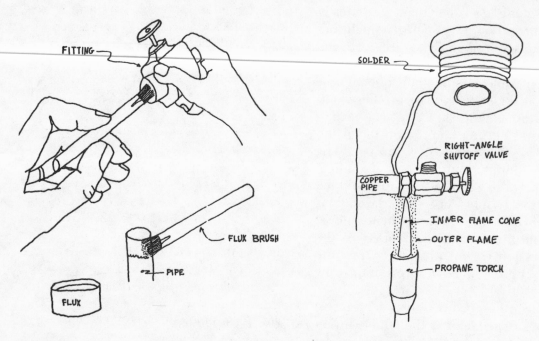

FIG. 4-20. APPLYING FLUX TO THE FITTING
AND PIPE

FIG. 4-21. SOLDERING A JOINT

dered. This is to protect it against fire. Also, unroll about 6 inches of solder and put a right-angle bend ½ inch in from the end. This is approximately how much solder it will take to sweat (solder) the joint.

When soldering shutoff valves, it is important to remove the valve stem, or at least turn the handle to the open position so that the plastic washer doesn't melt from the heat of the flame. The stem is removed by unscrewing the packing nut as shown in Fig. 4-13.

Now it's time to light the propane torch. Turn the knob counterclockwise a little, until you hear the gas hissing out. Hold the spark lighter right at the end of the nozzle and make a spark. The gas should ignite and form a flame. If the

flame lights for an instant, but pops and goes out, the gas is on too high. Turn it down a little. A torch can be lit with matches, but it's difficult and dangerous. The gas keeps blowing the match out. It is better to spend three dollars on a spark lighter.

Adjust the flame until the inner blue cone is 1 inch to 1½ inches long. The highest temperatures are produced at the tip of this blue inner cone. Train the tip of the blue cone on the fitting, the part of the shutoff valve that covers the supply pipe (Fig. 4-21). The idea is to heat up the female end of the shutoff valve until it's hot enough to melt the solder. You don't have to aim the flame at the pipe or melt the solder with the flame and let it drip onto the fitting. With the torch held in your weak hand and the roll of solder held in your strong hand, continue to train the tip of the blue cone onto the fitting.

Soon the flux will begin to melt and bubble. You can test to see if the fitting is hot enough by touching the solder to the joint between pipe and fitting every 5 seconds or so. When the solder sticks a little to the pipe, the fitting is almost hot enough. Wait a few more seconds and try again. The fitting is hot enough when the solder melts and is drawn into the joint. At this point, move the torch a few inches down the pipe away from the joint, as you allow ½ inch of solder to melt into the joint. Turn the torch off and you're done. It's important to not get so involved in the soldering that you forget where the flame is pointed. This is easy to do. Keep it trained on the pipe until the joint has been soldered.

The joint now should be leak-free. If, when you turn the water back on, you notice drops of water that you are sure are emanating from this joint, brush some flux around the joint between the pipe and fitting and melt a little more solder around the joint (remember, the water must be off for soldering and the pipe drained). If this doesn't do it, reheat the fitting until the solder melts and take it apart with Channellocks. Have a bucket of water handy in which to dunk the hot pieces. Begin the whole process again.

Clogs in the Drainage System

UNCLOGGING A DRAIN

There are many ways to unclog a drain, but always try the easiest methods first.

The plunger is the cheapest, easiest way to unclog a drain. It is easy to see why it is called the plumber's friend.

If there isn't water already in the sink, fill the sink with 2 inches of water (Fig. 4-22). Plug up the overflow drain hole near the rim by covering it with a wet cloth. Slide the plunger into the water at an angle, to ensure that water and not air is trapped in the bell. Position it over the drain and work the plunger up and down quickly ten to twelve times. If you are having a hard time maintaining suction between the plunger and sink bottom, coat the plunger rim with some petroleum jelly. The force created by the suction should loosen the clog so that the sink will drain. If the plunger partially loosens the clog, hot water may do the rest. Chemical uncloggers may also loosen the remaining clog, but don't use them if you have cast iron or steel pipes in the basement.

If a plunger doesn't free up the drain, disassembling the trap may work. Often

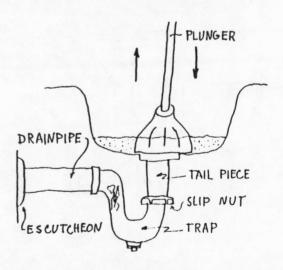

FIG. 4-22. UNCLOGGING WITH A PLUNGER

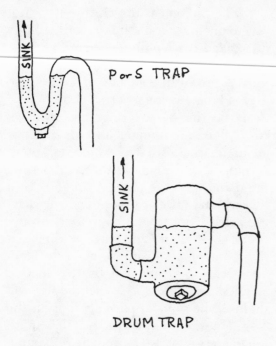

FIG. 4-23. TWO TYPES OF TRAPS

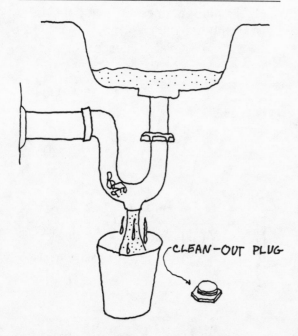

FIG. 4-24. REMOVING THE CLEAN-OUT

the clog will be in or near the trap. The trap is an intentional cul-de-sac built into the drain to prevent sewer gases from coming up through the drain and escaping into your house. Fig. 4-23 shows two types of traps: the P or S trap and the drum trap. It's the water that stands in the traps that prevents gases from backing up into the house. Most traps also have a clean-out plug that unscrews to allow access to the diamond ring that has been dropped down the drain and is causing debris to form a clog around it.

Place a bucket under the trap and loosen the plug (Fig. 4-24). A crescent wrench, Channellocks, monkey or pipe wrench will do the job. Once the water has drained out, probe around in the drain with a piece of wire, like a coat hanger, and try to fish out the clog. This can be pretty messy, so you may want to wear rubber gloves.

If the above methods don't unclog the drain, then the problem is between the trap and the place where the sewer pipe goes through the basement wall. A snake is the right tool for the job. They can be rented or purchased for under fifteen dollars (Fig. 4-3). There are also less expensive models like the one shown in Fig. 4-25, but the advantage of the ones with a container is that the dirty snake wire stays confined in one place.

Insert the snake into the trap cleanout and push it as far as it will go. To make the head of the snake rotate, tighten the set screw and turn the handle. The turning not only helps dislodge the clog but also aids the snake's progress around bends in the drain. If the snake encounters a blockage, push the snake in hard while turning the handle. Sometimes the snake will be stopped by a curve that it just can't weave through. In that case, pull it out slowly.

Reinsert the trap plug and see if the sink drains. If not, go down in the basement to the place where the snake was stopped and look for a nearby clean-out in the same drain line (Fig. 4-26). The modern plumbing code requires a clean-out for each horizontal run of drainpipe. Some older houses don't have this. Once a clean-out is found and the plug unscrewed, the snake can be inserted as before.

Chemical drain cleaners shouldn't be used on drainage systems that contain cast iron or steel pipes, because they can eat through the pipes. They are also not recommended for septic systems because they can upset the bacterial balance. Otherwise, they are convenient for small clogs that are near the drain.

Aerosol cans that contain air under pressure are available. Basically, they blow out the clog. This method is not recommended for drainage systems that contain plastic, cast iron, or tile pipes. The pressure can loosen the joints between pipes and create even more trouble.

TRAPS, TAILPIECES, AND SINK BASKETS

Often there is a slow, quiet leak in the pipes under the kitchen sink that goes undetected until you go looking for a new sponge at the back of the sink cabinet. These leaks are hard to pinpoint. Try running water in the sink and watch to see if droplets appear at any of the joints in the drainpipe under the sink. Fig. 4-27 shows the parts of a typical sink drain. The tail-

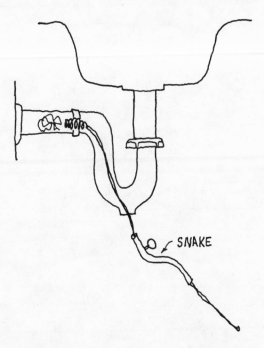

FIG. 4-25. UNCLOGGING WITH A SNAKE

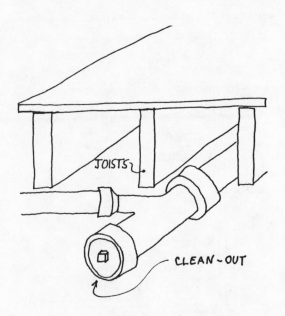

FIG. 4-26. CLEAN-OUT IN A BASEMENT PIPE RUN

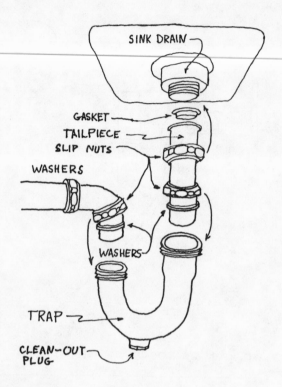

FIG. 4-27. PARTS OF A DRAIN

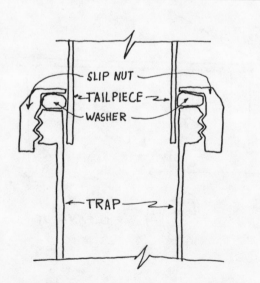

FIG. 4-28. HOW A SLIP NUT WORKS

piece is the straight piece of pipe that extends from the sink drain. The trap is attached to that. Slip nuts or coupling nuts hold the pieces together via a type of compression joint (Fig. 4-28).

A compression joint works like this. A slip nut and washer (in that order) are slipped onto the bottom end of the tailpiece. The bottom end of the tailpiece is inserted into the larger-diameter trap pipe, which has threads around its upper end. The slip nut screws onto these threads, and as it is tightened the washer is compressed against the tailpiece and against the top of the trap to prevent any leaks.

Before trying anything else, tighten all the slip nuts. This may squeeze the washers tighter against the pipes and stop the leak. Next check the trap plug and make sure water isn't leaking around it. If water is leaking, unscrew the plug, apply some pipe dope, and retighten it. If a leak persists, disassemble the parts as shown in Fig. 4-27 and replace the washers. Bring them down to the hardware store to be sure you get the right replacement ones.

ADJUSTING A LAVATORY POP-UP PLUG

Many a lavatory pop-up plug does not seal the drain well enough to keep water in the sink. Usually a small adjustment is necessary. Fig. 4-29 shows the mechanism and how the parts fit together. When you pull up the knob behind the faucet, a flat perforated metal strip called the clevis is also pulled upward. A pivot rod extends through a hole in the clevis and is moved upward as well. The rod also extends through the compression nut and into the drain tee, where it fits

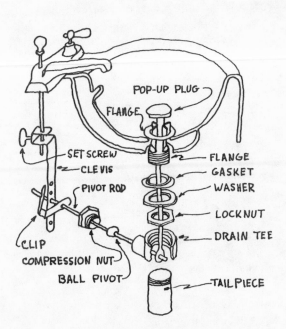

FIG. 4-29. HOW A LAVATORY POP-UP
DRAIN PLUG WORKS

the set screw. This exerts the maximum
force on the pop-up plug, helping it make
a tighter seal.

Toilets

EMERGENCIES

Probably the most common plumbing emergency is the toilet that is clogged and threatening to overflow. You can usually prevent it from overflowing by acting quickly. Remove the tank lid, reach inside the tank, and manually push the tank ball down until it seals against the valve seat at the bottom of the tank (Fig. 4-30). This will stop the flow of water into the bowl. Now there is time to get the plunger and unclog the toilet, as pictured in Fig. 4-31.

HOW A TOILET WORKS

The working parts of a toilet are in the tank. The tank fills up with water that comes through a supply tube under the toilet. It enters the tank through the inlet pipe and flows through the ball-cock assembly and into the tank via the filler pipe (see Fig. 4-30). Sometimes the filler pipe is a larger pipe around the inlet pipe and not a separate pipe. If you hold your fingers down near the bottom of the filler pipe while the tank is filling with water, you can feel it rush in. As the water level rises in the tank, the float ball rises with it. The float ball is attached by a rod to the ball-cock assembly, which is basically a shutoff valve operated by the float ball.

When someone turns the handle on the tank to flush the toilet, the trip lever moves upward, which lifts the tank ball. This sends all the water in the tank into the bowl via the ports around the rim and

through a hole at the bottom of the pop-up plug of the sink drain. True to its name, the pivot rod pivots around a fulcrum that is located at the compression nut to the drain tee. This means that when you pull up the knob to close the drain, the end of the pivot rod is pulled up. At the same time, the other end of the pivot rod that is attached to the pop-up plug is pulled down—and the pop-up plug with it. Thus, the seal is made.

To make a better seal between the pop-up plug and the chrome flange at the bottom of your sink, it is necessary to loosen the set screw that holds the clevis to the knob rod. Push the knob down until it is against the faucet fixture. Pull the clevis down as far as it will go and tighten

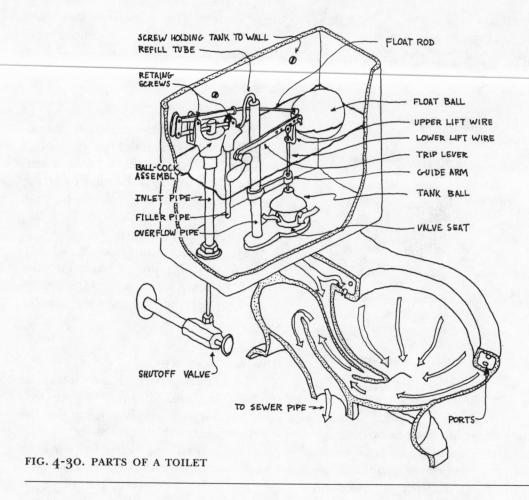

SCREW HOLDING TANK TO WALL
REFILL TUBE
RETAING SCREWS
FLOAT ROD
FLOAT BALL
UPPER LIFT WIRE
LOWER LIFT WIRE
TRIP LEVER
GUIDE ARM
TANK BALL
BALL-COCK ASSEMBLY
INLET PIPE
FILLER PIPE
OVERFLOW PIPE
VALVE SEAT
SHUTOFF VALVE
TO SEWER PIPE
PORTS

FIG. 4-30. PARTS OF A TOILET

pushes the contents of the bowl down the drain to the sewer pipe.

TOILET PROBLEMS

When the toilet runs continuously, the tank ball is not sealed against the valve. This allows water to constantly flow from the tank into the bowl and, therefore, keeps the float from rising high enough to turn off the inflow of water. Don't be confused by the terms tank ball and float ball. The tank ball is the ball at the bottom of the tank that is raised when the handle is pushed to flush the toilet. When it is raised, all the water in the tank flows into the bowl. The float ball floats on top of the water.

Flush the toilet while looking into the tank. Observe the lift wires and guide arm. If the tank ball doesn't drop freely back down or if it drops down and doesn't settle snuggly in the valve seat, the problem is in the guide arm and lift wires. Move the guide arm, which is held by screws, so that it is over the center of the valve seat. This should make the tank ball

seat better. Many times the lift wires are
bent and don't allow the tank ball to fall
unimpeded. If they are bent, they should
be replaced. New lift wires can be purchased at all hardware stores.

If the tank ball falls unimpeded, the
problem is in the ball itself or the valve
seat. Tank balls can get old and lose their
elasticity, which often causes a leak. Turn
off the water and flush the toilet. The tank
will not refill until the water is turned on
again. Remove the old tank ball. To do
this, reach your hand down into the tank
and unscrew the ball from the lower lift
wire. Take the old ball down to the hardware store and buy a new one.

If the toilet still runs, mineral deposits may have built up on the valve seat that
are preventing a good seal. Turn off the
water and flush the toilet. Sand around
the opening with a piece of emery cloth.

A high-pitched noise indicates that water
is continuously going through the ball-
cock assembly, which means that the float
ball is not turning off the water. Most
likely the problem is in the float ball itself.
It is not rising high enough to close the
ball-cock assembly. Check the water level
in the tank. It should be 1 to 2 inches
below the top of the overflow tube. If the
water level is higher, bend the float rod
down. This may stop the whistling. If the
float ball is made of hollow metal, check
to see if water has seeped into it. If so,
replace the ball. The metal kind will unscrew from the float rod.

If the toilet continues to whistle, the
problem is probably in the ball-cock assembly (Fig. 4-32). First try replacing the
washer as you would in any faucet that is
dripping. Turn off the water and flush the

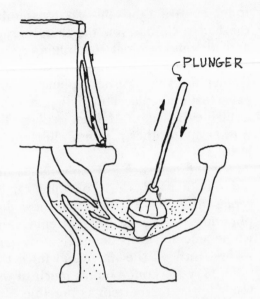

FIG. 4-31. UNCLOGGING A TOILET

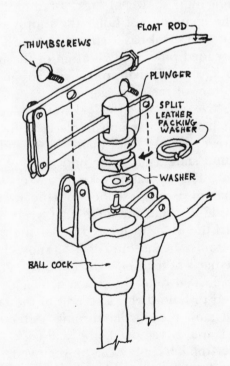

FIG. 4-32. REPLACING A WASHER IN A
TOILET BALL-COCK VALVE

toilet, emptying the tank. To disassemble the ball cock, unscrew the thumbscrews and lift out the float rod, plunger, and attached parts. The rubber washer, split leather packing washer, plunger, and valve seat are replaceable. They are often available in a kit. At least replace the washer and leather packing, while you're at it.

If the ball-cock assembly seems too old to bother with, the whole thing can be replaced. Fig. 4-33 shows the new diaphragm models available. To replace the whole assembly, it is definitely necessary to first turn off the water and flush the toilet. Try to sponge out as much of the water left at the bottom as possible. Remove the supply tube from the tank by loosening with a crescent wrench the coupling nut, shown in Figs. 4-6 and 4-18. The coupling nut holds the supply tube onto the shank base. The shank base is the threaded pipe at the bottom of the ball-cock assembly that protrudes through the bottom of the tank.

Next, remove the lock nut that holds the ball-cock assembly in place. It, too, is threaded onto the shank base and is found snug against the underside of the tank. This operation takes two wrenches: a pair of vise grips to lock onto the hex nut inside the tank and a crescent wrench to turn the lock nut located under the tank bottom. The inset in Fig. 4-33 shows how the parts fit together. Once the vise grips are locked onto the hex nut, you don't need to hold them. The wall of the tank will stop them from turning. After the lock nut is removed, the ball-cock and filler-tube assembly can be removed.

The new assembly is installed in the opposite order. Slip the inlet pipe gasket

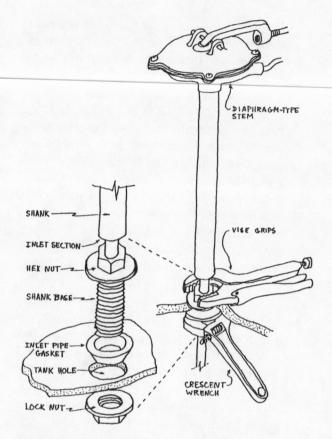

FIG. 4-33. REPLACING THE ENTIRE STEM

over the shank base and fit it through the hole in the bottom of the tank. Tighten the lock nut until the inlet pipe gasket is firmly pushed into the hole. Reattach the supply tube to the part of the shank base that extends down beyond the lock nut. Insert the nodule of the supply tube into the bottom of the shank base and tighten the coupling nut with a crescent wrench.

Replacing a Shower Head

A good way to save energy is to install a flow-restricting shower head. It reduces the amount of hot water used in a shower and can cut a hot-water bill in half.

Removing the old shower head calls for a monkey or crescent wrench (Fig. 4-34). If a pair of Channellocks or a pipe wrench is all you have, it is crucial to cover the teeth with tape before gripping the shower head. If you don't, the teeth will scratch the chrome. Turn the wrench counterclockwise to remove the head. Take the old shower head with you when you go to the hardware store to buy the flow-restricting shower head. Some shower heads have male threads and some have female threads. If the shower head you want does not match the old one in size or gender, the appropriate adaptors can be purchased right then. This will save you a trip later.

Coat the threads of the shower arm with pipe dope before installing the new shower head. Screw it on with a wrench.

If your shower arm is flared at the end and the shower head is attached by a nut, the whole assembly is one unit and must all be replaced in order to install a new head. The arm is screwed into a fitting in the wall. Unscrew the arm and take the whole assembly to the hardware store. Installing the new arm can be tricky if you can't see the fitting in the wall. Coat the threads with pipe dope and screw the arm into the fitting in the wall.

Hot-Water Tanks and Heaters

There are two kinds of hot-water tanks: those that heat the water electrically and those that heat it by gas. The electric ones come equipped with a thermostat that allows you to control the temperature of the hot water. This is very important for some disabled people, who can't feel the temperature of the water. Gas heaters allow you only to control how much hot water stays heated in the tank. If you or someone in your family is not able to feel the temperature of the water, it may be necessary to replace the gas hot-water heater with an electric one or to have a plumber install a thermostat on your gas hot-water heater.

LIGHTING THE PILOT LIGHT

It used to make me nervous to relight the pilot light on the furnace or hot-water heater. This was because I could never figure out which thing was the thermocouple. The thermocouple figures heavily in the directions pasted to the outside of every hot-water heater. They say that you are supposed to hold the match in front of the pilot gas nozzle, which is adjacent to the thermocouple (Fig. 4-35). In fact, the thermocouple is a wire with a thick-

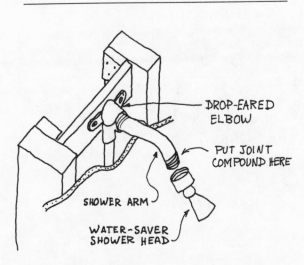

DROP-EARED ELBOW

PUT JOINT COMPOUND HERE

SHOWER ARM

WATER-SAVER SHOWER HEAD

FIG. 4-34. CHANGING A SHOWER HEAD

ened part that is touched by the pilot-light gas flame. It is located about ½ inch away from the pilot gas nozzle, which is a small ⅛-inch-diameter pipe.

First, locate the knob that has three settings: ON, OFF, and PILOT. The directions say to turn this knob to the OFF position and wait five minutes before lighting the pilot. This instruction created another area of confusion. I didn't understand how I could light the pilot light if the gas was off. After you wait the required five minutes and depress the reset button, you are sending a tiny amount of gas through the pilot-light nozzle. If, indeed, you hold the match between the pilot gas nozzle and the thermocouple, a flame will appear at the end of the ⅛-inch-diameter tube. That flame will heat up the thermocouple. After keeping the reset button depressed for one minute, the gas knob can be turned all the way to ON.

The thermocouple is a safety device. As it warms, it converts heat to electricity, which operates the solenoid valve. When this valve is open, gas is allowed to flow into the burner. The valve is open only when the thermocouple is hot. If the pilot blows out and the thermocouple cools, the solenoid valve closes off the gas to the burner. This prevents uncombusted gas from leaking into the house.

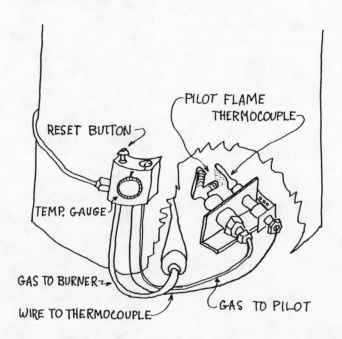

FIG. 4-35. HOW TO LIGHT A PILOT LIGHT

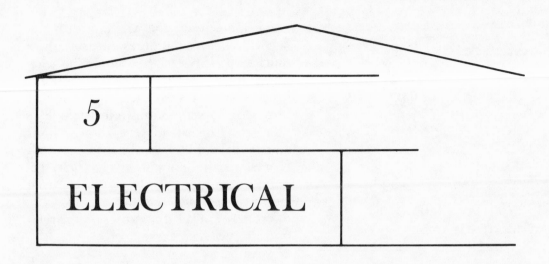

5

ELECTRICAL

A lot of people are leery of electrical repairs because they are afraid of getting a shock. However, if you always do your tinkering with the power off, then you are safe.

Perhaps you have had the unfortunate experience of thinking the current was off when it wasn't. If you had had a magic device called a voltage tester, there would have been no doubt (Fig. 5-11). For a mere $1.50 this little gem can be yours, and you will never be shocked again.

A Little About Electricity

There are three terms that are bandied about when people speak of electricity: ampere, volt, and watt. It's always been hard for me to remember which is which, so I use an analogy: Electricity flowing through a wire is similar to water flowing through a hose (Fig. 5-1). Let's say that the water hose has been rigged up so that the water that comes out turns a water wheel. When the faucet is barely open, a little water dribbles through the hose and turns the water wheel slowly. When the faucet is fully open, a lot of water rushes through the hose and turns the wheel faster. The more the faucet is opened, the greater the water pressure in the hose and the greater the flow.

It's the same with electricity. Greater pressure in the wires (volts) causes increased flow of electricity (amps) and results in more work done (watts). The amount of water flowing through the hose is analogous to the amount of electricity

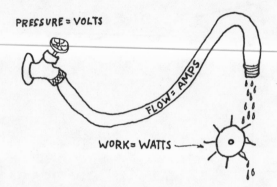

PRESSURE = VOLTS

FLOW = AMPS

WORK = WATTS

FIG. 5-1. ELECTRICAL TERMS

flowing through a wire. The ampere is the measurement of flow of electricity. It is often abbreviated amp. (Amps equal flow.)

When the water turns the wheel it is accomplishing work. We string wires throughout our houses so that the electricity flowing out the ends of the wires can do work. The amount of work electricity can do at any one moment is called a watt. (Watt equals work.)

To get the water to do more work for us and turn the wheel faster, we need to increase the pressure pushing the water through the pipe. This pressure is analogous to the voltage in a wire or circuit. A volt is the measurement of electric pressure or power. A flashlight battery is 1.5 volts and can barely create a shock. A car battery is 12 volts and can give a small shock. A 120-volt house circuit can give quite a jolt. (Volt equals pressure.)

There is one more related term: watt-hour. Remember, a watt is the amount of work that can be done at any one moment. The watt-hour is the measurement of work done over time. This is the measure-

ment of electricity that we're most familiar with because utilities measure how much electricity each household has used in watt-hours. Actually, because the watt-hour is such a small measurement, the term that appears on our electric bills is the kwh. This stands for kilowatt-hour and equals 1,000 watt-hours. A kwh represents the amount of electricity required to run an iron for an hour or an electric clock for a month.

There is a law that expresses the relationship between these terms:

$$\text{Amps} \times \text{Volts} = \text{Watts}$$
(rate of flow) (pressure) (work done)

The Electrical System

The electrical system of your house is like the nervous system in your body. The wires that run within the walls of a house are similar to the system of nerves that carry electrical impulses, which in turn activate our muscles to do work. One difference is that our bodies are complex biological machines that create their electricity via chemical reactions. Unless the house produces its own electricity with photoelectric cells or a windmill, the electricity for our houses is brought in via wires from the utility plant that produced it.

The electricity is carried to the house through two large power lines of 120 volts each. A third neutral line also comes into the house from the pole. All three then go to a panel box (not without first passing through the electric meter, of course), where the electricity is broken down into usable amounts and distributed throughout the house via circuits. A circuit is a wire pathway that brings electricity to lights, receptacles, and appliances (Fig.

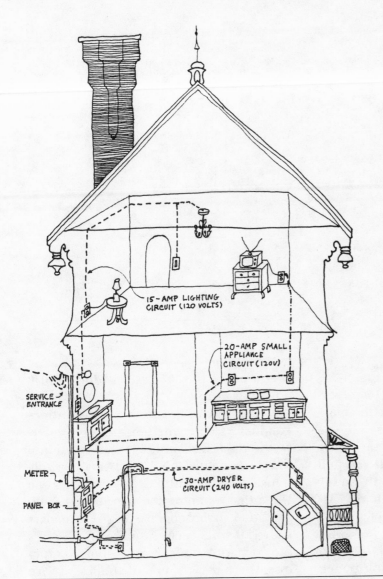

15-AMP LIGHTING
CIRCUIT (120 VOLTS)

20-AMP SMALL
APPLIANCE
CIRCUIT (120V)

SERVICE
ENTRANCE

METER

30-AMP DRYER
CIRCUIT (240 VOLTS)

PANEL BOX

FIG. 5-2. THE ELECTRICAL SYSTEM

5-2). There are many circuits in a house: several 15-amp lighting circuits that service the bedrooms and living areas; at least two 20-amp small-appliance circuits in the kitchen; and several single-appliance circuits that supply major appliances like the refrigerator, range, air conditioner, washer and dryer, dishwasher, fur-nace, water pump, water heater, and garbage disposal.

It is important to know where the panel box is in your house and to understand what is happening in it. There are two kinds of panel boxes: one with fuses (Fig. 5-3) and the more modern version with circuit breakers (Fig. 5-4).

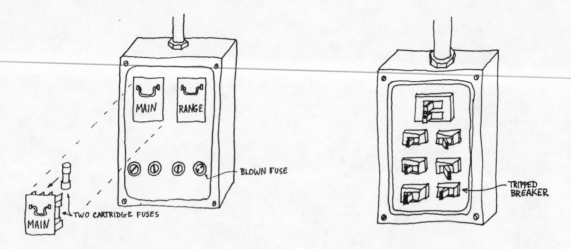

FIG. 5-3. PANEL BOX WITH BLOWN FUSE

FIG. 5-4. PANEL BOX WITH CIRCUIT BREAKERS

The panel box pictured in Fig. 5-3 is common in older houses with 60-amp services. The panel marked MAIN is the main disconnect for the whole house. If you pull it out, all power is cut off to the house —including the electric range. If you pull out the panel marked RANGE, only power to the electric stove will be cut off. Attached by clips to the MAIN panel are two 60-amp fuses—one for each hot wire coming into the house. Similarly, two fuses are clipped into the RANGE panel. These cylindrical fuses can be pulled out by hand and replaced. They are difficult to pull out by hand, so you may want to purchase a fuse puller. This is a plierlike tool made to grip cartridge fuses.

In newer boxes there are four large screws that hold the front of the panel box (including the door) to the box itself. It is safe to unscrew these screws to take the front off. It's also necessary if you are to see how the box works, but don't touch anything inside.

The two 120-volt service entrance conductors enter the box and go directly to the main disconnect (Fig. 5-5). If you flip the main disconnect to OFF, the whole house will be without power. The two wires that extend from the main disconnect to two bus bars energize the bars with 120 volts each. Another wire enters the box with the two insulated conductors. It is a bare, stranded aluminum wire called the neutral wire, which travels down the side of the box to the neutral bar. There should be a fourth and not quite so large wire in the box. It is a bare, stranded copper ground wire, which leads from the neutral bus bar out of the box and is attached to the water main and to a ground rod outside the house, thus grounding your house.

The two bus bars in your panel box

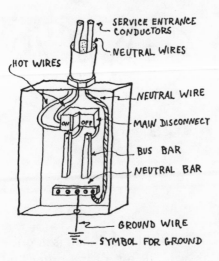

SERVICE ENTRANCE CONDUCTORS
NEUTRAL WIRES
HOT WIRES
NEUTRAL WIRE
MAIN DISCONNECT
BUS BAR
NEUTRAL BAR
ON OFF
GROUND WIRE
SYMBOL FOR GROUND

FIG. 5-5. THE SERVICE PANEL

may be totally covered by circuit breakers. These are black plastic switches that clip into one of the bus bars. There is one circuit breaker for each circuit. A circuit is a wire pathway in your house that leads from the panel box to several receptacles and back again. The tip of each switch is marked with a number like 15 or 20. This signifies the number of amps in that circuit. Only appliances that have an amp rating lower than that number can be plugged into that circuit. A circuit breaker is the safety switch for a circuit. If you overload the circuit, the breaker switch will flip open so that no more current can go over those wires until you correct whatever is wrong.

Overloading the circuit means that too many appliances have been plugged into that circuit, which required more amps than the wires are able to handle. Amperage, the flow of electricity over a

wire, creates heat. Too much heat in a wire can cause a fire. A circuit breaker detects the increased heat in the wires and turns itself off. A fuse does the same thing, except that instead of a switch being flipped, a thin metal strip within the fuse melts because of the heat. This interrupts the flow of current to the wires.

A lot of people put 30-amp fuses in the panel box to prevent fuses from blowing as frequently. This is a fire hazard. A fuse that is rated at a higher amperage than the circuit can handle will allow the fixtures and the wires in the wall to get dangerously hot before it blows. Put 15-amp fuses in lighting circuits and 20-amp fuses in small-appliance circuits.

When a fuse blows, it should be replaced; when a breaker flips, it should be reset. Unplug the offending appliance and go to the panel box. It should look like one of the boxes in Figs. 5-3 and 5-4. If a fuse is blown, unscrew it and replace it with one of the same amperage. The amperage is written on the face of the fuse. It's essential to keep several 15- and 20-amp fuses on hand. If you have a breaker box, look closely until you see the one switch that is out of line with all the others. Some circuit breakers have a small window near the base of the switch that shows red when the breaker has tripped. Flip the switch to OFF and then flip it to ON to restore the current.

Your utility bill has a lot of information on it, but the bottom line is how many kilowatt-hours you use per month. The utility company determines this by reading the meter monthly. If you are interested, you can keep track of your current usage per day by reading the meter.

The meter is usually outside the

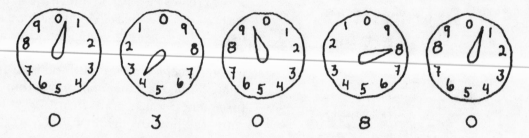

FIG. 5-6. READING AN ELECTRIC METER

house directly under where the wires from the pole connect to the house. It consists of five dials within a sealed glass cover. Read the dials from the left, writing down the number indicated by each pointer. There are a few rules to follow. When the pointer is between two numbers, write down the smaller of the two. If the pointer is exactly on a number, look at the dial to the immediate right. If the pointer of this dial has passed 0, write down the number indicated by the previous dial. If the pointer of the second dial has not reached 0, the number that should be written down for the previous dial is the next smaller one than indicated. To make it even more complicated, the numbering of the dials alternates between clockwise and counterclockwise. For example, the dials in Fig. 5-6 read 03080.

A SIMPLE CIRCUIT

Electricity travels in circuits. Electric current flows to the outlet and back to the panel box. Electrons don't actually flow to and from the panel box. One excites the electron next to it, and that one excites the electron next to it, and so on. It is similar to an open-ended pipe full of golf balls. If you push a golf ball into one end, another will fall out of the other end.

A simple circuit consists of a circuit breaker, three-wire cable, and a fixture (like a light or receptacle). A receptacle usually houses two electrical outlets into which appliances can be plugged (Fig. 5-7). The circuit breaker is clipped onto the bus bar. The cable for a typical 120-volt circuit contains two insulated wires and one bare copper wire. The plastic insulation on one wire is colored black and the insulation on the other is white. The black hot wire is inserted into the circuit breaker and held by a set screw. The white neutral wire is attached to the neutral bus bar. If you have a more recent system, the bare copper wire will be attached to an equipment-grounding bar, which is separate from the neutral bar. Otherwise, it will be attached to the neutral bar.

The plastic-covered cable runs to the receptacle, which is located within a plastic or metal receptacle box in the wall. Here the black hot wire is connected to the brass terminal screw, the white neutral wire is attached to the silver terminal screw, and the copper wire is attached to the green grounding screw. When the circuit breaker is on, electricity flows through the black wire to the receptacle and back to the panel box through the white wire. If you plug an appliance into this circuit and turn it on, the wheel in the meter will begin to revolve, indicating that you are using some electricity. Otherwise, the electricity just sits there waiting for you to use it. It isn't constantly flowing out of the receptacles.

The ground wire is there for your protection. If the hot wire accidentally slips off its brass terminal screw as it has in Fig. 5-8, the fixture becomes electrified and is potentially dangerous to anyone who may touch it. Luckily the ground wire is there to siphon off the current that has

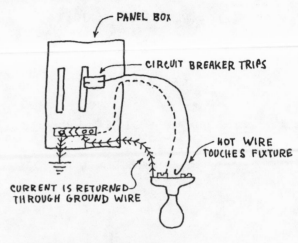

FIG. 5-8. A SHORT CIRCUIT

just electrified the light fixture itself. Electricity always takes the easiest route to ground and it loves copper wires. In this case the ground wire returns the current to the equipment-grounding bar or to the neutral bus bar, and the main ground wire carries the current into the ground, where it can do no harm. Meanwhile, the circuit breaker flips immediately, cutting off the flow of electricity, accompanied by flashes and noise at both receptacle and panel box.

HOW TO PLOT THE CIRCUITS IN YOUR HOUSE

Having a circuit map of your house greatly facilitates dealing with electrical emergencies. Making one is a very straightforward project, which is easier if you have an assistant.

First, draw a floor plan for each floor of your house. Note each receptacle, switch, and appliance, using the symbols in Fig. 5-9.

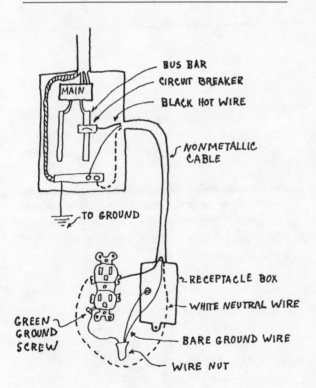

FIG. 5-7. A SIMPLE CIRCUIT

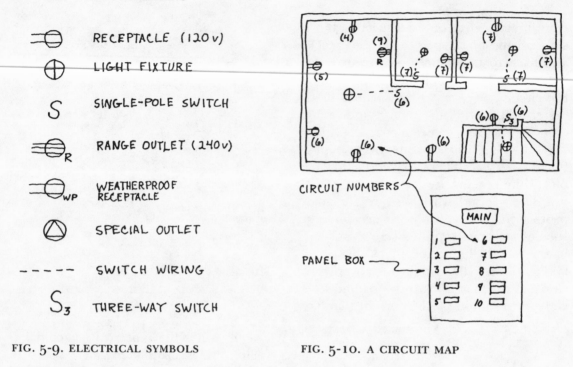

⊖ RECEPTACLE (120v)

⊕ LIGHT FIXTURE

S SINGLE-POLE SWITCH

⊖R RANGE OUTLET (240v)

⊖WP WEATHERPROOF RECEPTACLE

△ SPECIAL OUTLET

- - - - - SWITCH WIRING

S₃ THREE-WAY SWITCH

FIG. 5-9. ELECTRICAL SYMBOLS

FIG. 5-10. A CIRCUIT MAP

Second, go to the panel box and number each circuit breaker or fuse (Fig. 5-10). Some houses have subpanels; these circuits should be numbered also.

Third, have your assistant stand at the panel box and turn off one circuit breaker or remove one fuse. Then test each receptacle, light, and appliance in the house to see which are off. All receptacles and switches that are off are on this particular circuit. Write the number of the circuit on the floor plan beside the dead outlets. To determine if an outlet is dead, carry a small lamp with you. Test each half of the receptacle, because sometimes the top half will be on one circuit and the bottom half on another. This is common in kitchens and shops and is done so that a number of small appliances can be used near each other at the same time without overloading any one circuit. Remember to test each 240-volt circuit also. These are the double circuit breakers with their switches ganged together. In older houses, this is a pullout block with cartridge-type fuses. In some houses the 240-volt circuits go off only when the main is pulled (see Fig. 5-3). One large appliance like a furnace, range, or a central air conditioner is controlled by a 240-volt circuit breaker. After switching off a large circuit breaker, turn each appliance on to see which one is on that circuit.

When the map is completed, slip it in a plastic cover and hang it near the panel box for future reference.

An Electrical Tool Kit For Your Home

Doing electrical repairs requires a few specialized tools (Fig. 5-11). The voltage tester is not optional. It is necessary for safety and peace of mind.

PLIERS

Long-nose pliers can be used to bend or cut wire. They are good for reaching into electrical boxes and they are the right tool for the job when making the little loop at the end of solid copper wire that wraps around a terminal screw, as shown in Fig. 5-12. The terminal screw is the screw that attaches the wire to a receptacle, switch, or lamp.

Lineman's pliers are the right tool for twisting wires together.

When using a pair of pliers, hold them as shown in Fig. 5-13. Putting your little finger inside the handle allows more control in opening and closing the pliers.

WIRE STRIPPER

Depending on the model you get, this is a multipurpose tool. Usually it has two functions: stripping the plastic coating off wire and cutting wire. There are many sizes of wire and each has a number. The smaller the number, the larger the diameter of the wire. The most common wire sizes used in houses are sizes 10, 12, and 14. Each hole between the jaws of a wire stripper has a number which represents the size of wire that can be stripped in that hole. The holes are sized to cut only the plastic coating, not the copper wire itself.

When stripping wire, you want to remove about ¾ inch of insulation. Grip the

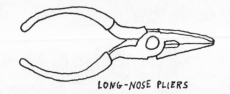

LONG-NOSE PLIERS

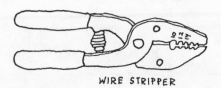

WIRE STRIPPER

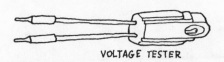

VOLTAGE TESTER

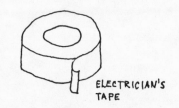

CONTINUITY TESTER

ELECTRICIAN'S TAPE

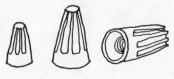

WIRE NUTS

FIG. 5-11. HOME ELECTRICAL TOOL KIT

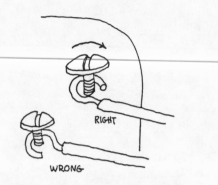

FIG. 5-12. WIRE ON TERMINAL SCREW

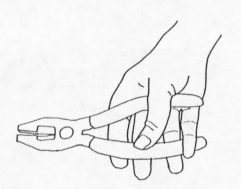

FIG. 5-13. GRIPPING PLIERS

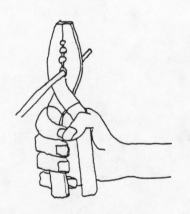

FIG. 5-14. USING WIRE STRIPPERS

strippers as you would a pair of pliers and close the jaws around the wire so that the wire falls into the correct size hole (Fig. 5-14). When I don't know the number of the wire, I begin with a hole that's clearly large enough, and work my way down in hole size until I find the hole that will cut through the insulation and not into the wire. Now squeeze the handles together and release. There should be a pleasing little click, not unlike recapping a pen. Rotate the stripper 180 degrees, squeeze again, and pull it toward the end of the wire. The ¾ inch of insulation should slip off.

VOLTAGE TESTER

This tool is a must. If you use it, it will protect you from getting shocked. When the two prongs are inserted into the slots in a receptacle, as in the left half of Fig. 5-24, the light in the voltage tester will glow if the current is on. This tool is well worth the $1.50 it costs.

CONTINUITY TESTER

This tool tests the integrity of switches and cords. It is inexpensive and a worthwhile addition to the toolbox, if you like to fix things like lamps instead of throwing them away. It should only be used on equipment that is unplugged or whose breaker or fuse is turned off.

ELECTRICIAN'S TAPE

The world is held together with tape, as most of us know. This particular kind is essential for splicing extension cords and has a thousand other uses as well.

WIRE NUTS

These are colored plastic screw caps

for wires. They are color-coded for size, and it is useful to have a few different sizes around the house.

Lamps and Lights

IF A LAMP DOESN'T LIGHT

Any number of things could be wrong when a lamp fails to light. The trick is figuring out which one it is. The method for doing this is called troubleshooting. Troubleshooting is moving down a list of questions until you discover the source of the problem. Always begin with the simple things first. If a lamp doesn't light, check it out in the following order.

1. Is the bulb blown?

2. Is the circuit breaker tripped or the fuse blown?

3. Examine the lamp.
   —Is the plug broken or has a wire come loose?
   —Is the cord broken?
   —Does the socket check out? Is a wire loose, is the switch broken, or is the circuitry within the socket itself bad?

Let's look at the last three problems and how to repair them.

FAULTY PLUG

Examine the plug (Fig. 5-15). Lift off the insulating disc. Are both wires wound tightly around the terminals and held securely by the screws as they should be? Are some strands of one wire squeezing out from under the screw and touching or almost touching the other wire? Often one of the wires frays like this or comes off the screw terminal because of constant yanking at the plug. This is a good reason

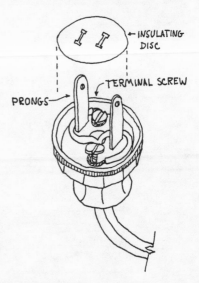

FIG. 5-15. PARTS OF A PLUG

to grasp only the plug when unplugging —not the wire.

Tighten the terminal screws if they are loose. If the strands of one wire have worked their way out from under one screw and are close to touching the other, loosen the screw and remove the wire. Straighten it out and retwist its strands. Form the end of the wire into a loop and fit it around the terminal screw as in Fig. 5-12. Placing the loop in this way helps tighten the loop as the screw is tightened. Use a pair of long-nose pliers to form the loop.

A plug should be replaced when the plastic housing is cracked or when one of the prongs is loose.

FRAYED EXTENSION CORD

Next, examine the length of the cord. If it is frayed or cut, you should either replace it with a new length of lamp cord or repair the break. Look closely at the

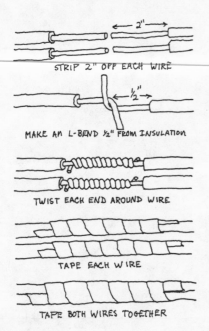

FIG. 5-16. SPLICING A WIRE

electrician's tape. Begin taping one tape's width back onto the insulation and wrap toward the splice, overlapping half the width of the tape each revolution. When you have taped over the insulation on the other end, spiral back so the spirals crisscross. Wrap three layers over each wire individually, and then tape both wires together with one layer of tape.

frayed place to see if any strands of copper wire are showing. If bare wire is visible on one wire, but none of the strands have been cut, the bare spot can simply be taped with electrician's tape. If the insulation has been scraped off both wires, pull the wires apart and tape each separately. Three or four layers of electrician's tape are adequate insulation.

If some of the strands have been cut, it's best to sever both wires in the cord and splice them together (Fig. 5-16). Strip 2 inches of insulation off all four ends. Make a right-angle bend in each wire about ½ inch from the insulation. Hold the intersection with pliers or your fingers while you twist each end around the main wire on either side of the intersection. Repeat for the other wire.

Wrap each wire individually with

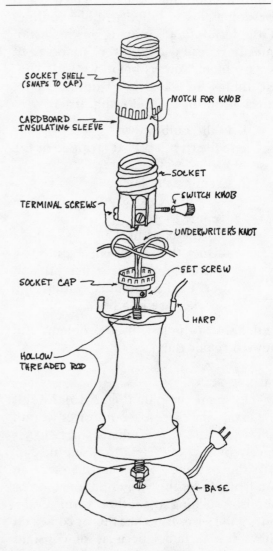

FIG. 5-17. PARTS OF A LAMP

REMOVING AND REPLACING THE SOCKET

Now comes the fun part. If the plug and cord are okay, you get to disassemble the lamp, because the problem is probably in the socket (Fig. 5-17).

Unplug the lamp and remove the shade and bulb. Press with your finger or a screwdriver on the socket shell where indicated in Fig. 5-18. Slip the socket shell and the cardboard insulating sleeve off

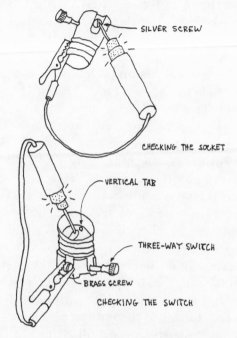

FIG. 5-20. USING A CONTINUITY TESTER

FIG. 5-18. REPLACING A SOCKET

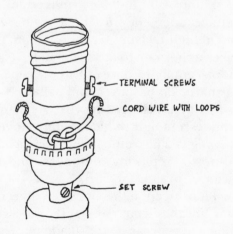

FIG. 5-19. INSIDE A SOCKET

the socket by lifting upward. This should reveal a socket with two wires attached to two terminal screws (Fig. 5-19). If one of the wires has come off its screw, this is probably the reason why the lamp won't light. Replace it and tighten the screw.

If nothing appears amiss, the problem is likely to be in the socket itself. Remove the wires and test the socket with a continuity tester (Fig. 5-20). Squeeze the alligator clip onto the metal shell that holds the bulb and touch the point of the continuity tester to the silver terminal screw. If the tester lights up, the continuity of the path of the neutral wire is okay. If it doesn't, there is a break in the neutral somewhere within the socket. Now attach the clip onto the brass screw and touch the brass tab at the bottom of the socket with the tip of the tester. When the switch is on, the light in the tester should glow. If it doesn't, there is a break in the path of the hot wire somewhere within the socket. If the tester lights on both tests, it is okay. If it fails to light on either test, it should be replaced.

If the circuitry is fine, check the switch next. Squeeze the alligator clip onto the brass terminal screw and touch the point of the tester to the tab that contacts the bulb in the bottom of the socket. Turn the switch off and on. The tester should light when the switch is on. If it doesn't, the switch is broken and the socket should be replaced. If the tester lights, but the lamp still doesn't work when it's reassembled, the problem may be that the tab at the bottom of the socket is not contacting the bulb. Unplug the lamp and pry it up with a knife.

Testing a three-way switch within a socket is similarly done. Clamp the alligator clip onto the brass screw. If the switch is in the first on position, the tester should light when its point is touching the small vertical tab at one side of the bottom of the socket. When the switch is in its second on position, the tester should light when its point touches the contact tab. When the switch is in its third on position, it should light when touched to either tab.

Every hardware store carries many kinds of sockets. As a matter of fact, look on a broken socket as an opportunity to install a three-way socket or a dimmer socket.

REPLACING THE SWITCH KNOB

The round on-off knob on most sockets is hard to negotiate if you have greasy fingers or if the strength and dexterity in

FIG. 5-21. REPLACING THE SWITCH KNOB

your hands is low for any reason. It is very easy to change this annoying design problem. The switch knob screws off and can be replaced by a paddle-type knob, which is much easier to grip (Fig. 5-21). Some people prefer a pull chain. These can be added by replacing the old socket, as described above, with one equipped with a pull chain.

TROUBLESHOOTING FLUORESCENT LIGHTS

Fluorescent lights go unfixed longer than incandescent ones do. They have an aura of high-tech mystery about them that makes us hesitate to tackle them. In reality fluorescent lights have only three replaceable parts: bulb, starter, and ballast. Now, it's true that this is two more parts than an incandescent light, which requires merely screwing in a new bulb. However, the procedure for replacing the ballast and the starter is straightforward.

Fluorescent lights operate differently from incandescent ones. Incandescent bulbs glow because the filament inside becomes so hot that it emits light. Fluorescent bulbs work because a surge of electricity created by the ballast or the starter excites the atoms of gas in the tube, causing it to emit ultraviolet waves. We can't see these waves, but when they strike the sides of the tube that have been coated with a phosphorescent material, the coating glows brightly.

Older fluorescent lights have both a starter and a ballast. Newer ones, called rapid-start or instant-start, have only a ballast. The ballast is a little transformer, and both it and the starter serve to generate the electrical surge needed to start a fluorescent light. Because fluorescent lights don't use heat to emit light, they are cheaper to use and give five to six times as much light per watt as an incandescent bulb. Fluorescent light used to be cold and harsh. Now you can purchase tubes that duplicate the warmth of incandescent light.

All the parts of a fluorescent fixture are replaceable. *Turn off the current or unplug the lamp before removing any parts.* Hardware or electrical-supply stores have bulbs, starters, ballasts, and tube holders. Be sure the wattage of the starter or ballast matches the wattage marked on the fluorescent tube. Take the old part to the store and get an exact replacement. The starter is the cheapest to replace, the tube is next, and the ballast is the most expensive. So when troubleshooting a fixture that won't light, replace the starter first, then the tube, and finally, if need be, the ballast (Fig. 5-22).

Not all fixtures have a starter. If the offending fixture has one, remove it by twisting one-quarter turn counterclockwise and pulling it out of its socket. The cover of the fixture does not have to be

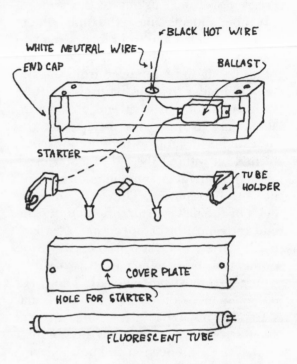

FIG. 5-22. ANATOMY OF A FLUORESCENT LAMP

removed first, because the starter sticks out through the cover plate.

There are two types of fluorescent tubes: those with two prongs at each end and those with one prong at each end. The two-prong type is installed by inserting both ends into the tube holders and giving the tube a quarter turn. Check to see that the tube is seated properly by tugging downward on the tube. If it's not seated, the tube will pull out. There are two little notches opposite each other on each end of most new tubes. They should be parallel with the tube holders when the tube is inserted properly.

Tubes with one prong at each end

are removed by pushing against one of the tube holders. One of the tube holders is spring-loaded and will move when you exert pressure against it. This allows the other prong to be removed from the stationary holder. If your fixture has a tube with one prong at each end, it is an instant-start fixture. This means that the tube lights instantly when the switch is turned on without the aid of a starter.

Tube holders sometimes break and need to be replaced. They slide into the ends of the metal fixture. Sometimes the end caps must be removed first (see Fig. 5-22). After you slide it out, the tube holder will be dangling from two wires, which also must be removed. The wires either snap in or are held by terminal screws. If no screws are visible, insert a small screwdriver or nail into the slot next to the wire's connection and pull the wire out. Take the tube holder to the store with you to get an exact replacement.

The ballast should be replaced as a last resort. Sometimes it is cheaper to buy a new fixture. First, remove the tube and the cover plate, which is held in place with two screws or a silver-colored friction clip. Remove the old ballast by cutting all the wires coming from it so that 5 inches of wire are still attached. Remove the two screws that hold the ballast to the metal fixture. In fluorescent table lamps the ballast is in the base. Take the ballast to the store and buy an exact replacement. The new one will have several wires of different colors all about 5 inches long, sticking out of it. Mount the new ballast before you connect the wires. Strip ½ inch of insulation from the end of each wire (Fig. 5-14 shows how to strip wires). Connect like-colored wires (red to red, blue to

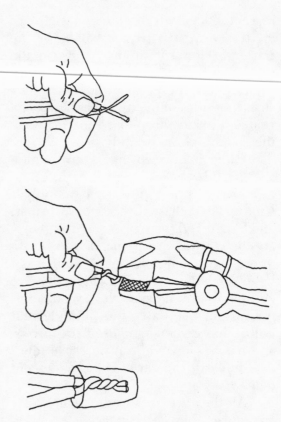

FIG. 5-23. PUTTING ON A WIRE NUT

blue) with one medium-sized wire nut for each set of two wires (Fig. 5-23). Make sure to check the connection by tugging on the wires with one hand while holding the wire nut with the other.

Receptacles, Lights, and Switches

Permanent electrical fixtures like receptacles, lights, and switches can break or become outdated. They can be replaced safely if two simple safety procedures are followed: *Turn off the current* and then *test to make sure the current is off.*

RECEPTACLES

A voltage tester is needed to check to see if the current is off. Stick the prongs of the tester into the vertical slots in the receptacle as in the left-hand drawing in Fig. 5-24. Have a friend flip the breaker on and off several times, while you watch the little light on the tester. It should go on and off also, if your friend has chosen the right circuit. Now have the friend turn the breaker or fuse off. It is important at this point that you make sure the prongs of the circuit tester are pushed deeply into the slots in the receptacle. If you can't get the light to go on, the electricity is off.

To replace a cracked receptacle, first remove the cover plate by unscrewing the single screw that holds it in place. After turning off the current, test to make sure it is off (Fig. 5-25). Testing is a double check to be sure you have turned off the right circuit.

Unscrew the mounting screws that hold the receptacle to the box. These screws are kept from falling out of the receptacle mounting strap by thin cardboard washers, so don't remove them. Pull the receptacle out as far as the wires will permit. Touch only the aluminum ears at the top and bottom, until you know the current is off.

Use the voltage tester again for a double check. Receptacles have two screws on each side and a single green screw toward one end. The green screw is the ground screw; the bare copper wire is attached to it. The screws on one side are brass and those on the other are silver. Only black hot wires are attached to the brass screws. White neutral wires are attached to the silver ones. Touch one of the legs of the voltage tester to a brass

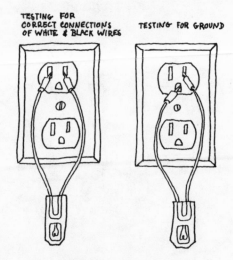

FIG. 5-24. TESTING FOR
CORRECT CONNECTIONS

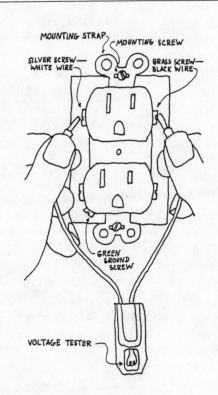

FIG. 5-25. TESTING TO SEE IF
CURRENT IS OFF

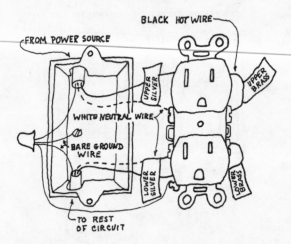

FIG. 5-26. REPLACING A RECEPTACLE

terminal screw and the other to a silver screw. If the current is off, the tester light will not glow.

When you have pulled the receptacle out, you should see something similar to Fig. 5-26. There are many variations on this wiring diagram, which depend on whether the receptacle is the last opening on the circuit or in the middle of it, whether half the receptacle is switched and the other half constantly on, or whether the upper half is on one circuit and the lower half on another, as is common in kitchens. To understand all these variations would take months of study. However, with a roll of masking tape and a pen you can mark the wires that connect to the receptacle, so that they can also be attached to the new receptacle without the worry of crossed wires.

Label each wire before removing it. Attach a piece of tape to the wire that is attached to the UPPER BRASS screw. Attach a piece of tape to the wire that is con-

nected to the LOWER SILVER screw, et cetera (Fig. 5-26). When all the wires have been removed, reconnect them to the new receptacle as directed by the tabs on each wire. Make sure that each wire is connected, as in Fig. 5-12.

After the receptacle has been wired, replace the fuse or switch on the breaker in the panel box and check your connections. If the receptacle has been wired correctly, and there is a bare grounding wire in the box to attach to the ground screw, both tests pictured in Fig. 5-24 should make the tester's light glow. If there is not a bare copper ground wire in the box, which is the case in older houses, the test pictured in the right-hand drawing does not apply.

SWITCHES

Installing dimmer switches gives a variety of lighting levels and helps conserve electricity. All lights except fluorescents can be put on dimmer switches. There are many new switches that either make life easier or save electricity: noiseless, time-clock, lighted-handle, or time-delay switches that allow you enough time to walk away before turning themselves off. The latest development in switch technology is a heat-sensitive switch that operates when a person goes in or out of a room.

Sometimes switches break and need to be replaced. First, turn off the current at the panel box. When you remove the cover plate of the switch, you will see one of the wiring configurations in Fig. 5-27. Test to see if the current is really off (Fig. 5-28). Touch one of the legs of the voltage tester to the box (if it's metal and a bare ground wire is connected to it) and

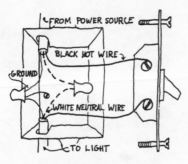

SWITCH IN MID-RUN

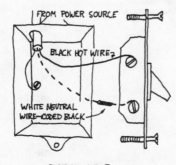

SWITCH LOOP

FIG. 5-27. WIRING CONFIGURATIONS
FOR SWITCHES

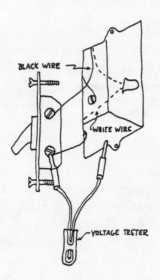

FIG. 5-28. TESTING A SWITCH

the other leg of the tester to each of the brass terminal screws. If the box is plastic, touch the tester leg to one of the bare copper ground wires. The tester should not light when touched to either screw. If the tester does light, you have turned off the wrong circuit.

If there is no ground wire in the switch box, the test can be done in another way. It may sound scary but it is perfectly safe. Grasp one prong of the tester between your thumb and forefinger and touch the other prong to both screws attaching wires to the switch. If the electricity is still on, a small glow can be seen in the light when the prong is touching the in-coming hot. No glow will be seen when the prong touches the switched hot. The reason you do not get a shock is that the bulb in the tester draws only a minuscule amount of current. Since the bulb glows dimly, do the test away from the light to help you detect the glow.

In Fig. 5-27, the diagram labeled "Switch in mid-run" occurs when the switch is located before the light in the circuit wiring. The diagram labeled "Switch loop" occurs when the light comes before the switch in the circuit. Once again, you do not need to know a lot about wiring to replace a switch. Get out your masking tape and label each wire. Single pole switches are easy because there are only two terminal screws on the switch and therefore only two wires to be connected. These are the switches that have ON and OFF marked on the toggle. As you look at the switch, the wire connector screws should be on the right side. When the switch is put in thus, the switch will be on when the toggle is up and off when it is down. Label one wire UP and the other

DOWN when holding the switch, so that it is ON when the toggle is up.

After labeling each wire, loosen the terminal screws and remove the old switch. If a similar switch is being wired in, attach the wires as indicated by the tape. If you are installing a dimmer switch, connect one of the switch leads (the wires hanging from the switch) to one of the wires you labeled, and the other switch lead to the other (Fig. 5-29). It doesn't matter which goes to which.

The switch leads will be stranded copper wire. The wires in the box will be solid copper. With a pair of pliers, straighten the solid wires. Cross the switch lead over the solid wire and wrap it tightly around (see Fig. 5-23). You can twist the wires with your fingers if they are stranded. If they are solid copper, use pliers. Finally, screw on one of the wire nuts provided in the dimmer switch box. Always check to see if a wire nut is on securely, by pulling each of the wires it holds. If one comes loose, unscrew the wire nut, twist the wires again, and replace the wire nut.

Timers are wonderful devices to put on appliances that use a lot of electricity, such as hot-water heaters. Timers can be set to heat the water only when the household needs it. A time-clock switch can be installed in place of a single pole switch only when it is a switch in mid-run. The reason for this is that the clock motor requires a neutral wire.

To install a time-clock switch, it is necessary to ascertain which black wire is coming from the power source and which one is going to the light. With the power off, unscrew the mounting screws and pull the switch out of the box as far as it will

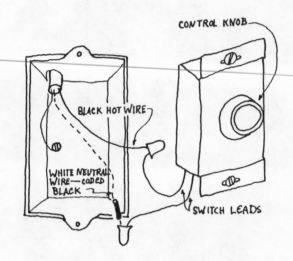

FIG. 5-29. INSTALLING A DIMMER SWITCH

come. Turn the power back on and turn on the switch. Perform the test pictured in Fig. 5-28. When the tester is touched to one of the terminal screws, it will light. The wire attached to this screw is the wire coming from the power source. Label it accordingly.

Turn the power off again and remove the old switch. Straighten the loops on each of the black wires with pliers. Connect the straightened loop from the power source to the black switch lead with a wire nut (Fig. 5-30). Connect the other black wire to the red switch lead, also with a wire nut. Remove the wire nut from the two white wires that are spliced together and twist the end of the white switch lead around these two wires and screw on the wire nut. That's all there is to it.

LIGHTS

If a light fixture fails to light, the problem could be in the fixture itself. First go down the troubleshooting checklist given on page 83. Turn off the current at the circuit breaker or fuse. Switching off the light is not enough, as it may leave some hot wires. Remove the light fixture by unscrewing the screws that hold it to the box in the ceiling (Fig. 5-31). Often fixtures are screwed to a fixture strip that is in turn screwed to the octagonal box. Don't let the fixture hang from the wires; support it from a hook fashioned from a piece of wire or a coat hanger.

Check to see if the black and white wires are firmly attached to the light fixture. If there are sockets on the fixture, check their integrity with a continuity tester, as described on pages 85–86. If the fixture has one central socket, it can be tested by clipping the alligator clip onto the brass screw and touching the tester to the silver screw. Remember to turn the switch to ON. If the tester fails to glow, the fixture itself is broken and should be replaced.

Unscrew the wire nuts (if there are any) that attach the fixture leads to the black and white wires coming from the power source. Attach the fixture leads from the new fixture in the same way: black to black and white to white.

Adapting a Doorbell for the Hearing-Impaired

It used to be that doorbells in the homes of hearing-impaired people had to be rewired to a light that would flash when someone rang the bell. Nowadays, many companies make a sound-activated light that flashes when it detects a noise in the room like a phone ringing, a doorbell, music, or voices. It has a sensitivity-con-

FIG. 5-30. CONNECTING A TIMER SWITCH

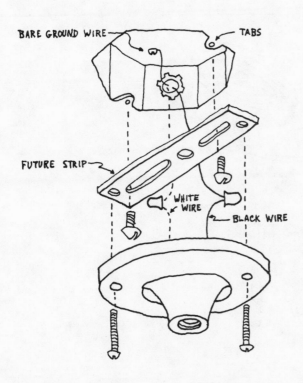

FIG. 5-31. ANATOMY OF A LIGHT FIXTURE

trol dial that can be adjusted to various sound levels. The lamp plugs into a standard 120-volt outlet. A lamp such as this costs from fifty to seventy dollars and is available through stores that carry supplies for the hearing-impaired.

Electric Ranges

Most repairs to an electric range should be done by a serviceperson. Replacing the burners, however, is easy to do yourself. If a burner fails to heat, the first thing that needs to be determined is whether the fault is in the burner or in the wires to the burner.

Turn off the electricity to the range circuit in case there are any loose wires in the range. Remove the suspect heating element from its terminal block (Fig. 5-32). Also remove a heating element of the same size that you know is working. Insert the suspect element in the terminal block from which the working element was removed. If the heating element heats, the fault is in the wiring of the other terminal block. If the element fails to heat, you can replace it yourself. Appliance stores that carry your brand of range will have them.

Some heating elements are inserted and removed from their terminal block like a plug (Fig. 5-32, top). Grip the element and pull. If the element comes out but is still attached to wires as in the lower illustration, the two screws will have to be removed to free the element.

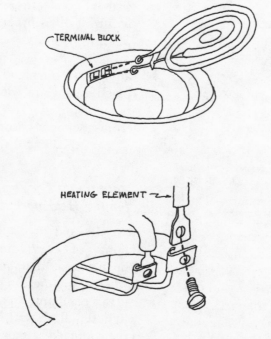

FIG. 5-32. REMOVING A HEATING ELEMENT FROM AN ELECTRIC RANGE

6

WALLS
AND CEILINGS

The Structural System

A basic understanding of walls, what they're made of, what's inside them, and what they support makes doing repairs around the home a lot easier. Walls are part of the structural system of a house. A wall consists of a skeleton of wood (called the framing) that is covered by a skin of some sort. In older houses the skin is plaster; in newer houses it's Sheetrock. There are two kinds of walls: load-bearing and non-load-bearing. Load-bearing walls support the snow on the roof and the furniture and people resting on the floors. Non-load-bearing walls can be removed and the house will not be affected.

The weight of things that houses are designed to support is transferred from one supporting member to another, until it finally reaches the foundation and is spread out over the ground by the footing, so that the house doesn't sink. The footing is to the wall what your foot is to your leg. Both spread the weight of what they are supporting over the ground, so that neither the house nor you will sink into it.

Let's take furniture and people for example. Chairs are arranged randomly on the floors of houses and their weight and the weight of the people who sit in them is held up by the joists (Fig. 6-1). A joist is a horizontal board that, when placed on edge and parallel to other joists, supports the floor of a house. The ends of the joists rest on the exterior walls and a beam supported by an interior wall. These exterior walls are called load-bearing, because they support the weight of

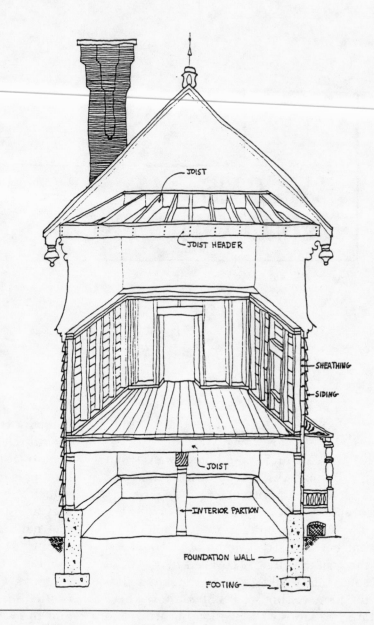

JOIST

JOIST HEADER

SHEATHING

SIDING

JOIST

INTERIOR PARTION

FOUNDATION WALL

FOOTING

FIG. 6-1. THE STRUCTURAL
PARTS OF A HOUSE

the furniture and people (live load) on the floors and transfer it to the foundation. The exterior walls on which the rafters rest and the walls directly below them are all load-bearing. The weight they support is that of snow, which can be 40 pounds per square foot.

Houses also have non-load-bearing walls that support only their own weight (dead load). If you want to remodel your house, it's important to determine which walls are load-bearing and which are not. Load-bearing walls can be removed if they are replaced by a beam capable of

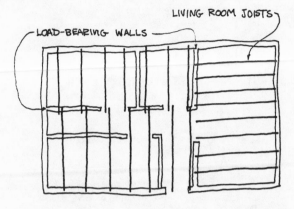

FIG. 6-2. LOAD-BEARING WALLS

supporting the weight they previously held. This might take some detective work, since joists can change direction even within a floor. If a house is more than 16 feet wide, there are probably two sets of joists that are supported in the middle by a beam or a load-bearing wall. Sometimes even within one floor, joists can change direction (Fig. 6-2). When a room spans the whole width of a house, as some living rooms do, the joists over this room have most likely been turned 90 degrees and are running parallel to the long side of the house.

THE PARTS OF A WALL

Fig. 6-3 shows the names of the parts of a typical wall. The vertical members, which transfer the weight the wall carries down to the foundation, are called studs. There are several different types of studs. A trimmer stud is placed on either side of windows and doors and is nailed to a king stud. The trimmer on either side of the door or window supports the header. The header is a small beam that supports the weight that the studs would have sup-

ported had they not been removed to make a window or door. The short studs under and over a window or door are called curtailed studs, since they don't reach from the bottom plate to the top plate. Many texts call them cripple studs, but I find this term objectionable.

In houses that are seventy years old or older, the studs are not necessarily evenly spaced. The sheathing and siding that was nailed to the studs in these houses were hand-cut and of random lengths, so even spacing wasn't crucial. With the development of mass-produced sheathings like plywood and gypsum board, it became imperative that framing members be orderly. That is when the convention of on-center spacing began. In houses built since 1930, the center of each stud is 16 inches from the center of

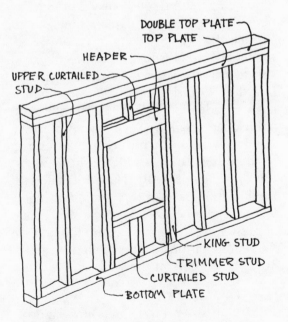

FIG. 6-3. THE PARTS OF A WALL

the ones next to it. This is a very important bit of information to anyone wishing
to hang anything on a wall. It means that
if you can find one stud, you can find all
the others on that wall and put your painting where you want it. In some well-
insulated houses built since 1970, the
centers of the studs in the exterior walls
are 24 inches apart, but those in the interior walls are still 16 inches apart.

Attaching Things to Walls

How you attach things to a wall depends on what kind of wall you have. If
you live in a house that was built since
1950, you have gypsum board walls (also
called drywall or Sheetrock walls). If the
house was built before 1940, the walls are
plaster and lath. Houses built during the
1940s could have either interior wall
finish or one or two others, the most nota-
ble being Homasote, or "kitty nose
board" as I like to call it. Homasote is
½-inch-thick 4×8 sheets of compressed
cardboard, and if you look at the edge, it's
soft like the fur on a cat's nose. Gypsum
board is ½-inch-thick 4×8 (or longer)
sheets made of a chalklike substance with
a thick paper skin on each side. A plaster-
and-lath wall is much thicker than either
of the others. In this wall finish, ¼-inch-
thick wooden slats called lath are nailed to
the inside surface of the studs, leaving a
½-inch space between each. Several coats
of plaster are then troweled on the lath so
that enough is pushed between the lath to
hold the plaster on the wall.

PLASTER-AND-LATH WALLS

If you still aren't sure which kind of
wall you have, look in nooks and crannies

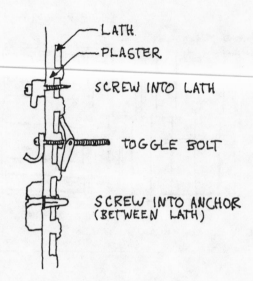

FIG. 6-4. ANCHORS FOR PLASTER

that may have gone unfinished, like the
stairwell to the basement or attic, inside
closets, under stairs, or around the attic
hatch. Plaster-and-lath walls are thicker
(¾ inch) than gypsum board, and therefore heavier things can be hung on the
wall between studs. A screw can be driven
directly into the wall because it's likely
that it will hit a piece of lath and hold
fairly well (Fig. 6-4). Screw anchors work
well if the screw is large and the load
heavier, or if the location is between laths.
Toggle bolts are ideal for hollow walls
with a rough interior surface, like plaster-
and-lath walls. The only hollow wall fastener that doesn't work well on this kind
of wall is the molly bolt (see Fig. A-5 in the
Appendix).

GYPSUM BOARD WALLS

Because gypsum board walls are
backed by wood only at the studs, screws
work as fasteners only when accompanied

by a screw anchor. If you are hanging a mirror, it can go anywhere on the wall, but where there is no stud, a screw anchor must be used. All the hollow wall anchors shown in the Appendix, Fig. A-5, will work on this kind of wall.

LOCATING STUDS AND JOISTS

If heavy things like bookshelves are to be hung from the wall, they must be fastened into the studs. Studs can be located by sliding a stud finder across the wall until the little magnetized arrow stands rigidly perpendicular to the wall

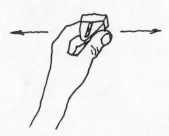

FIG. 6-5. USING A STUD FINDER

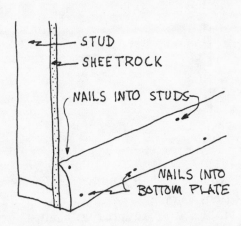

FIG. 6-6. LOCATING STUDS BY EXAMINING THE BASEBOARD

(Fig. 6-5). This works best on plaster-and-lath walls, because there is one nail per lath at every stud, so there is lots of metal for the magnet to sense. Drywall is nailed much less often—every 8 inches—so you have to slide the stud finder across a greater area to locate a stud. The stud finder locates joists also.

Another method is to look at the baseboard and determine which nails were nailed into the studs (Fig. 6-6). Remember there is a 1½-inch-thick bottom plate that runs horizontally along the bottom of the wall. Only the nails along the top edge of the baseboard are nailed into studs; the nails along the bottom edge are nailed into the bottom plate.

Once a stud is located, you can measure in multiples of 16 inches to either side of it and find any other stud in the wall. If you think you've found a stud but you're not sure you want to risk drilling a hole in the living-room wallpaper to find out, then "plumb down" to the baseboard and test for the stud by hammering in a small nail. To plumb down, use a level and hold it vertically against the wall next to the stud mark. When you have gotten the bubble in the middle of the vial, draw a very light, very short line along the side of the level near its bottom, shorter than shown in Fig. 6-7. Repeat this process, proceding down the wall until you reach the baseboard.

HANGING BOOKSHELVES

After locating the studs, mark each stud into which a support should be fastened. If the wall has studs 16 inches on center (commonly abbreviated 16 o.c.) and the books are heavy, you should place a shelf support at each stud. If the shelf

The labels in Figure 6-6 read: STUD, SHEETROCK, NAILS INTO STUDS, NAILS INTO BOTTOM PLATE

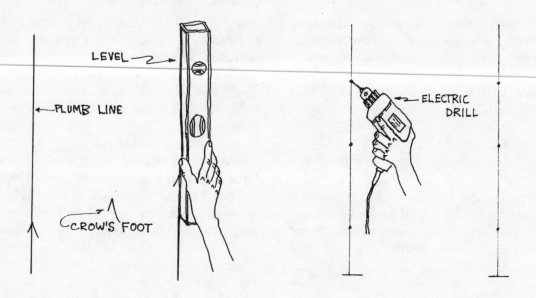

LEVEL

PLUMB LINE

CROW'S FOOT

FIG. 6-7.

ELECTRIC DRILL

FIG. 6-9

MOUNTING BOOKSHELVES

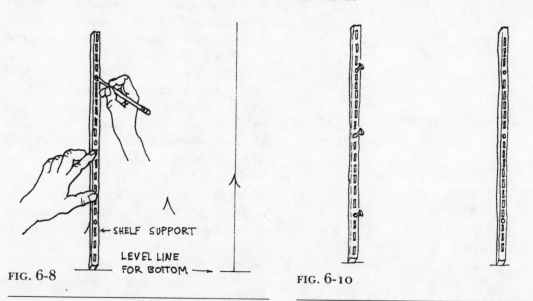

SHELF SUPPORT

LEVEL LINE FOR BOTTOM

FIG. 6-8

FIG. 6-10

itself is to be 2 inches thick or is to hold light knickknacks, then the supports can be placed 32 inches apart (Fig. 6-7). Hold the level vertically against the wall at each mark that indicates a stud over which there will be a shelf support and draw a light pencil line.

Hold a shelf support up against the wall and imagine how high you want the shelves to go and where the bottom of the support should be located to allow this. Draw a level line at the bottom of each vertical shelf-support line (Fig. 6-8). Hold the bottom of each support on the level line and along the vertical plumb line and mark the screw locations with a pencil or nail. Sometimes a pencil point is too big to reach through the hole and a nail is preferable.

Choose a bit that is a little smaller than the threads of the screw (Fig. 2-8) and drill holes with either an electric drill as in Fig. 6-9 or a push drill. When putting up the supports, start all the screws before driving any of them home (Fig. 6-10). Often when one screw in a series is driven home before the others are started, it's much harder to get the rest started in their holes.

INSTALLING GRAB BARS

Grab bars should be strategically placed to help the wheelchair user transfer from the chair to the toilet or tub. Because a lot of weight will be put on a grab bar, it must be firmly mounted into the studs of a wall. If the bathroom is finished in tile, the bar can be mounted directly on the tile, because it is resilient enough to support the weight of a large person. In this case, the only specialty tool you will need is a small masonry or glass bit that will drill through the tile. Select a bit a couple of sizes larger than the screws, so that they can pass easily through tile. With a bit a little smaller than the diameter of the screw (Fig. 2-8) drill into the wood stud.

If the bathroom is finished in drywall or if the grab bar flanges do not land over a stud, a backing board must first be mounted on the wall (Fig. 6-11). Fasten it

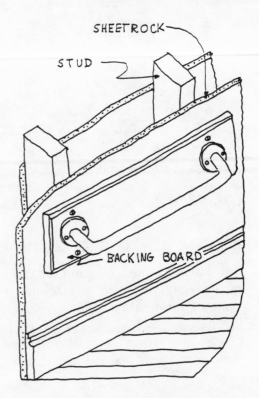

FIG. 6-11. INSTALLING A GRAB BAR

into the studs behind the drywall with two screws per stud. They should be no smaller than number 12 screws that are minimally 2½ inches long. When the backing board is secured to the wall, the grab bar is screwed into it.

HANGING PLANTS FROM THE CEILING

When hanging any but the lightest plants and lamps from the ceiling, it is best to fasten them into the joists. Locate the joists as described on page 99. Drill into the joist with a bit a little smaller than the diameter of the screw hook you are using (see Fig. 2-8). If, when screwing the hook in, it becomes difficult to turn,

FIG. 6-12. INCREASING LEVERAGE

thread a large nail or screwdriver blade through the hook and grasp that. It will act as a lever and increase your power (Fig. 6-12).

Repairing Holes in Walls and Ceilings

There's quite a demand for this type of patching, because people are constantly putting their pool cues or fists through walls. How you patch a hole depends on whether the wall is drywall or plaster and lath and on the size of the hole.

HOLES IN DRYWALL

The procedure for fixing a hole is different from that for a dent. If there is an actual hole in the drywall bigger than a half-dollar, a backer must be fastened to the inside of the wall before the drywall patch can be inserted. First, cut a square patch from another piece of gypsum board a little bigger than the hole.

Sheetrock is cut with a utility knife or a Sheetrock or keyhole saw (Fig. 6-13). If the piece to be cut is rectangular, the knife is the right tool for the job. The saws are good for cutting holes for electrical outlets in the middle of a piece of Sheetrock. They are pointed so they can be pushed through the Sheetrock to begin the cut. Lay a straightedge along one line on the Sheetrock. A straightedge can be any-

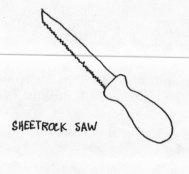

SHEETROCK SAW

UTILITY KNIFE

FIG. 6-13. TOOLS FOR CUTTING SHEETROCK

thing like a yardstick, the edge of a level, or a straight piece of wood. Draw your utility knife along the straightedge, scoring the paper and cutting into the gypsum a little (about ⅛ inch). Move the sheet so that the scored line is over the edge of a table or board and break the Sheetrock by pushing down gently. Finally, cut the paper on the other side of the sheet with the knife to disconnect the two pieces.

Place the newly cut Sheetrock patch over the hole and trace around it (Fig. 6-14). Using a keyhole or Sheetrock saw, cut along the lines you have just traced, making a nice square hole in the wall (Fig. 6-15).

Next, cut a backer 2 inches larger than the hole all around from a piece of wood. Using a paddle bit (Fig. 6-16), drill a hole in the middle large enough for your finger. Put blobs of mastic on the board

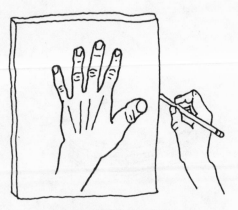

FIG. 6-14. PATCHING A HOLE IN
SHEETROCK

FIG. 6-16. PADDLE BIT

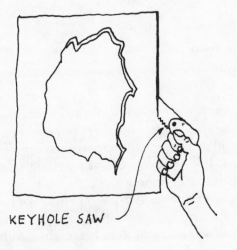

KEYHOLE SAW

FIG. 6-15

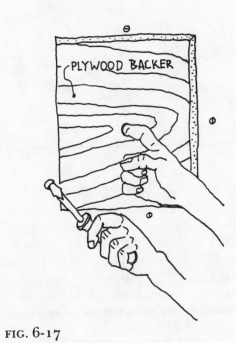

PLYWOOD BACKER

FIG. 6-17

all around near the edge. Mastic or construction adhesive comes in cans or in
tubes for use in a caulk gun. Because it's
larger than the hole, the only way this
piece of wood will fit through the hole is
by holding it diagonally. After slipping it
through, hold it tight against the inside
surface of the wall by slipping your finger
into the drilled hole and pulling (Fig.

6-17). Use number 6 or 8 screws that are
¾ to 1 inch long to hold it in place. Small
screws are needed because they don't require pilot holes. You don't have enough
hands to start a pilot hole for a bigger
screw.

At this point, it is probably best to let
the glue set, because the glue will be
stronger than the few screws you put in.

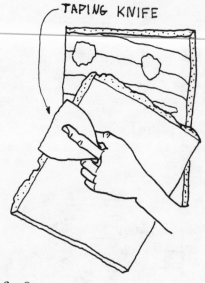

FIG. 6-18

FIG. 6-19. OPENING A 5-GALLON BUCKET

If you can't wait, proceed very cautiously and put only gentle pressure against the wood backer. Cut a piece of gypsum board ⅛ inch smaller than the hole (see pages 106–107). Put blobs of mastic on the back of it (the side with gray paper). With a putty knife, apply joint compound all around the edge of the patch and push it in place (Fig. 6-18).

Joint compound is similar in consistency to Spackle, but Spackle shrinks less and dries faster. Spackle is used to patch cracks and joint compound is used to plaster the joints in drywall. Gallons and gallons of joint compound are used to hide the joints in a new house and the cost would be prohibitive if it contained the chemical agents in Spackle that keep it from shrinking and help it dry fast. Spackle used to come in a box and had to be mixed; now it comes already mixed in

quarts and gallons. Joint compound comes in 1-, 2-, or 5-gallon buckets. A 2-gallon bucket will do most average-size jobs. If you have a lot of patching to do, the most economical size to buy is the 5-gallon bucket. A 5-gallon bucket of joint compound is one of the heaviest things you'll ever encounter. It weighs around 60 pounds. You need a screwdriver or chisel and a hammer to pry it open (Fig. 6-19). The lid has regular indentations all around it that must be cut. I use my all-purpose screwdriver.

With a wide taping knife, remove some joint compound from the container and smear it on the crack and over the entire surface of the patch (Fig. 6-20). Put enough on to completely hide the crack (1/16 to ⅛ inch thick). When it is dry, sand down the ridges with medium sandpaper wrapped around a block of wood (Fig.

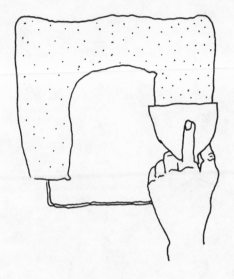

FIG. 6-20

SANDING BLOCK

FIG. 6-21

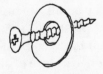

FIG. 6-22. PLASTER ANCHOR

6-21). If the patch still shows, apply more joint compound, this time feathering the edges out away from the patch. Sand between each coat. It usually takes three coats to completely hide a patch.

Small holes and dents don't need backers and that simplifies the process. Rough up the surface surrounding the dent with a sanding block. Fill the dent with joint compound. If the dent is very deep, put only a ¼-inch layer of compound in at a time, so it can dry. Finally, sand with medium sandpaper on a sanding block until the patch is smooth.

HOLES IN PLASTER WALLS

There are always places in old houses where the plaster is loose or has fallen down. This is caused by water leaking in near the spot over the years. When you paint a plaster wall, there are usually places that move when you touch them. You must decide if the plaster will hold or if it will fall down the next time someone bumps into it. It's a tough decision, because patching the plaster involves some work.

One trick to use on plaster that is marginally loose is to screw it to the lath. Putting a washer around the screw spreads out the force exerted by the screw and keeps the plaster from cracking (Fig. 6-22). Get a package of washers that have a middle hole that is big enough so that the head of a Sheetrock screw sits almost flush with the top of the washer. Slip a Sheetrock screw through a washer and, with a variable-speed drill equipped with a Phillips head bit, drive the screw into the plaster. Chances are that you will hit a piece of lath and the screw will hold

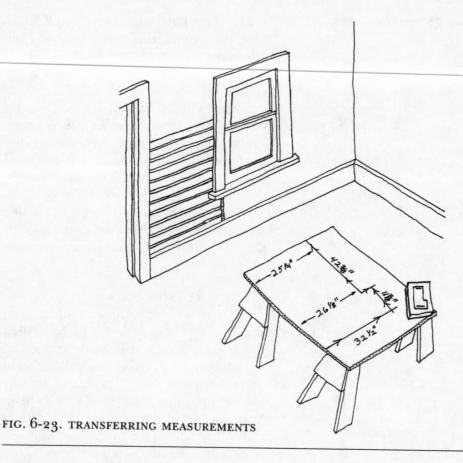

FIG. 6-23. TRANSFERRING MEASUREMENTS

snugly to the plaster. If you miss the lath you'll know it, because the screw will go right in without resistance. The washer will stick out from the wall about ⅛ inch, which is fine if you have a slew of them in one area and can hide them by plastering over them with joint compound. Otherwise, it's a good idea to hollow out a place for the washer so that it is flush with the surface. Use a grinder bit on a drill for this. Don't use a hammer and coal chisel (a chisel made to cut metal and stone) because the blows will loosen more plaster.

Where plaster has fallen or it has been necessary to pull it down and expose the lath, a drywall patch is needed. Three-eighths-inch Sheetrock is usually the thickness of the plaster that has been removed. It will be screwed into the studs directly over the lath.

Before this is done, the ragged hole must be made rectangular so that a piece of Sheetrock can be cut to fit in the hole. Use a coal chisel or an all-purpose screwdriver to dent the plaster in the shape of a rectangle. With a flat bar or the claw of your hammer, pull the loose plaster off within the dented rectangular perimeter.

Measure the dimensions of the hole

and transfer those measurements onto the piece of ⅜-inch Sheetrock. A lot of mistakes in measuring are made in spatial reasoning, the ability to see a shape as it is and transfer it elsewhere. To avoid these errors, I always draw the shape I'm measuring on a scrap of paper or board and write the measurements of each dimension near the appropriate line (Fig. 6-23). Measure at intervals along the length of the rectangular shape, because chances are that the sides of the hole are not parallel.

Screw the piece into the studs with Sheetrock screws and a variable-speed drill. The screws should be countersunk just below the surface, but not so far as to break the paper.

Using a drywall knife (4 to 6 inches wide), smear joint compound over each screw and on all edges, as in Fig. 6-20. Over each edge, apply a strip of drywall tape, which looks something like cash-register tape. Cut a piece of drywall tape to the length of the joint, center it over the joint, and embed the tape in the compound by drawing the taping knife along the joint. Press firmly enough to push the tape into the compound and to remove excess compound as the joint knife is drawn along the joint. With some joint compound on your knife, draw the knife along the joint, applying a thin skim coat over the tape. When this first coat is dry, sand out the ridges with a sanding block. Apply a second coat of joint compound to the tape and feather out the compound 2 inches beyond the edges of the first coat. When the second coat is dry, sand again and apply a third and final coat. It's difficult to hide the joints of a patch like this. More coats may be needed. The more you

feather the edges, the better the joint will look.

Plaster ceilings often have a rough texture. If the patch is in the ceiling, you will have to sand down the surface texture at least 6 inches around the perimeter of the area to be patched. If you don't, the taping knife will leave ripples in the joint compound every time it hits a bump. After you have made a smooth transition from patch to ceiling, the patch will have to be textured to match the ceiling. Texture paint is a type of paint to which a texturing substance like sand has been added. Applying texture paint over the patch will help it blend into the rest of the surface.

CRACKS

A rule of thumb for cracks is that most of them are structurally harmless unless they are getting bigger. A crack that changes cyclically with the seasons is caused by swelling of building materials as a result of temperature and moisture shifts and doesn't signal building damage. Horizontal and vertical cracks that are ⅛ inch wide and under are rarely a cause for concern. If the plaster has cracked in a regular pattern that looks like alligator skin or a map of Europe, this indicates failure of the plaster, not of the structure. The plaster will eventually fall down. Diagonal cracks are the ones that indicate that the building has moved in the past (Fig. 6-24). Tension cracks are most common in old houses, and the tops of the cracks actually point to the wall or column that has sunk. Compression cracks occur if the exterior walls sink but the interior columns stay put.

Even if the cracks do not indicate

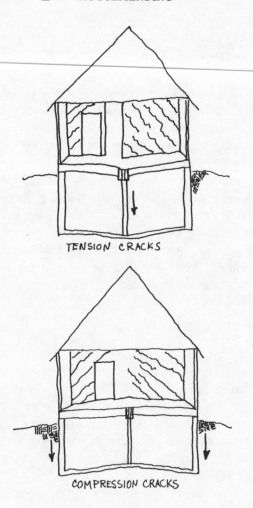

TENSION CRACKS

COMPRESSION CRACKS

FIG. 6-24. THE MEANING OF CRACKS

paintbrush dipped in water. Using a flexible putty knife, fill the entire opening with spackling compound. When it is dry, sand it smooth with fine sandpaper wrapped around a block of wood. All cracks should be primed before painting.

REPLACING AN ACOUSTICAL TILE

Whenever you put up acoustical tile, it's a good idea to save some leftovers in a corner of the attic, so that if one is damaged you have a replacement. First, cut around the offending tile with your utility knife (Fig. 6-25). You are cutting through the tongues and grooves that hold one tile to the next. After it has been removed, clean away any staples that remain in the furring strips to which the tile was attached. Furring strips are pieces of wood that are evenly spaced and attached to a surface to form a nailing base. Cut the tongue and groove edges off the back of the replacement tile, using a utility knife (Fig. 6-26). Spread mastic on the back perimeter of the tile and push it up into place, so that the glue makes the bond between tile and furring strips. If the tile is not held in place by friction from other tiles, a pole can be used to prop up the tile until the glue sets (Fig. 6-27).

Moisture Problems

There are many signs of moisture problems in a house: mildew on the walls, condensation on the windows in winter, and peeling exterior paint. If any of these occur, it means that there is an excess of moisture in your house and it's having trouble getting out. The cause of the high moisture levels can be any number of things: a damp crawl space or basement

damage to the structure, they are unsightly and should be filled before painting. Cracks that are 1/32 inch and under can be filled by using your finger to force Spackle into the crack. Larger cracks must be filled with Spackle, and to keep the Spackle in the cracks, they should be opened up a little. A can opener is a good tool for this. Drag the pointed end along the crack to widen its opening. Moisten the sides of the crack by painting it with a

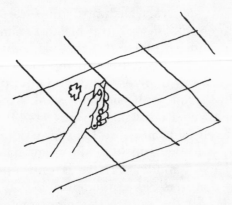

FIG. 6-25. REPLACING AN ACOUSTICAL
CEILING TILE

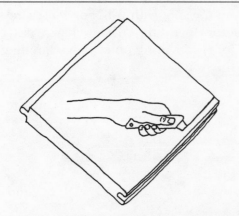

FIG. 6-26. CUTTING ACOUSTICAL TILE

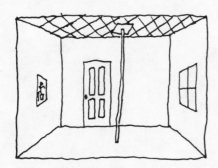

FIG. 6-27

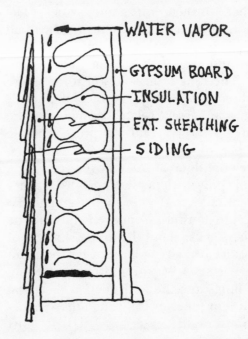

WATER VAPOR
GYPSUM BOARD
INSULATION
EXT. SHEATHING
SIDING

FIG. 6-28. MOISTURE CONDENSATION
WITHIN WALLS

that is transmitting water vapor into the house, a wet life-style (lots of showers, cooking with open pots, and drying laundry in the house), and drying firewood inside. High levels of moisture (above 30 percent relative humidity) never show up in old drafty houses. It's the tightly built new houses or the tightened-up old houses that exhibit these symptoms.

Mildew and peeling paint are caused by moisture condensation in the exterior walls (Fig. 6-28). Moisture is constantly passing through all exterior walls, whether it be in new houses or old. However, old houses were so drafty that the condensed moisture was carried away by the wind. When we tightened our houses by adding insulation, not so much wind rushed through the wall cavities. The moisture that condensed in the wall stayed there, causing peeling paint, mildew, and eventually rotting studs.

The long-term solution to moisture problems is to keep the moisture levels below 30 percent relative humidity in the winter. Cook with lids on pots, ventilate the bathrooms, don't dry wood indoors, cover the floor of the crawl space with a 6-mil. polyethylene sheet, and do whatever it takes to dry up the basement. To stop the moisture from even entering the walls, you can paint the inside surfaces of the exterior walls with vapor-barrier paint (see page 31). Most important is to plug any holes into the wall, such as electrical outlets or pipes. It is through these penetrations of the exterior wall that most moisture passes. Hardware stores carry packages of foam gaskets, which, when inserted under outlet and switch-plate covers, stop infiltration. It's also important to caulk around all pipes, vents, and interior window trim with silicone caulk (see "Priming and Caulking," pages 41–43).

Even with all those long-term solutions, you may still have the immediate problem of mildew. There is only one thing that gets rid of mildew and that's bleach. All the mildew cleaners on the market contain bleach in varying strengths. After these cleaners have been applied and the wall scrubbed, it is safest to paint the spot with B-I-N or white shellac before painting. Mildew has a nasty habit of reappearing unless you eliminate it in this way.

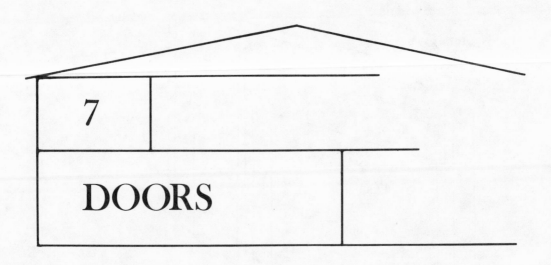

7

DOORS

Doors literally bridge the gap between the stud skeleton that is the functional part of a wall and the finished beauty of polished trim. The door itself is definitely part of the finish woodwork, but there would be no door if a hole had not been left in the wall during framing. The hole, into which the door will eventually fit, is called the rough opening. It is space bounded by the two trimmer studs, the header, and the floor (Fig. 7-1). Notice that the studs on either side of the rough opening are doubled. This is done for two reasons. Structurally, it is needed to compensate for the stud that was removed to make way for the door. The trimmer studs hold up the header and the header supports the weight that would have been held by the stud had it not been curtailed. The

king studs, which are the two full-length studs next to the trimmers, keep everything in line. The doubling also means that there is more wood behind a door opening to nail the door casing to.

The door jamb is inserted into the rough opening and is attached to the trimmer studs by means of skinny wedges made out of cedar shingles. The door jamb has three pieces: two side jambs and a head jamb. The trimmer studs can be a little out of plumb—that's why it's called a rough opening—but the side jambs must be exactly vertical. If the jambs are not vertical, the door will fall open or closed. I'm sure you have experienced the frustration of a refrigerator door that falls closed instead of just staying where you put it.

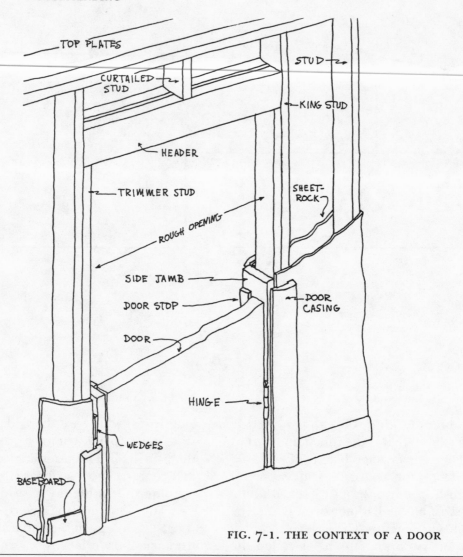

TOP PLATES

CURTAILED STUD

STUD

KING STUD

HEADER

TRIMMER STUD

SHEET-ROCK

ROUGH OPENING

SIDE JAMB

DOOR STOP

DOOR CASING

DOOR

HINGE

WEDGES

BASEBOARD

FIG. 7-1. THE CONTEXT OF A DOOR

The door is attached to the jamb by means of hinges. There are usually two, one at the top and one at the bottom. Large exterior doors usually have a third in the middle. The entire weight of the door is supported by the hinges. That is a lot of weight no matter what the door is made of. Add to this other mysterious forces that affect a door (Fig. 7-2), and you can understand why they tend to sag and form parallelogram-like shapes over the years. It's one of the reasons doors stick.

Types of Doors

There are two kinds of doors. The traditional type is the panel door. It consists of solid wood panels framed by stiles

FIG. 7-2. FORCES ACTING ON A DOOR

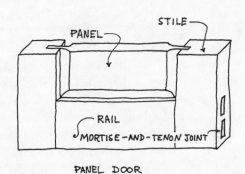

PANEL DOOR

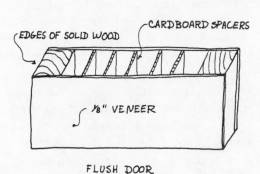

FLUSH DOOR

FIG. 7-3. TYPES OF DOORS

(vertical) and rails (horizontal) (Fig. 7-3). The panels are set into grooves in the stiles and rails, which are held together by mortise-and-tenon joints. This kind of joint has a lot of surface area, which allows a good glue bond. It is a very strong joint and it needs to be, when you remember the forces acting on a door. If you look at the edge of some doors, you may see the tenon.

The flush door is a more modern door. Most houses built since 1950 are equipped with them. They are made of two pieces of ⅛-inch-thick plywood on either side of a frame of solid wood. The plywood can be made of any wood, though pine, birch, mahogany, and oak are the most common. The door is hollow in the middle except for cardboard spacers which, by virtue of their tensile strength, keep the two sides of the door equidistant. (As an example of tensile strength, roll a piece of paper up into a cone, fasten it with a piece of tape, stand it on end, and place a book on the paper. The book will be held by the paper, which has temporarily become a column because of its tensile strength.)

Common Problems with Doors That Swing

When dealing with doors that stick, always remember that the door used to fit in the hole. There are many tricks to making a door swing freely again, so don't reach for the saw or plane first.

DOORS THAT STICK

Doors stick for many reasons: too many layers of paint, loose hinge screws, a bent hinge pin, swelling because of

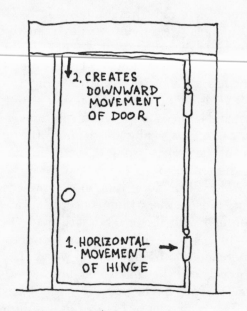

FIG. 7-4. HORIZONTAL MOVEMENT
TRANSLATES INTO VERTICAL

damp weather, or loose joints. It is your job to discern the reason. Always begin with the easy problems first.

If the door fits tightly into the jamb (with no gaps on either side), paint or wood will have to be planed off. But that is a last resort. If there is a ⅛-inch crack —even on one side—between the door and the jamb, the door can be repositioned within the jamb so that it does not stick.

Determine where the door is hitting the jamb. This tells a lot about which hinge is causing the problem. If the top of the knob side of the door is hitting the jamb, the problem is that the top hinge barrel is too close to the knob side of the door. If the top edge of the knob side of the door is hitting the head jamb, chances are that the bottom hinge is the problem.

Moving the hinge barrel away from the knob side of the door will free the door, because by moving the barrel horizontally you also move the top edge of the door down. When you are playing with one hinge, the door is held only by the other. Any movement you induce by tightening screws or inserting shims will pivot the door around the other hinge. This is how a horizontal movement at the bottom hinge can translate into a vertical movement up at the top, knob side of the door (Fig. 7-4). If the bottom of the door is hitting the jamb, the bottom hinge barrel must be moved away from the knob side.

A door can also have the opposite problem and not stay closed. As you close it, you will feel it resist your hand just as the door is almost closed. It will feel as if there is a spring between the door and jamb that is pushing the door back open. The hinge edge of the door is actually hitting the hinge-side jamb before the door is closed. When this happens, the door is said to be hinge-bound. The remedy is to move the barrels of both hinges away from the hinge side of the door.

All this movement is accomplished by inserting thin cardboard shims behind the hinges. It is amazing the effect a $\frac{1}{32}$-inch-thick shim can have. If the shim is placed toward the back of the hinge mortise, as at A in Fig. 7-5, the barrel of the hinge moves away from the knob side. If the shim is inserted behind the front edge of the hinge leaf, as at B, the barrel moves toward the knob side. When the barrel of the top hinge moves toward the knob side, the top half of the door moves toward the knob side. When the barrel of the top hinge moves away from the knob side, the top half of the door goes with it.

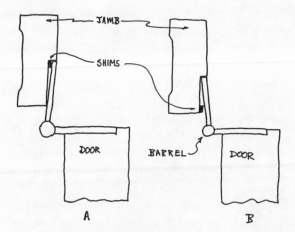

FIG. 7-5. SHIMMING A DOOR

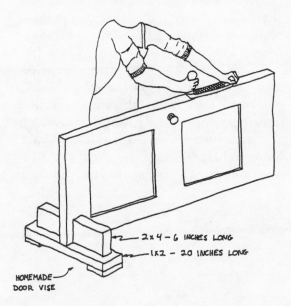

2 x 4 - 6 INCHES LONG

1 x 2 - 20 INCHES LONG

HOMEMADE DOOR VISE

FIG. 7-6. PLANING A DOOR EDGE

Sometimes the cause of a door sticking is as simple as loose hinge screws. If the hinge screws are loose, you may hear a bumping noise as the door opens and closes, because the hinges are actually

moving away from the jamb and back again. The solution, of course, is to find a screwdriver and tighten the screws.

PLANING OR SHORTENING A DOOR

The decision to take wood off a door should come only after the above solutions have been tried. There are two situations that usually require a door to be planed or cut: a too thick paint layer on the edge of a door and a door that drags along the floor because it is too long.

If tightening the hinge screws and shimming the hinges have not freed up the door, it's time to take some wood off the edge. If the amount to be taken off is very small (less than ⅛ inch), a plane can be used. If anything more than ⅛ inch must go, it's quicker to use a saw. Many times the edge can be planed in place. However, if you find planing at odd angles difficult, it is easy to take a door off its hinges. Once off, the door can be planed in a homemade door vise that will hold it firmly while you work on it (Fig. 7-6).

Taking Doors Off Hinges

To take a door off its hinges, open the door halfway. Place a wedge under the door toward the knob side. With a screwdriver in one hand and a hammer in the other, tap the hinge pin upward until it is free of the hinge barrel (Fig. 7-7). It is difficult to get your screwdriver under the head of the hinge pin if it is tight against the barrel of the hinge. Put the screwdriver tip firmly against the joint between the head of the pin and the barrel, and tap the handle of the screwdriver with the hammer. Sometimes a nail can be inserted into a hole at the bottom of the barrel, and by tapping the nail upward the hinge

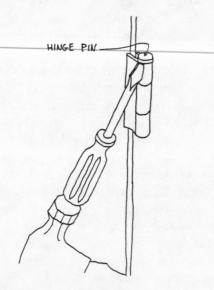

HINGE PIN

FIG. 7-7. REMOVING THE HINGE PIN

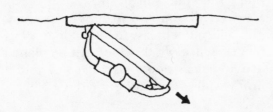

FIG. 7-8. REMOVING THE DOOR

pin will pop up enough to let you get your screwdriver under the head.

First remove the bottom hinge pin and then the top one. The wedge under the door should prevent it from falling down, although the door may shift when you remove the last hinge pin. The door is now free of its moorings. Stand facing the door with one hand on the knob edge and the other holding the hinge edge. Your hand should be able to fit around the hinge edge, because the door is half open. Move the door horizontally away

from the hinges until the hinge leaves on the door slide out of the barrel of the hinge on the jamb (Fig. 7-8). The door is now off its hinges and you can move it wherever you like.

Carrying Large Objects

There is a trick to carrying large objects like doors or pieces of plywood. The trick is to find the midpoint or balancing point of the object and lift it there.

As you stand holding the door, turn your side to the door, so that your strongest arm is behind you gripping one edge and your other arm in front of you gripping the other edge. Your strongest arm should be exactly at the balancing point—approximately the midpoint of the sheet (Fig. 7-9).

Grip the front edge with your weak arm about 1 foot below the midpoint. As you bend your knees, this arm rocks the door back onto your strong hand, which acts as a fulcrum as you straighten your knees to help lift the sheet. Shift the door onto your back a little so that the shoulder

FIG. 7-9. CARRYING HEAVY THINGS

blade of your strong-arm side is in contact with the sheet. In this position, with a little practice, you can carry doors, sheets of plywood, ladders, and the like.

If you are carrying something and it feels excruciatingly heavy, you are doing something wrong. You are probably not lifting at the midpoint. Put the object down and try again to locate the balance point.

SAWING OFF A DOOR BOTTOM

While the door is still on its hinges, determine how much the door needs to be shortened. If the floor around the door is level, the door can be cut off evenly along the bottom. If one side of the door is closer to the floor than the other, you can make the door bottom look more even by cutting more off the side of the door that is closer to the floor.

Lay the door on a pair of sawhorses or across two chairs (Fig. 7-10). As an example, let's say you need to take ¼ inch off the door bottom. Measure ¼ inch up from the bottom on the knob side and make a mark. Because the door bottom may be uneven, make the measurements for the cut *from the top of the door,* not the bottom. Measure from the top of the door down to the mark you made on the knob side. Now measure this same distance from the top of the other side of the door and make another mark at the bottom. Connect the two marks and you have the line you should cut along.

It is important to score the wood with a knife just above this line so that the wood around the cut doesn't splinter when the saw goes through. Lay a straightedge about ⅛ inch above the line and cut into the wood about ⅙ inch deep.

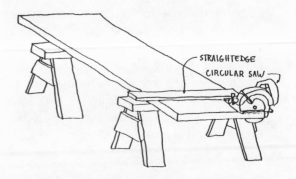

FIG. 7-10. CUTTING OFF A DOOR BOTTOM

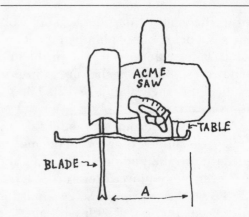

FIG. 7-11. BLADE OFFSET FROM EDGE OF TABLE

This is especially important to do on a flush door, because it is so easy for the veneer to splinter when it's sawed.

Never cut off a door without using a guide. Measure from the edge of the table of the saw into the part of the blade that is closest to the edge (distance A in Fig. 7-11). The table of the saw is the metal plate that rests on the wood. Lay a straightedge above the cut line by this much (usually around 3 to 4 inches) and clamp or nail (with fine nails) the straightedge in place (see also Fig. 2-21).

Now you are ready to cut. Hold the edge of the saw table tightly against the straightedge as you saw across the door. If you have measured correctly, the blade should be sawing along the cut line. You should be pushing the saw forward but also into the straightedge at the same time. For a full explanation of the circular saw, turn to pages 17–19.

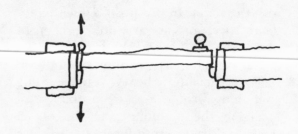

FIG. 7-12. WHY DOORS CLOSE BY THEMSELVES

DOORS THAT SWING OPEN OR CLOSED BY THEMSELVES

When a door doesn't stay where you put it, the jamb is not plumb. The problem is not being out of plumb in the direction parallel with the wall; the problem is being out of plumb in the direction perpendicular to the wall (Fig. 7-12). The solution is to move the hinges in or out so that the door becomes plumb. For instance, the upper hinge can be moved more toward the middle of the jamb and the lower hinge moved toward the edge.

To do this, the hinge screws must be unscrewed, the screw holes plugged, a larger hinge pocket mortised out, if necessary, and new screw holes drilled for the newly positioned hinge.

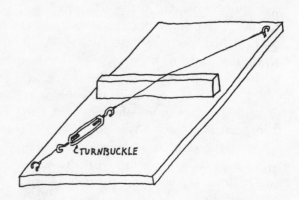

FIG. 7-13. CORRECTING A WARP IN A DOOR

WARPED DOORS

There are three ways to correct a warp in a door. One is to lay the door flat and put weight on it for a few days. This means taking the knob off (see pages 120–23). Another is to lay the door on two sawhorses and place weights on top of the door in order to bend it the other way. A third method is useful when the door is twisted. Screw hooks into diagonally opposed corners of the door and string a wire and turnbuckle between the two (Fig.

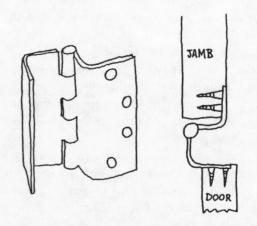

FIG. 7-14. SWING-CLEAR HINGES

7-13). Place a 2×4 under the wire. By tightening the turnbuckle, the two corners of the door will be pulled up and the warp corrected after a few days.

SWING-CLEAR HINGES

A door with standard hinges intrudes into the open space between the jambs about 1 to 2 inches. Sometimes widening the opening by this amount is important. Swing-clear hinges are designed to swing a door completely clear of the opening (Fig. 7-14). For wheelchair users, they can make the difference between passing through a doorway gracefully or with scraped knuckles. They are available through Stanley Hardware.

Knobs, Strikes, and Latches

When knobs stick or doors refuse to latch, it is sometimes a problem with the lockset. The lockset consists of the knob, spring mechanisms, and the strike plate. These problems are usually solved by replacing springs or adding lubrication.

DOORS THAT WON'T LATCH

Often the latch bolt won't seat itself into the strike plate because the bolt isn't centered on the hole in the plate. The house may have settled and caused movement of the door or the jamb. The easiest solution is to enlarge the hole in the strike plate or to move it. If the latch bolt is just grazing the strike, it will be easiest to use a file to enlarge the hole (Fig. 7-15).

Strike plates are usually mortised into the jamb. (In this sense, the word "mortise" is a verb meaning to chisel out.) In other words, part of the jamb has

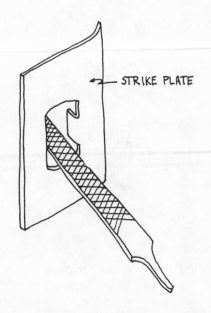

FIG. 7-15. FILING DOWN THE STRIKE PLATE

been chiseled out for the strike so that it will sit flush with the surface of the jamb. Moving the strike plate involves chiseling out a little more wood. Fig. 7-16 shows how to mortise out a hinge pocket. The procedure is the same for strike plates. First, trace around the hinge leaf (A). Then indent that perimeter line using a chisel with the bevel facing toward the hinge pocket (B). Tap the chisel into the wood, as in C, with the chisel bevel up. Go as deep as the hinge leaf is thick. Then, with the bevel down and beginning at the same end of the hinge pocket where you started before, tap the chisel lightly to clear out the chips (D). Finally, smooth the bottom of the pocket with the chisel bevel up. (For the correct way to hold a chisel, see Fig. 9-10, p. 158.)

When the plate has been moved, the

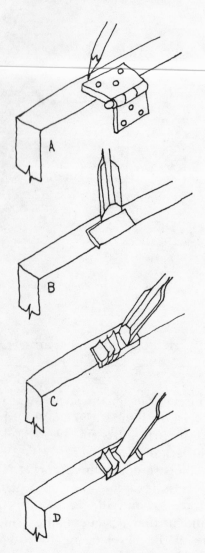

FIG. 7-16. MORTISING OUT A HINGE
POCKET

matchsticks, or whittled plugs so that new screw holes can be drilled without the bit slipping into the old holes.

Sometimes the latch bolt doesn't spring out far enough to seat itself into the strike plate. This can be caused by dirt, a faulty spring, or the lockset's being screwed together too tightly.

There are basically two kinds of locksets: mortise and tubular. Mortise locks (Fig. 7-17) usually have a large rectangular plate around the knob, whereas tubular locks (Fig. 7-18) have a circular rose plate. The rose plate is the circular metal plate that surrounds the base of the knob and rests against the door. When you look at the edge of the door, mortise locks will have a larger face plate (3 to 6 inches) than tubular locks (under 2 inches long).

To free up a stuck lockset it is usually necessary to take the lock off the door and then take it apart. Before doing that, try fiddling with it. Turn the knob hard one way and then the other. If it's a tubular lock, loosen the rosette screws and the face plate screws just a little. This may do the trick.

You may think that taking something apart is scary because you fear never getting it back together. But if you save all the screws and parts and *remember or jot down what goes where,* you'll be able to succeed where all the king's horses and all the king's men couldn't. Just work systematically and stay in your most calm and rational state of mind. Remember that the worst thing that can happen is that you may have to call a locksmith or take your dismantled lockset to him or her for assistance.

chiseled-out place where it used to be is revealed. This can be filled with wood filler or drywall compound. As always, when a hinge or plate is moved, the old holes should be filled with toothpicks,

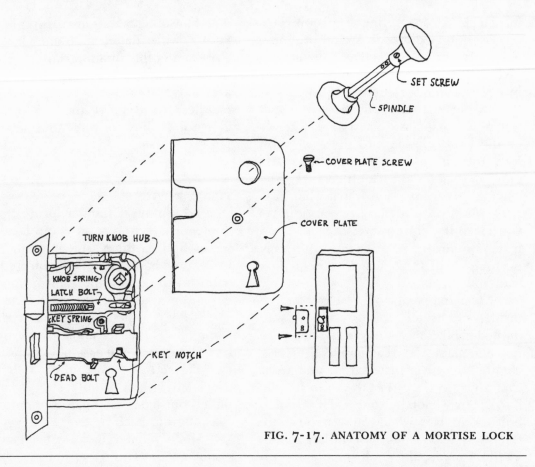

FIG. 7-17. ANATOMY OF A MORTISE LOCK

MORTISE LOCKS

To remove a mortise lock from a door, first unscrew the set screw in one of the knobs and slide the knob (some twist off) off the spindle. The other knob and spindle can now be slid out of the lockset. Next, unscrew the two screws that hold the face plate onto the edge of the door. The black box can now be pulled out of the door. Grasp the latch bolt or face plate and pull. If there is resistance, push a screwdriver through the hole where the spindle was and push the screwdriver toward the edge of the door. This should force the black box out a little so that it can be removed.

Lay the black box on a table. On one side of it you should find a cover plate screw or screws. Unscrew these and carefully remove the black metal cover plate. Now just look at the parts for a minute and compare what you see with Fig. 7-17. Locate the three springs. Two are flat metal springs and the latch bolt spring is the coil type. The most common problem with mortise locks is broken or misplaced springs. Do the flat springs weave correctly around the nubbins that hold them in place? Are any springs broken? Have any been jiggled loose? Are all the moving parts seated correctly? You may be saying "How would I know?" You'll know by observation. Stay calm and keep looking. Make the mechanisms work and watch what happens. Insert a screwdriver or the knob spindle into the turn knob hub, turn it, and watch how the parts move in relation to each other. Insert the key in the key hole and watch what happens when you turn it. One caution: As you make the parts move, prevent them from popping out of place by periodically pushing them back into the metal box with your finger.

Clean the years of dust out of the insides of the lock with a cotton swab dipped in oil. Spray some lubricant on the moving parts and reassemble the lock. Tighten the cover plate screws and see if everything works. Insert the knob spindle into the turn knob hub and see if the latch bolt springs back when you turn the knob. If it doesn't, loosen the cover plate screws a little. Remove the knob spindle and insert the mortise lock into the door. Slide the knob spindle through and replace the other knob. Situate the knob so that one of the holes in the spindle is visible through the set screw hole in the knob handle. There are several holes in the spindle so that it can adapt to doors of varying thickness. The set screw should be screwed through the set screw hole in the knob and into the hole in the spindle. Finally, replace the face plate screws.

A lot of people have trouble gripping a knob. There are a couple of things that can be done. One is to dip the knob in liquid rubber or some other grip-increasing material that makes it easier to turn.

The other solution is to replace the knobs with handles. Some hardware stores and rehabilitation centers can supply the handles. If replacement handles aren't available, locksets equipped with handles are. Remove the old lockset as above and follow the directions for installing the new one.

TUBULAR LOCKS

To remove a tubular lockset from a door, unscrew the rosette and face plate screws and set them aside in a safe place. Place one hand on one knob and one hand on the other and pull in opposing directions away from the door. The knob that is not attached to the spindle should come off. The other knob can be jiggled free of the latch bolt assembly and slid out (see Fig. 7-18). Now nothing is holding the latch bolt assembly and it can be pulled out from the edge of the door by grasping the latch bolt.

Some tubular locks come apart by removing the knob that doesn't contain the push-button lock. This type of lock has no rosette screws. Instead, the removable knob will be held onto the spindle by a small rectangular catch that slips through a corresponding rectangular hole in the shank of the knob. The knob is removed by depressing this metal catch until it is below the surface of the knob shank and then pulling the knob off. The rest of the dismantling is as above.

Examine the parts. If they are dirty, clean them with a cotton swab dipped in oil. Lubricate the moving parts with light oil or graphite. If the lockset goes on an exterior door and you live in a cold climate, use graphite—the cold weather

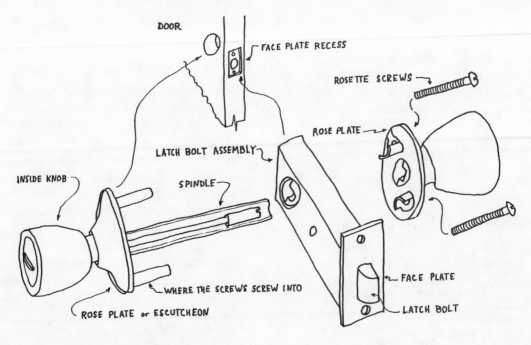

FIG. 7-18. ANATOMY OF A TUBULAR LOCK

makes oil useless as a lubricant. Turn the knob to work the lubricant into all the parts. After lubricating, if the latch bolt does not spring back when it is depressed, the problem is most likely a bad spring within the latch bolt assembly. Take the latch bolt assembly to a hardware store and replace it.

When all parts have been cleaned and lubricated, replace the lockset. First, insert the latch bolt assembly. Then slide the spindle through its hole in the latch bolt assembly. Finally, slip the other knob over the spindle and screw in the rosette and face plate screws. Turn the knob a couple of times each way. If the latch bolt doesn't spring out as it should, loosen the

rosette screws a little. If that doesn't do it, loosen the face plate screws a little. If that doesn't work, the lock will have to be replaced or taken to a locksmith.

Replacing the lockset will be a lot easier if you purchase a lockset with the same hole-size requirements as the one you are discarding. The holes drilled in a door for a lockset vary from 1½ inches to 2⅛ inches in diameter. To drill such a large hole requires a special bit called a hole-saw bit (see Fig. 10-11). Furthermore, it is very difficult to drill a larger hole where there is already a large hole because there is no pilot hole to keep the bit steady. It is best to avoid all this and replace the lockset with a similar one.

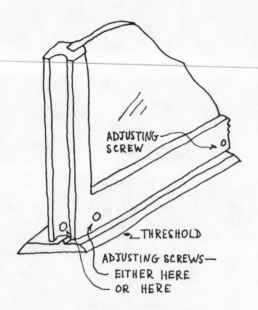

ADJUSTING SCREW

THRESHOLD

ADJUSTING SCREWS—
EITHER HERE
OR HERE

FIG. 7-19. ADJUSTING A SLIDING DOOR

Problems with Nonswinging Doors

There are several kinds of nonswinging doors: sliding, bifold, and pocket. Sliding doors are most commonly found on closets or used as the entrance to patios. Bifold doors are the most common kind of closet door. Pocket doors slide into the wall and are used when there isn't room for a door to swing. Most of the problems with these doors arise from their going out of plumb.

You can tell when a sliding door is out of plumb by pushing it almost closed and looking to see if the door edge is parallel to the jamb or not. If it isn't, the door should be adjusted (Fig. 7-19). A sliding glass door moves on concave wheels, like pulley wheels, that straddle a track. The wheels can be moved up or down by turning the adjusting screws that are located

at the bottom of the door—one on the left and one on the right as you face the door. Some models have the adjusting screws on the edge of the door, others on the face of it.

If there is an uneven gap between the door and the jamb (wider at the top than at the bottom), the adjusting screw under the lock should be turned counterclockwise, so that that end of the door will move downward. This will widen the gap at the bottom of the door and make the door more plumb. The screw on the nonlock side of the door can also be used. If it is moved clockwise, that end of the door should move upward, thereby moving the top lockside edge of the door toward the jamb. The two screws should be used together until the door edge is parallel with the jamb.

When a sliding door is very hard to move, it has probably come off its track. Kneel down and actually look at what is happening under the door. Usually lifting the door as you push it back on its track does the trick. If this doesn't work, unscrew both adjusting screws all the way so that you have as much room as possible to lift the door, and try again.

Bifold doors are hinged to each other but not to the jamb. They swing from top and bottom pivot pins at one side of the door (Fig. 7-20). There is a roller protruding from the top edge of the knob side of the door. The door does not hang from this roller; its function is merely to keep the top of the door in the track. These pivot pins fit into a holder that can be adjusted to plumb the door. Usually it is the pin at the top that can be adjusted for plumb. The pin at the bottom can be adjusted for

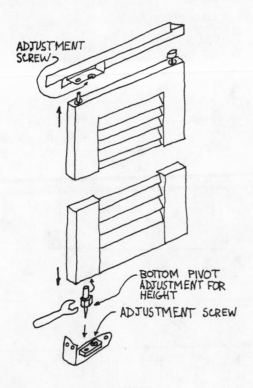

FIG. 7-20. BIFOLD DOOR

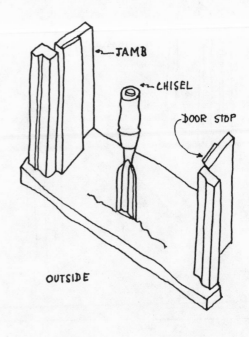

FIG. 7-21. REMOVING A THRESHOLD

height. A small crescent wrench is the tool needed for adjusting the height of the door. A screwdriver is usually called for to adjust the position of the top pivot. By unscrewing the holding screw, the pivot slides freely in the upper track. Moving the pivot toward the jamb moves the knob end of the door upward.

Other Door Problems

REPLACING A THRESHOLD

The threshold of an exterior door gets a lot of wear and weather. It is common for them to rot out or wear down so thin that they need to be replaced.

To remove the old threshold, first open the door wide or remove it from its hinges. If the door stops are removable, remove them. Some door stops are nailed on, but others are integral to the jamb, as in Fig. 7-21. Try to remove the threshold in one piece by prying up with a crowbar. If it extends under the jambs, the threshold will be harder to remove because it is attached by hidden nails through the jamb bottoms and into it. If the threshold is rotten enough, hitting it with a hammer to push it horizontally out from under the jambs may dislodge it. Otherwise it will have to be removed in pieces. Splitting the threshold with a chisel into small pieces that can be worked free is one method (Fig. 7-21). Sawing the threshold

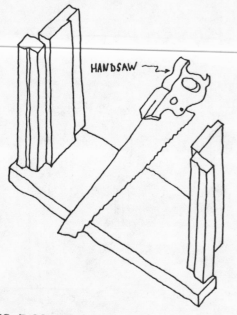

FIG. 7-22

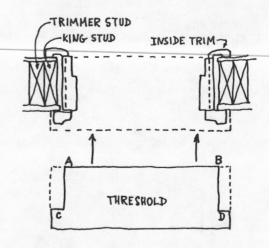

FIG. 7-23

into two or three pieces is another (Fig. 7-22).

The reason you want to try to get the threshold out in one piece is that then you can use it as a pattern for the new one (Fig. 7-23). Thresholds can be purchased at lumberyards. They are made of oak or pine and they come unfitted. It's up to you to cut the notches appropriate to your particular door. The ends of the old threshold can be placed on the uncut threshold and traced around. The cuts may be started with a circular saw but must be finished in the corners with a handsaw.

Before sliding the new threshold in under the jambs, snip off any nails protruding down from the bottom of the side jambs. Lay a large bead of caulk down on the rough sill before you install the new

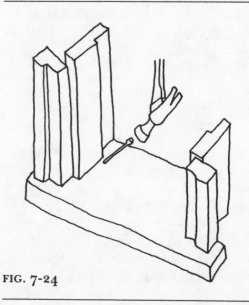

FIG. 7-24

threshold, to prevent air infiltration. The new threshold should look like the one in Fig. 7-23. The width between the notches (distance A–B) should easily fit between the trimmer studs with a ½-inch space on either side. Points C and D should fit tightly up against the sheathing. When the threshold has been tapped into place, it should be nailed, as in Fig. 7-24. Set the nails and seal the holes with caulk or paint.

STORM AND SCREEN DOORS

A typical problem with aluminum storm doors is that they don't close properly. These doors are subject to the same forces that act on other doors. They can sag because of a loosening of the frame screws on the upper hinge side.

A storm door is hung in an aluminum frame that fits inside the exterior trim of the door. The frame also has a flange that extends out over the face of the trim and is screwed to it (Fig. 7-25). If the door has sagged so that the bottom hits the threshold, the solution is to tighten the screws on the upper hinge side of the frame. It may be necessary to remove several of the upper screws in order to push the frame tighter against the trim. Remember that there are screws into both the edge and the face of the trim.

Another common problem with storm doors also involves screws. Often the wind will catch these doors, and the screws anchoring the spring or door closer will be torn loose. The door closer is the aluminum tube that looks like a bicycle pump and pulls the door closed. The remedy for this is to put a wood plug into the old screw hole, relocate the door closer bracket slightly, and drill new holes for the screws.

INSTALLING WEATHERSTRIPPING

There are several different kinds of weatherstripping (Fig. 7-26). The kind that is the longest lasting and most effective is spring metal or plastic molded in

FIG. 7-25. A SAGGING SCREEN DOOR

the shape of a **V**. The metal is nailed onto the top and side jambs, bridging the gap between the jamb and the edge of the door. The plastic **V**-strip comes with an adhesive backing, but it should be nailed or stapled every 12 inches because the adhesive often fails to hold through the winter.

To apply **V**-strip weatherstrip, first open the door completely. Obviously, it is better to do this in the summer when it's warm than at the last minute. Not only will you stay warmer, but the adhesive on the back of the plastic **V**-strip adheres much better when it's warm.

Cut a piece for the top jamb that runs the full length from side jamb to side jamb. Both the metal and plastic **V**-strips are installed with the open end of the **V** toward the great outdoors. The metal strip should be nailed with the nails provided in the predrilled holes. After the

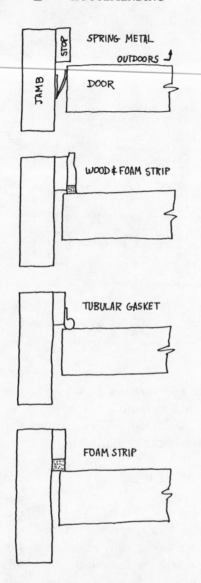

FIG. 7-26. WEATHERSTRIPPING

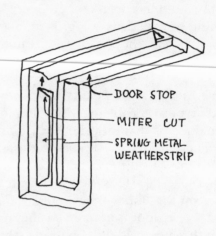

FIG. 7-27. MITER CUT ON V-STRIP

protective paper has been peeled off the back of the plastic strip, it is pushed against the jamb, which should be clean and dry. Tack the strip down every 8 inches with small brads.

The pieces of weatherstrip for the side jambs should be mitered at the top (Fig. 7-27). This means cutting the spring flap at a slight angle so that the spring flap of the side piece rests lightly against the spring flap of the top piece when both are slightly compressed.

The bottom of the door needs a different kind of treatment. Fig. 7-28 shows several options. The door sweep is the easiest to install. To install it, nail or screw it to the side of the door where the hinge barrels are. When the door is closed, the rubber blade or nylon brush should touch the threshold along its entire length.

The other two treatments for a door bottom may require the door to be shortened. See "Sawing Off a Door Bottom," pages 117–18. To install a door shoe, the door may have to be removed from its hinges. If the existing space between the door bottom and the threshold is perfect to allow the shoe to be installed and the rubber gasket to compress against the threshold when it is closed, then the door does not need to be shortened. If the

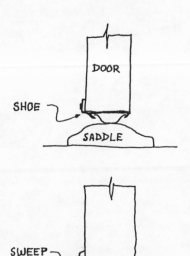

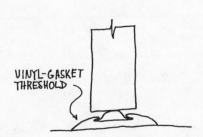

FIG. 7-28. DOOR-BOTTOM TREATMENTS

space is so large that after the installation of the shoe, the rubber gasket doesn't contact the threshold, a shim should be added to the door bottom to bring the shoe closer to the threshold (Fig. 7-29).

Another way to deal with the draft under a door is to install an aluminum threshold with a vinyl gasket (saddle). This is also a good way to cover a partially worn threshold. The door must be removed, but before you do this, place a piece of tape on the face of the door near the bottom and another across from it on the face of the door stop (Fig. 7-30). Make a pencil mark across the two before removing the door. The marks will serve as a reference point from which to measure when deciding how much of the door must be shortened to accommodate the new threshold. Measure from the mark on the door stop to the top of the rubber gasket. Now measure this same amount plus ⅛ inch down from the mark on the door. This is the cut line for the bottom of the door. The extra ⅛ inch assures that the door will compress the rubber gasket.

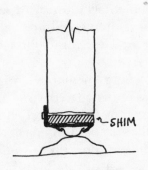

FIG. 7-29. MAKING A DOOR LONGER

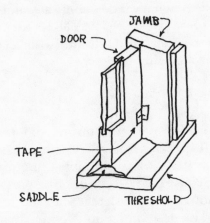

FIG. 7-30. INSTALLING A NEW SADDLE

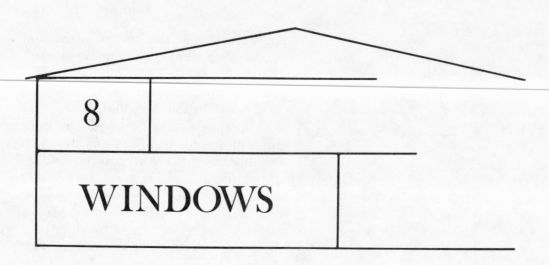

8

WINDOWS

Windows are holes through the walls of a house. They bring a view of the outside in but keep the elements out. Since the windows are the thinnest part of the house, this is where the elements occasionally leak in. Rain is obvious when it finds its way in through a window, but the wind is not so obvious. Houses lose 30 to 40 percent of their heat through cracks—most of them around the windows.

Types of Windows

Windows come in several different styles (Fig. 8-1). The most common up until the 1970s was the double-hung window. It consists of two sashes (the part of a window that opens) that slide up and down. The design of a double-hung window allows only half the area of the win-

dow to open for ventilation. Yet double-hung windows are the most prone to infiltration.

The most common window today is the casement. It has the advantage of having all its area openable for ventilation. The sash, which is hinged at the side, opens by turning a handle. It is the tightest type of window. Some companies are making casement windows with very good weatherstrip systems and infiltration ratings as low as 0.25 cfm (cubic feet of air per minute).

The awning or hopper window is often placed under a fixed pane. This type can be hinged at the top (called an awning) or at the bottom (hopper). They can also be tightly made with low infiltration ratings. This style of window is popular in houses designed for people in wheel-

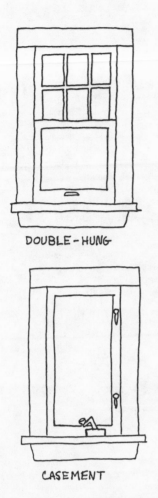

DOUBLE-HUNG

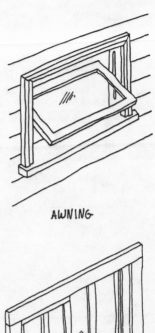

AWNING

CASEMENT

SLIDER

FIG. 8-1. THE DIFFERENT TYPES OF WINDOWS

chairs because the handles and opening mechanism are placed low, where they can be easily reached.

The slider has two sashes, but one is usually fixed, as in a sliding glass door. One sash slides horizontally by the other so that only half of the total window area can be used for ventilation. This type of window is seen infrequently.

HOW A WINDOW WORKS

The old double-hung window is by far the most complicated kind of window, equipped as it is with secret pockets in the wall, counterweights, and pulleys. Modern versions have springs instead of counterweights and no pockets in the wall are required, which makes these a lot more energy efficient. Generally, this type of

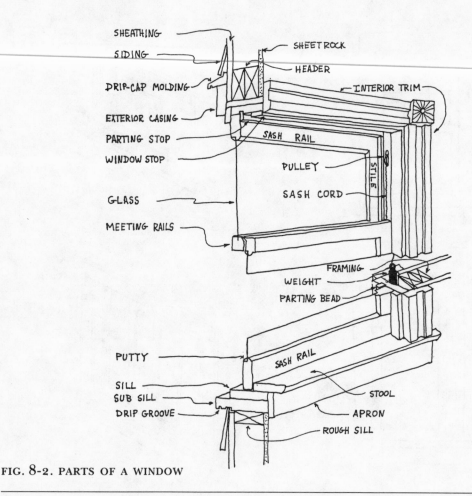

SHEATHING

SIDING

SHEET ROCK

HEADER

DRIP-CAP MOLDING

INTERIOR TRIM

EXTERIOR CASING

PARTING STOP

SASH RAIL

WINDOW STOP

PULLEY

STILE

GLASS

SASH CORD

MEETING RAILS

FRAMING

WEIGHT

PARTING BEAD

PUTTY

SASH RAIL

SILL

SUB SILL

STOOL

DRIP GROOVE

APRON

ROUGH SILL

FIG. 8-2. PARTS OF A WINDOW

window is not as tight against infiltration as the casement window.

The parts of a double-hung window are illustrated in Fig. 8-2. The upper sash is exterior to the bottom sash so that there will be no water leakage at the meeting rails where the two come together. The bottom sash and the top sash are separated by a vertical molding appropriately called the parting bead or stop. This piece creates two vertical tracks for the windows to slide in. It can be slipped out of its groove in the jamb (it is not nailed) so that the top sash can be removed. Both sashes are connected by a chain or cord to a counterweight that slides up and down in a pocket in the wall. The weights allow the bottom sash to stay up when you raise it. If it doesn't do so, the counterweight has probably come loose and is lying at the bottom of the wall pocket.

Before you start to reattach the weights in your double-hung windows, consider replacing the counterweight sys-

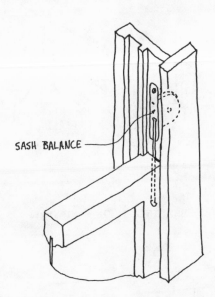

SASH BALANCE

FIG. 8-3. A SASH BALANCE INSTALLED

tem with a sash balance (Fig. 8-3). It is a more energy-efficient system, since it allows you to fill up the weight pockets with insulation. Another solution is to let the weatherstrip hold up the sash. Many kinds of weatherstripping, like spring metal or aluminum track, hold the window tight enough so that it stays where you put it.

To reconnect the weight, remove the panel that is in the lower sash track near the bottom. It is approximately 1½ inches × 5 inches and is held in place only with a small nail. When the panel is removed you can see into the secret pocket where the weights are. Remove the weight and feel around for the cord. Pull the cord out through the hole the panel covered. Tie the cord onto the weight and slip both back into the pocket. If the cord has long since disappeared or has been pulled out

of the pulley at the top of the track, tie a small weight onto a piece of string and thread it through the hole over the pulley. Grab the weight once it shows through the panel hole. Tie the other end of the string to the new sash cord and pull it through the panel hole.

The cord may be so old that it needs to be replaced. For this the bottom sash must be removed. This can be done by removing one side of the window stop. (The window stop consists of two side pieces and one top piece of interior molding that hold the sashes in place. They are sometimes held in place by screws so they can be easily removed.) The bottom sash should slip out. There are grooves in the edges of the sash into which the sash cord is fastened. Tie a knot in the end of a length of sash cord (cotton rope with a nylon center) and insert it into the groove. Tie the other end of the cord onto the weighted string and fish it through the panel opening, as described above.

A casement window opens by means of a handle. As you turn it, two sets of gears move and operate a lever outside that opens the window. This type of window is locked closed with one or two handles. Windows with one handle close to the bottom are easiest for disabled people to operate.

KEEPING A WINDOW WORKING

Windows stick for any of three reasons: the sash wood has become swollen as a result of an increase in humidity (a seasonal problem), paint or dirt has accumulated in the sash tracks, or the installation of weatherstripping has made the window too tight. First, make sure the tracks are clean. Use an old chisel to clean out the paint buildup in the corners of the sash track (against the parting stop and the window stop). With a sanding block that fits into the track, sand down the paint buildup on the edges of the track. If all this doesn't allow the window to move freely, remove the parting stop and window stop and plane them down a bit. If the window is still tight, remove the sash and plane it down. See pages 24–25 and Fig. 9-14, page 159, for how to use a plane.

Leaks

When you think about it, it is a miracle that windows don't leak more often. The main reason they don't is because of the flashing over the window (Fig. 8-4). This is a small piece of metal or vinyl that fits over the exterior window casing and up and under the siding. As the rain travels down the siding and reaches the top of a window, it hits the flashing and drips off it onto the ground. Rain cannot get in the sides of a window if the joint where the siding meets the exterior window casing is well caulked. The only place left for rain to get in is under the sill. But notice in Fig. 8-2 that there are two notches on the underside of the windowsill. The little one is a drip groove that causes any water traveling up the underside of a sill to drip off at that point. (Yes, water can travel uphill—that's why leaks are so insidious.) The second notch allows the siding to be tucked up under the sill so that blowing rain won't penetrate here. This joint should be caulked also. How to caulk is explained on pages 41–43.

When rain leaks in around a window

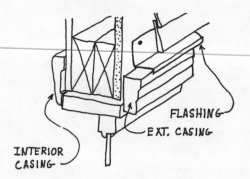

FIG. 8-4. FLASHING OVER A WINDOW

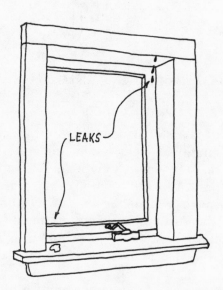

FIG. 8-5. LEAKS AROUND A WINDOW

(Fig. 8-5), check the three areas mentioned above: drip-cap flashing and the well-caulked sides and bottom. If everything is as described above, the leak is not coming from the window but from farther up the wall or, more likely, from a leak in the roof (see Chapter 10). When water is dripping in from the head jamb, the rain is getting in through the top of the window or above (the roof). When water appears near the sill, the leak is above that or is being driven in under the sash by heavy storms. If your inspection of the window exterior turns up old caulking or no drip-cap flashing, this is the problem.

The top of a window leaks either because there is no drip cap or because the piece of siding above the drip cap is pressed tightly against the flashing. Water can work its way uphill between two surfaces that are close together through capillary action. There should be a good ⅛ inch of space between the flashing and the butt edge of the siding.

To install drip-cap flashing over a window, gently pry up the piece of siding above the window and remove the nails. Slip the flashing up under the siding and tap the siding back into place. Do not nail the siding through the same holes. Nail the siding at least 1 inch above these so that the nails just catch the upper edge of the flashing. Always remember to nail flashing only near its upper edge—nail holes admit water, which defeats the purpose of the flashing.

Sash Problems

STICKING

Windows are always getting painted shut. To free the lower sash, place a stiff putty knife or window bar against the joint between the sash and the window stop and tap it with a hammer (Fig. 8-6). This breaks the paint seal. If more is needed, you may pry the bottom sash upward—but never from the inside. Prying from the inside leaves divots in the wood-

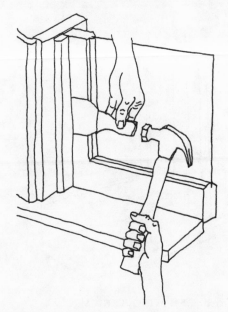

FIG. 8-6. BREAKING THE PAINT SEAL ON A SASH

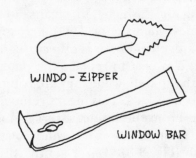

WINDO-ZIPPER

WINDOW BAR

FIG. 8-7. WINDOW TOOLS

work. Go outside and insert the pry bar under the lower sash and pry against the sill. The paint seal on a window can also be broken with a window-preparation tool (Fig. 8-7). It cuts through the paint layers as you move it along the seam in long strokes.

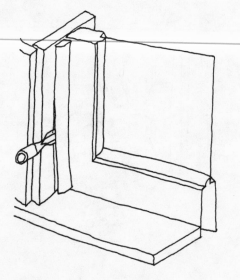

FIG. 8-8. REMOVING THE SASH

REPLACING A PANE OF GLASS

If a pane can be replaced without removing the sash, by all means do so. Sometimes when the broken pane is in a second-story window or is otherwise inaccessible, it is best to replace the pane of glass with the sash, while they are lying on a nice work surface. This means removing the sash. From the inside, insert a chisel into the seam between the window stop and jamb (Fig. 8-8). Tap it gently with a hammer, trying to get the chisel under the stop. Begin at one end and work toward the other. Pry up the stop on one side of the window. The sash should slip out now. If the sash cords are still attached, pull them out of the grooves in the sash and knot the ends so that the cords don't get pulled into the wall pocket by the counterweights.

Removing the old putty used to be the hardest part of replacing a pane of

glass, but there is a way to make the job easier. Paint the old putty with lacquer thinner and wait five to ten minutes. The lacquer thinner penetrates under the putty and breaks the rock-hard seal. The old putty can now be lifted away in long chunks with a putty knife. Removing old, rock-hard putty is one of the most frustrating and time-consuming jobs there is, but putty is easy to scrape off if it no longer adheres to the wood. It is well worth going to the trouble to get the lacquer thinner.

When the sash wood is clean and free of putty, measure the inside dimension of the depression in the sash where the glass rests (see Fig. 8-9). Glass comes in standard sizes, like 9 × 13, for use in multipane window sashes. If your pane is a standard size, the hardware or glass store may have it precut. If not, measure from the shoulder of the rabbet on one side to the opposite shoulder, and then from the top to the bottom shoulder. The glass should be cut ⅛ inch smaller than these dimensions. For instance, if the area where the glass will rest is 12 inches × 14 inches, the piece of glass should be cut 11⅞ inches × 13⅞ inches, so that there

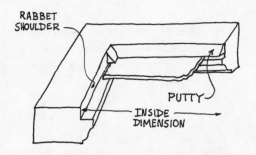

FIG. 8-9

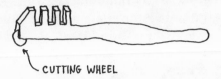

FIG. 8-10. GLASS CUTTER

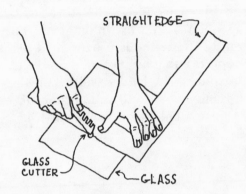

FIG. 8-11. CUTTING GLASS

is room for the pane to expand and contract with the change of seasons.

To cut a piece of glass to the proper dimensions, first lay it down on a clean (no grit), flat surface—preferably covered with carpet or cloth. Measure off the dimensions and mark them on the glass with a felt-tipped pen or crayon. Clean the glass along the cut line with gas or paint thinner. In our example, measure off 11⅞ inches from the left edge at both the top and the bottom. Gently lay a straightedge on the glass connecting these two marks, and with a glass cutter score the glass. A glass cutter is a pencil-like tool equipped with an extremely sharp metal wheel that actually is hard enough to scratch glass (Fig. 8-10). You hold it like a pencil or

between the index and middle finger and, with firm steady pressure, run it along the straightedge to cut the glass (Fig. 8-11). Do not go over your scratch line; it will dull the glass cutter. If there are portions along the line where no scratch occurred, go over just these parts, being careful not to touch the part of the line that has been scratched.

Lay the scored piece of glass over the edge of a table so that the score lines up with the edge. Hold the measured piece firmly against the table's surface and push down with a quick, sharp motion on the unsupported waste piece. It should break off cleanly along the scored line. If it doesn't and there are some irregular breaks, grasp them with a pliers and break them off in the same way.

Paint the edges of the rabbet with linseed oil or thinned exterior paint to prevent the absorption of the oil in the glazing putty into the sash wood. Lay a small bead of glazing compound (it has the consistency of soft clay) on the edge of the rabbet on which the pane will rest. Place the glass on it and press the glass into the putty. With a screwdriver, push glazing points (approximately 6 inches apart) into the sash to hold the glass in place (Fig. 8-12). The points have little shoulders

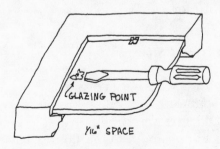

FIG. 8-12. REPLACING THE PANE

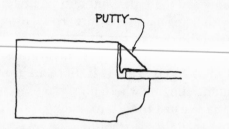

FIG. 8-13. PUTTYING A WINDOW

that the point of a screwdriver can push against. They should be pushed into the wood until the shoulder stops them.

It is the glazing points that actually hold the glass in; the putty keeps the water out. Roll some putty into a snake-like shape in your hand and press it into the corner formed by the glass and the shoulder of the rabbet (Fig. 8-13). Continue around the entire perimeter. It is okay if it looks like a child has done this. Now smooth the putty out with a putty knife. Hold the putty knife at an angle and run it along the putty. The angle at which you hold the putty knife determines the angle of the putty. If the angle is too shallow, the putty will extend into the glass too far and be visible from the inside.

After the putty has dried for a week it can be painted. Allow the paint to overlap onto the glass at least $1/16$ inch to seal it against rain.

Screens and Storms

REMOVING WOODEN STORMS AND SCREENS

Older storm windows and screens are made of wood. Some houses have a complete set of each. The windows are all numbered with thumbtacks with embossed numbers on them and the storms and screens are numbered to match. When it is time to exchange the storms for the screens, the screen number is matched to the window number.

The wooden frames are easy to remove. They are hung from two hooks on the exterior head casing of the window (Fig. 8-14). This allows the storm to be swung open on warm winter days. The bottom of the frame is usually held by a hook and eye that are fastened on the inside of the sill. A ladder will be needed when removing second-story frames (see how to use a ladder on pages 43–45).

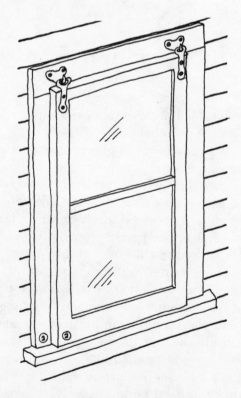

FIG. 8-14. WOODEN STORM WINDOW

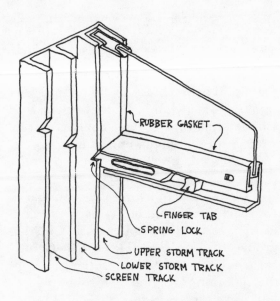

FIG. 8-15. ALUMINUM COMBINATION
STORM WINDOW

CHANGING COMBINATION STORMS

Most houses nowadays are equipped with combination storm windows. They are an improvement over the wooden storms as far as convenience goes, but they are not necessarily an improvement in energy efficiency. Only the more expensive models are made tight enough to prevent air infiltration.

Combination storms usually work on a three-track system (Fig. 8-15). The outer track holds the upper storm, the middle track holds the lower storm, and the inside track carries the screen. Each aluminum frame slides up and down within the track and locks in place where there is a notch. To move the storm sash, the finger tabs at both sides of the sash must be pushed away from the notch to release the spring locks. Once free, the aluminum sash can be pushed up or down

until the spring locks find another notch. The finger tab is difficult for many people to get their fingers into. It also requires a lot of finger strength to pull against the spring-loaded lock. For people who find these tasks difficult, interior storms may be the answer. They are available from energy stores.

In winter, the upper storm should be in the upper part of the outer track and the lower storm should be in the lower part of the middle track. The screen is stored in the upper part of the inside track. When summer comes, push the storm in the middle track up into the upper half of the window and bring the screen down from its winter storage area down to the lower half of the inner track.

REPLACING SCREENING IN WOOD AND ALUMINUM SASH

To replace screening, carefully pry up the screen molding that holds the old screen in a wooden sash (Fig. 8-16). Save it and use it to hold down the new screen. If it breaks as you are removing it, more can be purchased at the lumberyard. Just ask for screen molding. Cut the new screen 2 to 3 inches bigger than the old

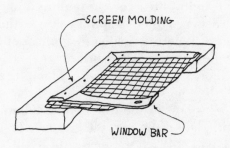

FIG. 8-16. REMOVING THE OLD SCREEN

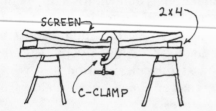

FIG. 8-17. REPLACING SCREENING IN WOODEN FRAMES

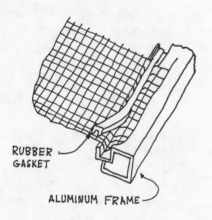

FIG. 8-18. INSTALLING SCREEN IN ALUMINUM FRAMES

screen. This excess will give you something to hold on to when stretching the screen tight. Bowing a wooden frame (Fig. 8-17) before stapling down the screen will aid a wrinkleless application. Place the frame on a flat surface and place 2×4 blocks under both ends. Clamp the middle of the frame to the flat surface, creating a bow in the frame. Staple both ends in place using a staple gun (see Fig. A-6, page 214). Now release the clamp; the screen will be pulled taut. Staple the screen down on the sides under where

the screen molding will go, pulling it tight as you go. Finally, tack the molding in place.

Replacement screen comes in many materials: nylon, brass, or aluminum. Aluminum or nylon is appropriate for wooden frames. The type that is easiest to work with in aluminum frames is the nylon screen, because it is easily compressed by a rubber gasket.

Cut a piece of nylon screen so that it overlaps the aluminum frame by several inches. Insert the rubber gasket in the groove on one side (Fig. 8-18). Gently stretch the screen and insert the gasket in the side opposite. A screen roller, which looks like a pizza cutter, is helpful in inserting the rubber gasket. Repeat for the remaining sides.

REPLACING GLASS IN ALUMINUM FRAMES

Aluminum storms consist of four pieces of aluminum channel held together by four corner locks (Fig. 8-19). The pane

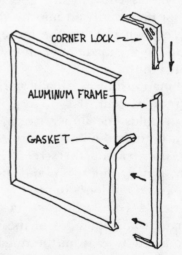

FIG. 8-19. REPLACING GLASS IN ALUMINUM STORM WINDOWS

of glass is wrapped in a rubber gasket that fits into the aluminum frame. To determine the size of a replacement pane, measure the broken shards if they are available. If not, measure the inside dimension of the rubber gasket within the channels. One leg of the frame will have to be pulled off to allow the new glass to be inserted. Grip one end of a leg with a pair of pliers and pull. Repeat with the other end. Wrap the new pane in the rubber gasket and insert it in the three-sided frame. Finally, tap the last leg into place with a hammer—gently.

PATCHING SCREENS

When the cat claws the screen to tell you it wants to come in, every claw enlarges the screen holes so that mosquitoes can get in. Instead of getting rid of the cat for the summer, fill the little holes with

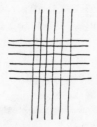

FIG. 8-20. A SCREEN PATCH

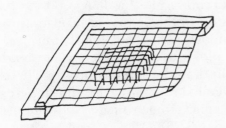

FIG. 8-21. MESHING THE PATCH INTO THE SCREEN

clear nail polish or glue. Acetone-based glue works best on plastic screen.

For large holes, make a patch out of another piece of screen. It can be sewed in place with fine wire or thread. Another way to attach a patch is to unravel a few of the edge strands (Fig. 8-20), bend the remaining ends down at a right angle (Fig. 8-21), and mesh the patch into the rest of the screen. Finally, bend the ends back to hold the patch on. Wire screen must be used for this method of patching because the plastic screen doesn't stay bent.

Windows As Heat Drains

WEATHERSTRIP

If a window can remain closed all winter, it can be caulked shut with a clear caulk that will peel off in the spring. Clay rope is also effective. The window can even be painted shut, as many people do with the upper sash of double-hung windows. The only kind of weatherstrip that really keeps out infiltration while allowing the window to operate is the metal or plastic V-strip (Fig. 8-22).

Metal V-strip has a longer lifespan than does plastic, but it is more expensive. The metal strip is held on with small brads. The plastic strip comes with adhesive on the back. Just peel off the paper tape and stick it on. I would also tack it down with brads or staples, because the adhesive sometimes gives out.

The hardest place to weatherstrip is the meeting rails of a double-hung window. Raise the lower sash as far as it will go and lower (if possible) the upper sash enough to expose the meeting rail. Apply the V-strip to the interior side with the open end pointing down. The open end

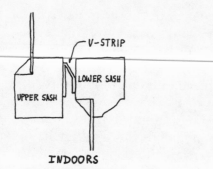

INDOORS

V-STRIP

LOWER SASH

UPPER SASH

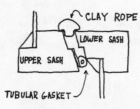

CLAY ROPE

LOWER SASH

UPPER SASH

TUBULAR GASKET

MEETING RAIL

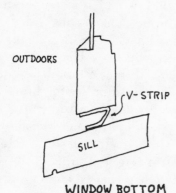

OUTDOORS

V-STRIP

SILL

WINDOW BOTTOM

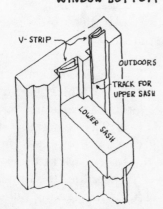

V-STRIP

OUTDOORS

TRACK FOR UPPER SASH

LOWER SASH

FIG. 8-22. INSTALLING WEATHERSTRIP

should always point toward the outside (see Fig. 8-22). Some meeting rails are skinny and it's very difficult to attach weatherstrip. Clay rope or tubular gasket is best in these cases, though the clay rope will have to be replaced every time you open the window.

The piece of weatherstrip on the bottom of the bottom sash is the easiest to install. Raise the lower sash and nail or stick it in place.

The side pieces can usually be installed without removing the sash. Many people have long since painted the upper sash shut, which leaves only the two sides of the lower sash to weatherstrip. Cut two pieces of **V**-strip so that they are 3 inches longer than the lower sash. Raise the lower sash as far as it will go and install the pieces of **V**-strip in the track. Bend the piece of weatherstrip and push it up behind the bottom edge of the sash. Make sure the plastic **V**-strip is in place before you remove the paper covering the adhesive. Tack most of the strip in place while the sash is raised, and tack the part that was covered after the sash has been lowered.

WINDOW INSULATION

A lot of heat escapes your house through the windows because they are so thin and conduct heat well. A good way to put a stop to this is to add insulation to the windows. The insulation is put over the windows at night when you would normally draw the curtains anyway. There are several kinds. Three are shown here: pop-in panel, roman shade, and window quilt (Fig. 8-23). All are available from energy stores and the first two can be made at home with kits.

Pop-in panels consist of a piece of rigid insulation board with foam glued around the perimeter to assure a tight fit against the jamb. A slipcover of attractive material can be made to fit over the insulation board. When not being used, they can be stored behind the sofa. Kits are available through Aerius Design, Kingston, New York.

A roman shade is made of four layers: an aluminized film and ¼-inch-thick batting sandwiched between two layers of cloth. The curtain is fixed at the top and raised by means of a cord. The edge seal is provided by magnetic tape. A piece is attached to the interior casing (the tape has adhesive on the back), and another piece of equal length is attached to a piece of half-round molding the length of the shade. When the shade is down, the two pieces of half-round molding are placed over the magnetic strips on either side of the window, thereby holding the shade in place by magnetic force.

A good edge seal is very important in window insulation because it helps keep the infiltration down. Window quilts have one of the best edge seals. They are an extruded plastic track into which the edges fit. Dealers usually install window quilts, but homeowners can buy the components and do it themselves.

Reaching Shades

Shades are difficult to operate if you're in a wheelchair. There are two solutions. One is to lengthen the cord on the shade so that when the shade is in its raised position, the end of the cord is still reachable from a sitting position. The

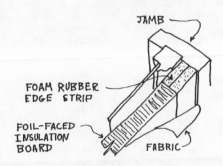

POP-IN PANEL

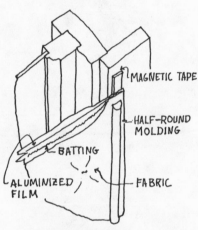

ROMAN SHADE

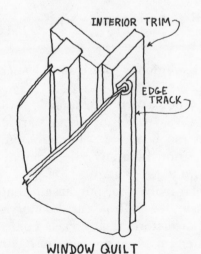

WINDOW QUILT

FIG. 8-23. TYPES OF WINDOW INSULATION

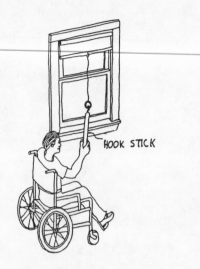

FIG. 8-24. USING A HOOK STICK

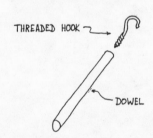

FIG. 8-25. HOOK STICK

other solution is to use a hook stick (Fig. 8-24).

A hook stick is a valuable tool. It is basically an extension of one's arm. Hook sticks can be made at home or the local occupational-therapy department can make one for you.

To make one, purchase a length of ½-inch dowel from the lumberyard or hardware store. The dowels come in 3-foot lengths. You may be more comfortable with a 2-foot stick. Into one end of the dowel, screw a hook, which you can also purchase at the same store (Fig. 8-25). It should be one with wood threads on it. You may have to drill a pilot hole for the hook if it is large. Drill a hole several sizes smaller than the shank of the hook, because you will be screwing the hook into end grain and threads don't hold as well there. The other end of the stick is the handle and it can be dipped into liquid rubber for extra gripping power.

Replacing Counterweights

The counterweight system in double-hung windows is not energy efficient because it requires empty pockets in the wall where the weights travel. There can be no insulation in these pockets. A more energy-efficient method for keeping window sashes where you put them is to fill the pockets with insulation and replace the counterweights with a sash balance (see Fig. 8-3).

The weights are removed through the access panel in the lower part of the track, as described on pages 132–33. Remove the pulleys by unscrewing the two screws that hold them each in place. Insert the spring balance and screw it into place. Remove the lower sash as was described on page 136. Screw the attaching flange into the groove in the sides of the sash and hook the spring-loaded tape to it. Replace the sash, and you have a window that stays up by itself but doesn't waste as much energy.

Another solution to the counterweights is replacement track. They are available from hardware stores and lumberyards and serve both as weatherstripping and as a means of keeping the window up.

9

FURNITURE AND CABINET REPAIR

We live our daily lives in, on, and around furniture. A well-designed piece that works can make an everyday routine such as getting dressed a joy. A dresser with drawers that stick can set the day off to a frustrating start. You owe it to your peace of mind to try to fix such things.

Troubleshooting

To fix something, you must determine not only what is wrong but what is causing the problem. You may have noticed that a cabinet door or drawer is sticking. The critical question is why. The answer is obtained through observation. Move the door back and forth. Pull the drawer in and out. Watch what happens. Try to observe details. Where is it rubbing? Is the hinge pin bent? Is a piece of hardware broken or damaged? Are the joints loose? Are screws loose? Are the hinges loose? Do the wheels turn easily? Is the wood warped? Are the tracks smooth and parallel? Is it square?

Use all your senses. What about noise? Are there any squeaks? Do you smell anything out of the ordinary? Are the runners rough? Are there uneven places?

Only after you observe the cause, or causes, can you begin to fix the problem. This chapter provides the basic techniques for repair. Some repairs will go beyond the scope of this book or will involve a complex combination of problems. Get advice from your newly acquired friend down at the hardware store. Bring the piece with you, if you can.

Home Remedies for Stains and Repairs

There are so many remedies for stains that I have decided to organize them into a table. Because some household chemicals mentioned in Table 2 can react to a particular finish, it is a good idea to know what the finish is.

The way to identify a finish is to see what dissolves it. Shellac is one of the most common finishes, so start with the solvent that dissolves it—denatured alcohol. On a part of the piece that no one ever sees, rub an area with a rag dipped in solvent. If the finish is dissolved by denatured alcohol, it is shellac. If the finish is softened by denatured alcohol, it is a shellac-lacquer finish, which can be dissolved by a mixture of half denatured alcohol and half lacquer thinner. A lacquer finish will be dissolved by rubbing with a rag dipped in lacquer thinner. Varnish and linseed oil will be dissolved by turpentine or mineral spirits; and oil stain by turpentine, naphtha, kerosene, or paint thinner. Some old chairs have been painted with milk-based paints. Ammonia is the only way to get this off.

One remedy for a surface with many small scratches is re-amalgamation of the finish. With a rag damp with the solvent that dissolves the finish, wipe the surface lightly until the scratches disappear. You are actually dissolving the very top layer of the finish and filling in the scratches.

If a stain has not penetrated completely through the finish, you may be able to remove it. If the stain has reached the wood, the finish must be stripped, the stain removed, and the spot or entire surface refinished. Shellac and lacquer finishes are not resistant to alcohol and water. This is why pieces of furniture finished in these ways are often protected with wax. Wax can protect the finish from a spill left for several hours.

When a stain is near the surface of a finish, a common method of removal is to sand it out. There are many different abrasives of various textures. When removing a stain, always begin with the finest texture and work up the scale to the rougher ones, until one works: cigarette ash, rottenstone, pumice (FFF is finer than FF), steel wool (0000 is finer than 000), and sandpaper (9/0 is finer than 8/0). Rottenstone is a powdered abrasive made from decomposed limestone, and pumice is finely powdered volcanic glass. These abrasives are usually used with oil. Almost any oil will do except a petroleum-based oil, because it will react with the finish. For instance, several of the remedies for removing water spots mentioned in Table 2 involve the use of abrasives: rubbing the spot with 000 steel wool and furniture polish, or rubbing with rottenstone and oil. For the latter, pour a little salad or linseed oil on the surface and sprinkle rottenstone powder on it. Rub with a soft cloth until the scratch has disappeared.

Dents are depressions in the wood caused by the impact of an object that may or may not break the finish. Deeper dents may tear the wood fibers and are discussed on page 153. The cure for a dent is to swell the wood fibers to their original size. The application of moisture and heat will do the trick for shallow dents in softwoods and some hardwoods. Cover the dent with a damp cloth folded over several times and press a heated iron against the

Table 2.

HOME REMEDIES FOR STAINS

MATERIAL	STAIN	CAUSE	REMEDY	RESTORE FINISH	COMMENTS
Wood (finished)	White spots	Unknown	1. Rub with a cloth dipped in cigarette ash and lemon juice or salad oil; or 2. Rub with cloth dipped in rottenstone and salad or linseed oil along the grain; or 3. Rub with cloth wet with naphtha (lighter fluid); or 4. Daub surface with cloth dampened with spirits of camphor or peppermint.	1. Wipe off, rewax. 2. Wipe off, rewax. 3 and 4. Rub with rottenstone and oil, rewax. Rottenstone is powdered decomposed limestone and is available in hardware and paint stores.	Shellac and lacquer aren't resistant to water or alcohol—wipe up spills immediately. Don't use petroleum-based oils; they will harm surface.
		Alcohol (medicine, beverages, perfume)	1. First, try #1 above; or 2. Rub with finger dipped in silver polish; or 3. Rub with cloth damp with a few drops of ammonia; or 4. For old spots or where spill wasn't wiped up immediately, try #2 under White spots (unknown); or 5. Wipe spot lightly with cloth damp with naphtha or turpentine.	1. Wipe off, rewax. 2. Wipe off, rewax. 3. Rewax immediately. 4. Wipe off, rewax. 5. If surface roughens, rub with 000 steel wool dipped in paste wax or oil.	Wax helps protect shellac and lacquer finishes from water damages.

Table 2. (*Continued*)

MATERIAL	STAIN	CAUSE	REMEDY	RESTORE FINISH	COMMENTS
Wood (finished)	White spots	Heat	1. Try #2 or #4 under White spots (unknown); or 2. Wipe spot lightly with cloth damp with camphorated oil. Don't use fuzzy cloth.	1. Wipe off, rewax. 2. Same as #5 under White spots (alcohol).	If the heat has penetrated deep into the surface, these solutions won't work and the surface must be refinished.
	Black spots	Water that has penetrated the finish.	Finish must be removed over spots or over the entire surface. Bleach with a solution of oxalic acid (2 ounces of crystals in a half gallon of warm water) or rub spot with a rust stain remover that contains oxalic acid.	Refinish surface.	Oxalic acid is available at hardware stores. Wear gloves and eye protection when working with oxalic acid. Tubes of stain remover are available in drugstores.
	Ink that has penetrated the finish		1. Blot up immediately, pat spot with damp cloth. Don't rub; or 2. Rub spot lightly with cloth damp with mineral spirits. Rinse with clean water; or 3. Try #2 under White spots (unknown); or 4. Rub spot with 0000 steel wool and mineral spirits in the direction of the grain.	1. Wax and polish. 2. Wax and polish. 3. Wax and polish. 4. If this damages the finish, refinish.	If the ink has soaked through the finish into the wood, the finish should be stripped entirely or just over the spots.

Material	Stain	Cause	Treatment	After-treatment	Comments
	Foggy haze	Moisture	1. Rub with cloth dipped in a solution of 1 tablespoon vinegar in 1 quart water. Let dry; or 2. Rub surface with 0000 steel wool dipped in boiled linseed oil. Rub with the grain.	1. and 2. Apply 2 coats of hard furniture wax, buff.	A white haze often develops on furniture with old shellac-lacquer finishes.
	Paint, tar, or grease		1. If fresh, remove with appropriate solvent: water for latex paint, mineral spirits for oil-base, gasoline for tar, and detergent for grease. 2. If dry, cover spot with linseed oil and let sit until paint is soft. Lift paint with a sharp putty knife, but don't scratch surface. If residue remains, rub with rottenstone and oil.	1. Rewax and polish. 2. Rewax and polish.	Linseed oil is available at paint and hardware stores.
	Wax or gum		Harden the substance by touching it with ice wrapped in cloth. When hard it should lift off with your fingernail. Then rub the spot with 0000 steel wool dipped in mineral spirits.	Wax the spot and polish the entire surface.	
Wood (un-finished)	Rust, water, concrete stains	Condensation from glass, leaks around window	Rub spot with rust stain remover containing oxalic acid or mix 2 ounces oxalic acid crystals in a half-gallon of warm water. Brush solution onto stain and let stand 15 minutes.	Rinse with cold water.	Wear gloves and eye protection with oxalic acid. Oxalic stain remover is available in tubes and works very well on wood as well as cloth.

Table 2. (*Continued*)

MATERIAL	STAIN	CAUSE	REMEDY	RESTORE FINISH	COMMENTS
Marble	Organic	Coffee, tea, fruit, tobacco, ink, iodine	Cover stain with a thick paste of powdered whiting and hydrogen peroxide (hair bleach). Add a few drops of ammonia, and keep the paste damp by covering it with plastic wrap for a few hours.	Rinse with water.	Powdered whiting is available at paint stores.
	Rust	Nails, lamp base, metal ashtray	Cover stain with a paste made from powdered whiting and a rust-reducing agent.	Rinse with water.	
	Oil	Milk products, hand cream, modeling clay	Cover stain with a paste made of powdered whiting and equal parts of acetone and amyl acetate. Let dry.	Rinse with water.	Acetone (nail polish remover) and amyl acetate are available in drugstores.
Concrete	Oil or rust		1. Cover stain with a paste of salt and lemon juice; or 2. Scrub stain with benzene and a stiff brush; or 3. Cover stain with a poultice of 1 part sodium citrate, 6 parts water, and enough powdered whiting to make a paste. Let sit for one week while keeping poultice moist.	For all remedies: Rinse with water.	Benzene and sodium citrate are available in drugstores.
Brick	Tar, oil		Remove bulk of tar with a heated blade, then test to see which solvent works on	Hose off with water. Traces of whiting left	Carbon tetrachloride is available in

		the stain: mineral spirits, gasoline, carbon tetrachloride, or kerosene. Wet area with the solvent that dissolves the stain best and cover the stain with a poultice of powdered whiting and the solvent. Allow it to dry.	on the brick will weather away.	hardware stores and drugstores. Use only in well-ventilated rooms.
Porcelain	Organic	1. Rub stain with carbon tetrachloride; or 2. If stain persists, mix a strong solution of 1 part oxalic acid and 8 parts water. Scrub stain with a brush dipped in this solution.	Rinse with water.	Carbon tetrachloride is available in hardware stores and drugstores. Use only in well-ventilated rooms.
Tile grout	Organic	Scrub grout with a toothbrush dipped in household bleach or kerosene. Let sit for 5 minutes.	Rinse with water.	
Carpet	Nongreasy food, alcohol, blood, washable ink, urine	Sponge with a detergent and vinegar solution. If blood-stain persists use trichloro-ethylene. Use puppy-stain remover or carbonated water on urine.		Wipe up stains immediately. It enhances stain removal.
	Grease, tar, crayon, chewing gum, paint	Scrape off as much as possible. Moisten sponge with dry-cleaning fluid or trichloroethylene and wipe toward the center to avoid leaving a ring.		Cleaning fluids are available at drugstores and hardware stores.

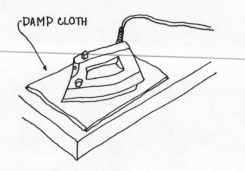

FIG. 9-1. STEAMING OUT A DENT

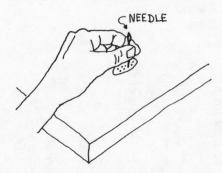

FIG. 9-2. SWELLING A DENT WITH THE AID OF A NEEDLE

cloth (Fig. 9-1). If one application doesn't bring the dent flush with the rest of the surface, repeat a couple of times. If the dent is in hardwood, stronger medicine may be needed. Try a commercial wood sweller, which can be purchased at the hardware store.

On stubborn depressions, try driving a pin or needle ¼ inch deep into the wood of the dent (Fig. 9-2). Remove the pin with a pliers. Cover the dent with a damp cloth and apply heat as before. The holes will allow the moisture to penetrate deeper into the wood and swell more fibers. The holes shouldn't show if you used the pliers to pull the pin straight out. If none of these remedies removes the dent, the hole will have to be filled as described on pages 153–54.

Some light scratches do not go through the finish. These can be filled in any of several ways. Rubbing the nut meat of a black walnut or Brazil nut over the scratch forces the nut meat and oil into the scratch. The oil may darken the scratch enough so that it disappears. Linseed oil, when rubbed into a scratch, may have the same effect. Don't use petroleum-based oils; they will harm the finish.

The scratch can also be carefully colored with shoe polish or iodine to match the finish. Apply the appropriate color shoe polish (brown for walnut, cordovan for mahogany, and tan for light-colored woods) with the tip of a toothpick wrapped with cotton or a small artist's touch-up brush. If the color you apply is darker than the finish, wipe the scratch with a cloth dipped in naphtha until the color matches. For a scratch in red mahogany, dip a small brush in iodine and paint it in the scratch. Dilute the iodine with denatured alcohol until the correct shade is reached for lighter woods. If the finish is shellac, the denatured alcohol may react with the finish. So be careful to paint just within the scratch. If you don't want to bother with these homemade coloring agents, apply oil-base stain with an artist's brush. Choose an appropriate color and thin the stain with a recommended thinner. Apply one coat and let it dry. If it's not dark enough, apply another coat until it is the right shade, each time letting the stain dry. Wax with a hard paste wax and buff.

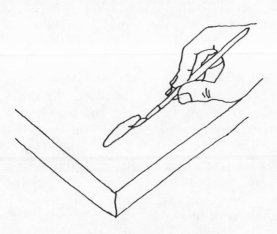

FIG. 9-3. SPOT FINISHING

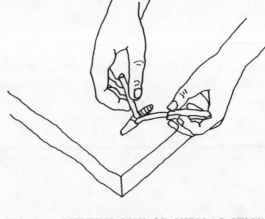

FIG. 9-4. MELTING WAX OR SHELLAC STICK
INTO A DENT

Medium scratches can be stained and filled with shellac, using a small artist's brush (Fig. 9-3). Dilute a small amount of the appropriate color oil stain with a little turpentine or thinner. Apply the stain to the scratch with an artist's brush. Let each coat dry about fifteen minutes, and apply another coat until the color matches the surface. With the same brush, fill the scratch with clear shellac and let it dry for four to five hours. If the shellac dries to a level below the surface, apply another coat. Sand the patch smooth with 8/0 sandpaper, and finish by rubbing the area with rottenstone and oil. You can rub with your fingers or with a soft cloth. Wipe and wax the entire surface.

If the surface is marred by many small scratches, rub the surface lightly in the direction of the grain with 0000 steel wool dipped in paste wax, then buff. Repeat if the scratches still show.

Filling scratches of any depth is done with fillers. There are several: wax stick, shellac stick, and wood putty (or plastic wood). Of the three, wax sticks or pencils are easiest to use. They come in different shades to match various woods: mahogany, walnut, colonial maple, and so on. Select the shade that matches the surface or mix two shades together to obtain an exact match. You can either mix the wax by breaking off small pieces and kneading them together in your hands, or you can actually melt the two shades together over heat. If the scratch is not too deep, the wax can be rubbed across it until the scratch fills up with wax. Scrape the excess off with a plastic credit card. Deeper gouges may require melting the wax into the groove (Fig. 9-4). Heat a curved knife (a grapefruit knife will do) over carbonless heat: an electric burner, alcohol lamp, or propane torch. The other sources you may be tempted to use, such as a candle or a gas burner, will deposit soot on the knife and discolor the wax. After heating the knife, hold it with the curve pointing down over the groove. Touch the wax to the knife. It will melt and flow into the groove. Melt enough so that the wax filling the groove rises above the rest of the surface. When the wax is cool, use a single-edged razor blade to scrape off the excess wax, so that the patch is level with the rest of the surface. Smooth down any irregularities with your finger.

A large patch may be obvious because the grain of the wood doesn't continue through it. This can be remedied by painting the grain on with a small artist's brush dipped in oil paint or stain. A wax patch can be left like this, but it may bleed into the surrounding surface. To make the patch more durable, spray a light coat of polyurethane or varnish over the spot, or brush a wash coat of shellac or polyurethane (a one-to-one mixture of shellac and denatured alcohol or polyurethane and its recommended thinner) over the entire surface. Blend this into the rest of the finish by rubbing with 0000 steel wool dipped in oil. Wax the entire surface with a paste wax.

Plastic wood is a popular filler. Its drawback is that it is opaque when dry and may stand out from the rest of the finish. It is excellent for painted surfaces and is available in hardware and lumber stores in cans and tubes. If it is crumbly, it can be brought back to life by adding the solvent recommended by the manufacturer. It can be stained to match the surface with oil stain. If the plastic wood is stained before it is put in the gouge, color it darker than the surrounding finish because it will lighten as it dries. It can also be applied in its natural hue and stained after it has dried. Make sure all wax, polish, or grease has been removed from the gouge. Pack the plastic wood into the depression with a putty knife until it is a little higher than the surface. It will shrink a bit while it dries and when it has, use fine sandpaper to sand the patch down until it's flush with the surface.

A finish similar to the rest of the surface can be applied to the patch with an artist's brush (see Fig. 9-3). If the finish is shellac, carefully brush on some clear shellac, feathering it into the surrounding finish. When it has dried, buff the patch with 0000 steel wool, and then wax the whole surface.

A permanent patch appropriate for fine furniture can be achieved with shellac stick. This is shellac hardened into stick form and it is available in several shades. It is difficult to find in hardware stores but can be obtained through woodworker supply stores and catalogs.* The procedure for using stick shellac is the same as for wax sticks, except that when the patch has been melted into the groove, a heated putty knife is pulled across the patch to level it. Scrape off any excess with a razor blade. The patch doesn't have to be covered with shellac to make it more durable —it is shellac. Rub the patch and surrounding area with 0000 steel wool dipped in oil to smooth it into the surrounding surface and give it a dull sheen.

A surface scorch in the finish can be removed by rubbing the spot with 0000 steel wool and mineral spirits. The abrasive steel wool will wear away the

*Among these are: Frog Tool Company, Ltd., 700 West Jackson Boulevard, Chicago, Illinois, 60606; Garrett Wode Company, 161 Avenue of the Americas, New York, New York, 10013; and Lee Valley Tools, Ltd., 2680 Queensview Drive, Ottawa, Ontario, Canada K2B 8J9.

scorched part of the finish. Wipe the surface clean and wax.

For severe burns that penetrate the finish, all the charred wood must be removed before the spot can be refinished. This is done with a curved-tipped knife (Fig. 9-5). The curved blade on a pocket knife will do. Carefully scrape away the blackened wood, but don't scratch the wood underneath or it will show through the patch. Now sand the edges of the spot to blend them in with the surrounding area. Use fine sandpaper and be careful not to scratch the finish outside the feathered area. Wet the sanded area with water to see if you have sanded away all the char. If the water makes it look burned again, you should sand some more. Finally, clean the area with a cotton-tipped toothpick dipped in naphtha.

All this will leave a depressed area, which, if small, can be swelled as described above (see Figs. 9-1 and 9-2). The larger gouges will have to be filled with wax, shellac, or wood putty (see Fig. 9-4). If the surface is veneered and the burn penetrated through the veneer into the base wood, the veneer should be patched as described on pages 156–58.

FIG. 9-5. SCRAPING OUT A BURN

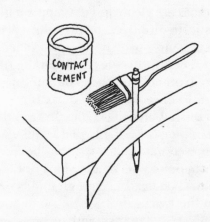

FIG. 9-6. RECEMENTING PLASTIC LAMINATE

COUNTERTOPS

Plastic-laminate counters are made by gluing 1/16-inch-thick sheet plastic to a plywood or chipboard base. Sometimes the sheet plastic will come unglued. This happens especially around the edge. The remedy is to reglue it and the correct glue for this job is contact cement. It comes in cans and can be brushed on with a throwaway brush. Contact cement is water soluble while it's still wet, so the

brush can be cleaned up in warm water. Make sure both surfaces (the surface of the wood and the underside of the plastic) are clean and dry. Place a pencil between the wood and the plastic to keep them separated, while you brush contact cement on both (Fig. 9-6). Let both surfaces dry until they don't feel tacky to the touch. Remove the pencil and push the two surfaces together. Rub firmly over the whole area with the heel of your hand. That's all there is to it.

A common problem with tile countertops is loose tiles. This is a regluing problem and the right glue for the job is mastic. Mastic comes in either cans or caulk tubes. It is a heavy-duty construction adhesive that doesn't need to be clamped. Remove the offending tile and clean off all the old adhesive and any dirt or grease from both the back of the tile and the wood surface. With a putty knife, chip away the grout that may be still attached to the tile. If this proves difficult, soak the tile in warm water and try again. When all surfaces are clean and dry, apply a glob of mastic to the back of the tile, spread it evenly, and push the tile into place.

After the mastic has dried the tile can be regrouted. Mix the grout mixture with water to the consistency of creamy yogurt, and push it into the cracks around the tile with a piece of flexible plastic (like a margarine-container lid) that has been cut to the shape of a rectangle. This homemade tool will be flexible enough to force grout into the cracks, but it won't mar the tile. Remove the excess with a sponge and finish off the grout joints by running your finger over each one.

For remedies for stains on plastic laminate, tile, and butcherblock countertops, see Table 2, pages 147–51.

VENEER PATCHES

Many pieces of furniture are not made of solid hardwood but are composed of sheets of thin hardwood veneer glued over a lesser wood. The veneer on older furniture can be $\frac{1}{20}$ to $\frac{1}{8}$ inch thick, but veneers of $\frac{1}{28}$ to $\frac{1}{40}$ inch are more common. Some veneered pieces are very beautiful. The grain is matched so well that you can't tell it's veneer. Other pieces are decorated with contrasting veneers in patterns and shapes. These fine pieces are certainly worth repairing well. The common problems with veneer are chips and blisters.

Blisters or bubbles in the veneer usually occur in older pieces. A blister is caused by glue failure. The old glues made of animal hide were not as strong as our modern ones.

Small blisters can be flattened with the application of heat. Cover the blister with a clean cloth and press the area with a medium-hot iron. Remove the iron as soon as the blisters have flattened. The heat softens the glue and revitalizes it. Leave the cloth in place and pile heavy books over the spot for twenty-four hours.

Larger blisters must be reglued. Cut the blister open by making a single cut through the veneer with a sharp craft knife (Fig. 9-7). Do not cut perpendicular to the grain or the cut will be visible later. The closer to parallel with the grain the better. Peer into the blister and scrape off all the old glue. Use a vacuum to remove the scrapings. Squirt a little yellow carpenter's glue into the blister. With an artist's brush, spread the glue evenly over all surfaces that will eventually come together. Press the blister down and if the two sides of the cut overlap, carefully shave one side with a craft knife or single-edged razor blade (only a little at a time) until they meet neatly. If the veneer is stiff and obstinate, apply heat with a medium-hot iron. Then use a roller, such as a roll-

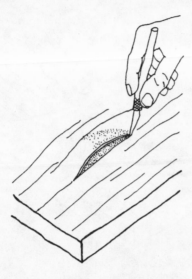

FIG. 9-7. REPAIRING A VENEER BLISTER

FIG. 9-8. ROLLING THE REGLUED AREA

ing pin, a wallpaper-seam roller, or large glass bottle to firmly press the veneer onto the surface (Fig. 9-8). As you roll, wipe away the excess glue that will squeeze out with a warm, damp rag.

When the veneer is adhering to the surface, cover the area with a piece of wax paper. Place a block of wood a little larger than the blister over the repair, and pile on heavy books. The wood block will concentrate the weight of the books onto the reglued spot. Allow the glue twenty-four hours to dry, and remove the books. If the paper sticks to the seam, pare it away gently using a chisel with the bevel down. The correct way to hold a chisel for this kind of shaving is shown in Fig. 9-10. Holding the bevel down allows the chisel to skim along the surface instead of cutting ever deeper into the wood, as it does when it is used with the bevel side up. Refinish the area as described earlier.

Chipped Veneer

When veneer has been chipped, a patch must be cut and glued in place. If veneer of the same wood is used and you work carefully, the patch will scarcely be visible. Veneer can be purchased at woodworker's supply stores and hobby shops in pieces as small as 1 square foot.

Locate a spot on the new sheet of veneer where the grain pattern matches the chipped area. Lay this part of the sheet over the chipped area so that the grain is going in the same direction. With a craft knife and a ruler, cut a diamond-shaped piece out of the new sheet of veneer (Fig. 9-9). Press firmly enough so that the same diamond shape is also scored into the veneer around the chip.

Put the diamond-shaped patch aside and turn your attention to removing the damaged veneer within the diamond scored into the surface. It is important

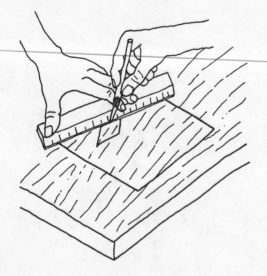

FIG. 9-9. CUTTING A VENEER PATCH

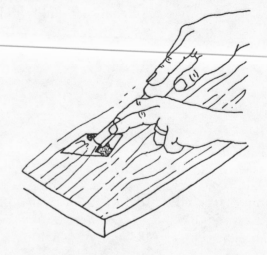

FIG. 9-10. USING A CHISEL

that the scoring has cut completely through the veneer. Use a chisel with the bevel down to pare away the veneer (Fig. 9-10).

Try the diamond patch in the hole. If it doesn't fit easily, sand a little off the appropriate edge by running the veneer patch lightly along a fine file or across the face of a sanding block. (See pages 25–26 and Fig. 2-36 for how to make a sanding block.) Do not sand by hand or you will compromise the straight edge of the patch. When the patch fits, spread yellow carpenter's glue onto the bottom of the hole and press the patch into place. Set the glue by rolling a rolling pin over the patch firmly and weight with books as described above. When the glue is dry, sand the patch with a sanding block until it is flush with the surface (Fig. 9-11). Identify the type of finish as described on page 146 and build up layers of that finish over the patch.

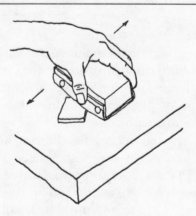

FIG. 9-11. SANDING THE PATCH WITH A SANDING BLOCK

The Moving Parts of Furniture and Cabinets

Furniture and cabinets are the repositories for all our material possessions. If we want a shirt, a dish, a can of cat food, we open a drawer or door to get it. We never give them a thought when they work smoothly, but we hate them when they stick or when a knob falls off in our hands.

DRAWERS

Drawer knobs are attached in two ways: by a wood screw that is screwed into the drawer front or by a machine screw that is held by a nut on the inside of the drawer front (Fig. 9-12). (See Fig. A-2, page 211, for the difference between wood and machine screws.) If there is a nut on the inside of the drawer front and it's loose, cover the screw head with your thumb and press the knob tightly into the drawer front with one hand, while you screw the nut on with the other. If the nut keeps coming loose, insert a locknut washer (see Fig. A-2) between the nut and the inside of the drawer front.

If a knob held by a wood screw is loose, it is probably because the screw is fitting loosely in the hole bored for it in the drawer front or knob. The remedy is to make the screw hole smaller. Dip several toothpicks in white or yellow glue and stick them in the hole (Fig. 9-13). Break them off flush with the surface and drive in the screw.

Drawers run on guides of either wood or metal. Newer drawers have manufactured metal guides. A faulty guide is often the cause of sticking, but not always. Drawers stick for several reasons. Sometimes they are too full and one of the contents is wedging the drawer closed. In the spring and summer the added moisture in the air causes the wood of drawers to swell and not fit between their guides. The hardwood guides of older drawers can become rough and uneven from wear. Finally, the

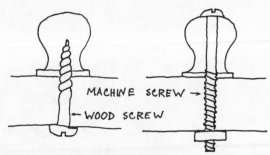

FIG. 9-12. DRAWER KNOBS

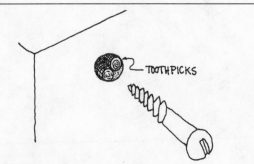

FIG. 9-13. TOOTHPICKS AS PLUGS

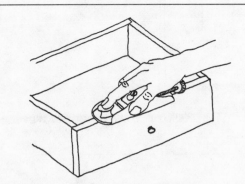

FIG. 9-14. USING A BLOCK PLANE

constant stress of pulling on a drawer can cause the joints to loosen.

A couple of things can be done for a drawer that swells with the seasons. If you notice that the top of the drawer front is rubbing in its frame, planing the spot may free up the drawer (Fig. 9-14). (For more

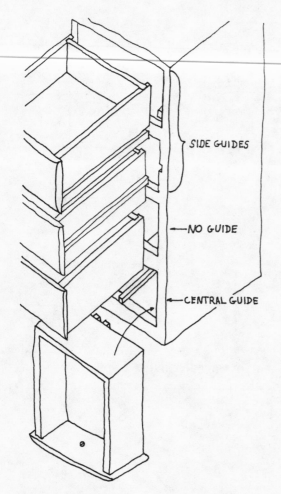

SIDE GUIDES

NO GUIDE

CENTRAL GUIDE

FIG. 9-15. ASSORTED WOODEN-DRAWER
GUIDES

travel is rough or if the guides are rough. There are many types of guides (see Fig. 9-15) and they all can stick.

If the guides are made of wood and are rough, sand down the roughness with medium-grit sandpaper. Sometimes waxing the runners and guides with paraffin helps drawers slide more easily. If one of the pieces is loose, renail it in place, but be careful to set the nail below the surface of the wood (see Fig. 3-6). You can usually discern the correct position of loose or fallen pieces because their location is outlined by darker-colored wood. Look for nail holes too; they are clues that something used to be nailed in that place.

Problems with metal guides have more to do with alignment and wheels that don't turn freely. The side guides are of better quality than the center guides, and the only thing that will go wrong with them is a screw coming loose, which causes one of the guides to move out of place. Just replace the screw. Once in a while a wheel may get stuck. Look to see if some thread has wrapped around the axle. The application of some household-grade oil may help the wheel turn more freely.

There are many types of oils. A household oil such as 3-in-one is an all-purpose lubricant for wheels, hinges, and moving parts. For locks and moving parts that will be subject to low temperatures, graphite is the best lubricant. Oil will thicken in cold weather and lose its ability to lubricate. Graphite is not a good choice for drawer guide wheels because it is a black powder and will stain the clothes in the drawer. Penetrating oils are excellent for loosening nuts or screws that are in metal. They penetrate down around the

on planes, see pages 24–25.) If everything seems to be swollen, pull the drawers out halfway and put a small lamp with a 60- to 75-watt bulb inside the cabinet. The heat from the bulb will dry out the wood and restore free movement.

Pull the sticking drawer out and examine the runners on the bottom of the drawer. Also look inside the cabinet and notice if the wood on which the runners threads, allowing the nut to be turned. Rust-dissolving oil is similar to penetrating oil, but it comes in gallons, so that you can place the rusty, frozen parts into the oil to soak.

It's easy for center guides to get out of alignment. When this happens, the drawer will be hard to pull out because the sides are rubbing on the face frame. The face frame is the wood surrounding a drawer or door. It is made up of many horizontal (rails) and vertical pieces (stiles) of wood. Remove the drawer. This is done much as you would remove a file drawer, by lifting the back as you move the front up and down until the drawer is free. Examine the screws that hold the center guide in place. Are they tight? Is the guide in the center and parallel with the sides of the cabinet? Realign it if it's not. The wheel brackets located on the bottom of the drawer and the inside of the face frame can also be loose and can be causing the drawer to bind. Tighten them.

A drawer has loose joints if you can move the back from side to side a little while you hold the front stationary. This is called racking: the tendency for joints to go out of square (Fig. 9-16). It can happen to houses, cabinets, drawers, or picture frames. The drawer must be rectangular in shape to slide smoothly. First, try regluing the drawer while it's still assembled. Squeeze glue into all the loose joints. Realign the drawer so that its corners are square. An easy way to do this is to measure the diagonals (inside corner to inside corner). If the diagonals are equal, the drawer is square (Fig. 9-17). If the joints are particularly loose, the drawer may

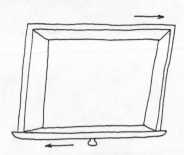

FIG. 9-16. RACKING

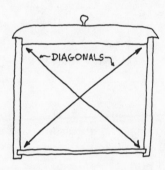

FIG. 9-17. SQUARING A DRAWER

have to be clamped while the glue dries. Pipe clamps are best for this job. They consist of a viselike handle and end stop mounted on a piece of pipe (Fig. 9-18). At one end of the pipe there is a handle, which, when turned, tightens the clamp. At the other end is a sliding stop that locks into place when a lever is depressed. Place the clamp on the drawer, snug the sliding stop against the drawer side, and turn the handle until the drawer joints become tight. If you don't have any clamps, use a glue with gap-filling capability, like epoxy.

Clamps are useful to have around (Fig. 9-19). A C-clamp can clamp as much as can fit between its jaws. C-clamps come

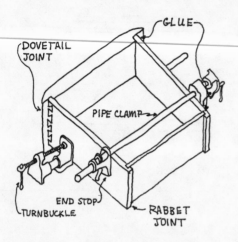

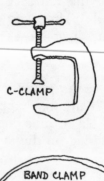

FIG. 9-18. CLAMPING A DRAWER

in different sizes to accommodate various needs. A band clamp is used for clamping irregular objects. It can be wrapped around frames and table legs. There are many specialized clamps. A frame clamp is designed to clamp the corners of a frame while glue dries. Spring clamps, which come in many sizes, are handy for clamping materials to a surface.

If regluing the drawer while it is still together fails to work, you will have to take it apart. Knock the joints apart by hitting the sides of the drawers with a hammer. Place a scrap of wood against the drawer wood so that the hammer won't damage the drawer.

DOORS ON FURNITURE

Hinges are usually the problem when doors bind. Their pins can become bent by children swinging on the lower doors of kitchen cabinets. The screws that hold hinges on can also loosen by this or more

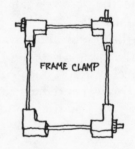

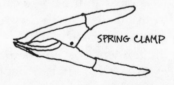

FIG. 9-19. CLAMPS

conventional use, thereby causing the door to stick.

First, notice where the door is hitting the frame. A door that swings properly fits within the frame but does not touch it. *Try the easiest solution first.* Read the section on

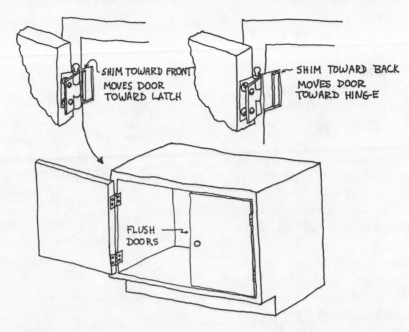

SHIM TOWARD FRONT MOVES DOOR TOWARD LATCH

SHIM TOWARD BACK MOVES DOOR TOWARD HINGE

FLUSH DOORS

FIG. 9-20. THROWING HINGES

"Troubleshooting" at the beginning of this chapter. If the door is rubbing at the bottom on the latch side, the hinge screws of the top hinge may be loose, making the door sag and rub. Next, check the hinge pin. A bent pin can cause a door to rub or just to swing hard. If the pin is bent, replace it with a new one or a small common nail. If you take the pin along to the hardware store, they will be able to fix you up with something that will work.

You might think that now is the time to get out your plane and take some wood off the door, but that should be the last resort. The door used to fit in the opening and it probably can be made to fit there again just by changing its location—not its size. The exception to this is a door that has seventeen layers of paint and is sticking because of the thickness of the

paint. The paint on the edge of the door should be taken off either with a rasp or a surform plane. A rasp is a coarse file made for grating wood. A surform plane is a plane with a rasplike bottom instead of a blade. The use of both these tools is described in chapter 2.

If nothing has yet solved the problem and the door in question is a flush door, the top hinge will have to be "thrown" away from the latch (see Fig. 7-5 and related text, pages 114–15). A flush door is one set within the frame (Fig. 9-20). Throwing the hinge means moving the barrel. This is done with shims made of cardboard that are placed behind the leaf of the hinge to move the barrel either toward the latch side or away from it. This movement, brought about by the insertion of a thin piece of cardboard, is usually enough to stop the door from rubbing. If the cardboard sliver is inserted behind the front edge of the top hinge leaf, the top of the door will move toward the latch. If the cardboard is placed behind the inside edge of the hinge, the top of the door will move away from the latch. This holds true for the bottom hinge also.

Cabinet doors are usually of two types: flush or overlapping. The most common kitchen cabinet door is the overlapping type. Doors that lap over the face frame are usually rabbetted so that only half of their thickness laps over the face frame. A rabbet is a two-sided groove cut out of the edge of a piece of wood. The cardboard shim trick only works on flush doors. Rabbetted doors have surface-mounted hinges that are visible. To move a rabbetted door so that the rabbetted edge does not rub on the edge of the face frame, the hinges must be moved (Fig. 9-21). As you would expect, you must move the hinge in the same direction as you want the door to move.

If the top edge of the door is rubbing, move the top hinge toward the latch. This has the effect of lowering the top edge of the door because the door is essentially pivoting around the bottom hinge. (If this doesn't do the trick, move both hinges down.) Because the hinges will be moved such a small distance ($\frac{1}{16}$ to $\frac{1}{8}$ inch) the screws will tend to slip back into the original holes. Insert wooden plugs or toothpicks into the old holes and drill new ones. The new holes may overlap the old ones, but the wooden plugs will keep the drill bit from slipping off center.

If the door still binds after you have tried all of this, plane a little wood off the edge of the door that is rubbing.

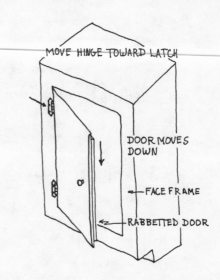

FIG. 9-21. ADJUSTING OVERLAPPING DOORS

Latches are often so covered with paint that they don't work. Chip some paint away with your all-purpose screwdriver, or take the latch off and apply paint stripper. Who knows, you may find solid brass under all the coats of paint!

One difficulty in removing the latch is that the slots in the screws are also covered with paint. You must scrape the paint out of the slots with your utility knife or with a small screwdriver before you even try to unscrew the screws.

Loose Joints

Loose joints are caused by either glue failure or the loosening of hardware fasteners. Try the simplest solutions first. If glue can be injected into the joint without taking the joint apart, all the better for you. Hardware stores carry different glues packaged in syringe-type containers. Try to avoid using metal fasteners like angle braces on furniture. They may be all right for a bookshelf or a chair that's out on the porch, but they are the last resort for living-room furniture.

Many table legs are held to the tabletop by means of metal brackets (Fig. 9-22). Usually one large screw holds each leg to the table. If a table has wobbly legs, tighten these screws first.

Chair legs and rungs come to a dowel shape at the ends, which are inserted into holes drilled in the underside of the chair seat. This is a type of mortise-and-tenon joint. The chair leg is the tenon and the hole into which it fits is the mortise (see Fig. 9-23). Because of stresses like people leaning back in chairs, these joints can be-

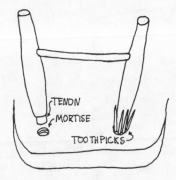

FIG. 9-23. TIGHTENING A LOOSE DOWEL JOINT

come loose. If the joint won't pull apart, try injecting some epoxy or wood glue into the joint. There is also a product called Chair-Loc, which isn't a glue. It swells the wood fibers and then deposits a solid material in the expanded fiber so that the joint stays tight. If chair legs are so loose that they easily pull out of their sockets, wipe some yellow glue or Chair-Loc on the dowel end and in the socket, and reassemble. After drying, the chair should be as good as new.

If a chair leg or rung is so loose that you can move it back and forth within the socket, wrap the leg end with thread soaked in glue and replace the leg in the socket. After the glue has dried for twenty-four hours, the chair can be used. Epoxy glue has gap-filling capability, so it is a good choice of glue for this job.

Here is a remedy for a very loose chair tenon that won't come apart because it's pinned or because it just won't. Dip in glue toothpicks or thin wedges that you have whittled off an old board and hammer them into the mortise around the

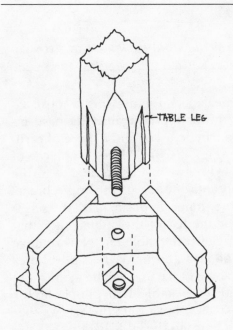

FIG. 9-22. TABLE-LEG BRACKET

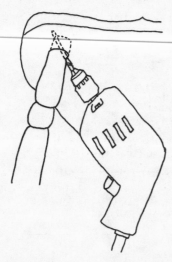

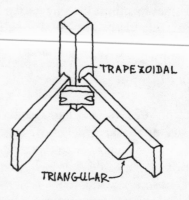

FIG. 9-25. GLUE BLOCKS

FIG. 9-24. PINNING A DOWEL JOINT

chair leg (Fig. 9-23). Place them carefully so that the leg stays centered in its hole. When the glue has dried, break off the protruding ends or trim them with a utility knife.

In the same situation but where appearance matters, drill a small hole at an angle through the chair leg and into the seat. Drill from behind so that the hole doesn't show. Select a finish nail that is slightly larger in diameter than the hole you drilled, hammer the nail into the hole, and set it (Fig. 9-24).

Tabletops are attached either by metal braces or glue blocks. Glue blocks are used on better furniture. They are triangular-shaped pieces of wood that are glued to the tabletop and the upper rails at their intersection (Fig. 9-25). Trapezoidal blocks are used at the corners of tables to strengthen them and to keep them square. If they are loose, reglue them.

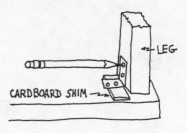

FIG. 9-26. DRAWING DOWN A TABLETOP

A neat trick for drawing a loose tabletop down tightly against its base involves an angle brace and a piece of cardboard (Fig. 9-26). Place a piece of cardboard between the underside of the tabletop and one leg of the angle brace. While the shim is in place, mark the screw holes for the leg of the angle brace that will be against the table leg. Now remove the cardboard and mark the screw holes for the angle brace that will be against the underside of the table. Drill pilot holes for all the screws, but insert the screws that hold the brace to the table leg first. As the screws are driven through the angle brace into the underside of the tabletop, they will pull the top tightly against the leg assembly.

It is common for chair rungs or chair backs to crack. The more feathered the break, the stronger the glue joint, because there is a lot of surface area to which the glue can bond. Spread glue on both parts, or if they are not fully broken, inject it or use a vacuum cleaner to suck glue down into the joint. To do the latter, use the vacuum attachment with the smallest opening. Place it against the bottom of the crack, so that as you pour glue onto the crack from above, the vacuum sucks the glue down and into the joint.

Yellow glue or epoxy are good glues for this job. Wrap the joint with wax paper, then cloth, and clamp. If the broken part is a round rung, automotive hose clamps make excellent clamps (Fig. 9-27). If the part is rectangular, wrap the joint with twine and, with another piece of twine, draw the legs together.

If a chair or table leg breaks, it should be doweled, because a leg carries so much weight. A dowel joint is the strongest way to repair furniture. Drill a small hole into one surface of the break and drive a finish nail into it. With a pair of pliers, nip off the nail so that only $\frac{1}{16}$ inch protrudes from the surface (Fig. 9-28). Carefully align the two parts and push them together so that the protruding nail makes a mark on the other part. Pull the nail out with the pliers. Drill a dowel-sized hole into the nail marks on each leg of the break. These holes should be about 2 inches deep and should be drilled very carefully. It is helpful to have a friend watch from a few feet away to tell you if you aren't drilling the hole straight in.

Cut a dowel that is the same diameter as the hole, to a length that is $\frac{1}{2}$ inch shorter than the depths of the two holes

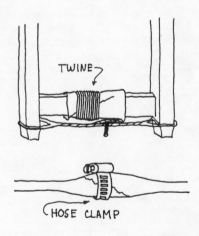

FIG. 9-27. CLAMPING IRREGULAR PARTS

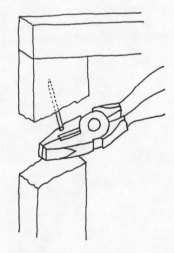

FIG. 9-28

combined. Sand or file the dowel ends so that they are tapered. Hold the dowel with a pair of pliers and squeeze. Channellocks are a great tool for this (see Fig. 2-25). The wood will be imprinted with teeth marks from the jaws of the pliers. Do this over the entire surface of the dowel. These depressions will allow the glue to spread around the surface of the dowel and will make the glue bond stronger. Of course, you could go to the hardware or lumber store and buy a ready-made dowel, but then you wouldn't have had the fun of making one yourself.

Spread yellow glue over the dowel and the surface of the break, and squirt some into the holes. With a hammer, tap the dowel into one hole and push the other part of the break onto the dowel (Fig. 9-29). If the holes have been drilled accurately, the two pieces should fit together well. If they are offset a little, pull the joint apart and remove the dowel. The dowel will probably have to be pulled out with the aid of pliers. Wipe off the glue so that it doesn't set, while you fix this little problem.

I would do one of two things—whichever is quickest. Either file down the dowel so that its diameter is smaller by approximately the amount the pieces were offset when you first put them together, or go to the store and get a smaller dowel. When you are ready, assemble the pieces without glue and see if they will fit. This should be possible now because the dowel will be loose in the holes. If everything fits, reglue and assemble as before, but this time use epoxy; it will fill the gaps around the dowel.

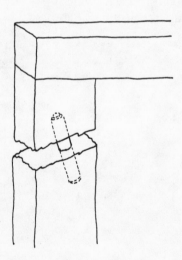

FIG. 9-29

10

EXTERIOR AND BASEMENT

Water Is Probably the Problem

Most of the damage done to the exterior of a house or its basement is caused by water. Imagine a house enduring many rainstorms. Consider the kind of exterior skin that would keep the rain out, but allow water vapor formed daily by the occupants to escape. The intersections of the many different materials used in house construction are the sources of many leaks. Water often enters where the roof meets the chimney, where the walls meet the roof, and around windows.

It's a wonder houses don't leak more often. Over the centuries that people have been building themselves dwellings, we have learned a few rules about how to keep the weather out:

1. The roofing and siding of a house are usually applied in rows or courses. Each course must lap over the course below it. This keeps the water out. It doesn't matter if the roof is made of thatch, slate, or asphalt shingles; water can't get in if everything above overlaps everything below (Fig. 10-1).

2. All protrusions (chimneys, skylights, windows, and vent pipes) through the waterproof covering of a house (roofing and siding) must be flashed. Flashing can be made of rubber, thin metal, or asphalt-impregnated felt and is used to form the watertight joint between the protrusions in a roof and the roofing itself. The flashing has to conform to rule 1 also. When someone has inadvertently installed it incorrectly, which often happens at the intersection of a roof and wall (Fig. 10-1), you can bet there is a leak there.

3. Usually water travels downhill, but

169

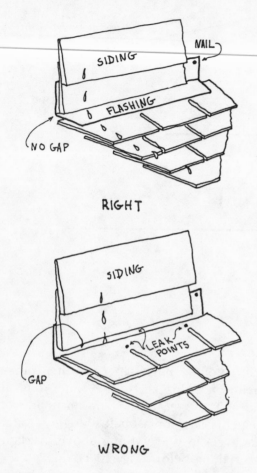

FIG. 10-1. OVERLAPPING PREVENTS LEAKS

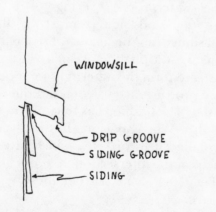

FIG. 10-2. DRIP GROOVE

it can travel uphill by capillary action. Capillary action plays a part in many leaks. Since water can move uphill between two surfaces that are close together, one way to prevent this is to build into leak-prone areas a place from which the water can drip. The drip groove on the underside of a windowsill is an example of this (Fig. 10-2) and the drip-cap flashing over a window is another (see Fig. 8-4).

ROT AND INSECTS

Rotten wood is wood that has decayed. Decay doesn't happen for no reason. It is caused by decay-causing fungi, which grow on wet wood and take their nourishment from it—thereby decaying it. There are four conditions that must be present for rot to occur.

1. A source. Decay-causing fungi are everywhere. They are propagated by microscopic spores that travel in the air. They are in the room with you now.

2. Moisture. The fungi need wet wood to feed on. They can live only on wood that comes in direct contact with water, not wood that swells up merely because there is a high vapor content in the air.

3. Temperature. These fungi need a temperature of 50 to 120 degrees in order to live and grow. Unfortunately this is pretty easy to achieve in the summer in most climates and all year round in others.

4. Darkness. The fungi love the dark. Unfortunately, in basements and under porches, where rot is likely to occur, there is not very much light.

If you take away any one of these conditions, rot cannot occur. Most of them you can't control. The only one you can control is moisture. If you dry up your basement or crawlspace by diverting water away from the house with a swale (Fig. 10-3) or by extending the downspouts farther out from the house, the rot that had begun will cease because the fungi will die.

The way to prevent rot is to keep an eye out for telltale signs of moisture or fungi. Peeling paint or stains on wood means that water has been present. Some forms of fungi are white and actually can be seen. When any of these signs are noticed, steps to dry up the area must be taken. The term "dry rot" is misleading, because no rot is dry. If the wood appears rotten or weak and is dry, the decay happened sometime in the past. If the wood is dry, further rot cannot occur.

Sometimes, no matter what you do, the wood will continue to get wet. Porches, decks, and mudsills are almost impossible to keep dry. Treating the wood in these areas with a wood preservative or sealing it with paint helps prevent rot. Some preservatives are toxic and dangerous to use. One of these is pentachlorophenol. This chemical is the active ingredient in Penta, a wood preservative. The fumes have been shown to be carcinogenic. It's best to stay away from this one. Green Cuprinol contains zinc naphthanate, which is much less toxic. Another solution is to use pressure-treated wood. This wood looks green and has had preservatives forced into it to take the place of the water in the fibers and cells. Fungi can't live on such wood and insects don't want to eat it.

There are two types of insects that

FIG. 10-3. A SWALE DIVERTS WATER AWAY FROM THE HOUSE

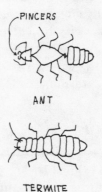

FIG. 10-4. KNOW YOUR INSECT

eat wood: carpenter ants and termites (Fig. 10-4). Of the two, termites are probably the worse because they feed on the wood. Carpenter ants just chew enough up to make a nest for themselves. They look like ants except that they have large pincers in front of the mouth. Carpenter ants eat only wet wood. Drying out the particular area in which the ants have built their nest and spraying them with insecticide will usually get rid of them. But consulting a professional exterminator is always a good idea in such cases.

Termites need water to live, but they can eat dry wood and obtain their water from the soil where they make their nest. They either burrow into a house through wood posts that are in contact with the ground or build mud tunnels against the foundation wall. These mud tunnels are a sign that termites may be in the house. Termites, who abhor light, travel back to the ground through these tunnels once a day to obtain water. If the tunnels are destroyed, the termites will die. In the spring, other signs of termites can be observed—a swarm of flying insects or a pile of discarded wings near a foundation wall. Termites have a very short flying stage in their life cycle and discard their wings at the end of it. If evidence of termites is found, call an exterminator.

LOCATING LEAKS

Leaks are often hard to find because the drip that you see isn't always directly below the leak (Fig. 10-5). Water can travel along a rafter or joist until it comes to a knot or crook in the wood. The water will collect in this low spot until there is enough to cause a drip. The best time to find a leak is when it is raining. Trace the path of the water back from where it is dripping to the leak in the roof by working your way up to the attic. Look for wet spots, drips, and water running along the rafter or joist. When you find the spot, mark it with a crayon. When the weather clears, go up in the attic again, find the crayon mark, and pound a nail up through the sheathing and the roofing. The nail will be visible from the top of the roof and will denote which shingle is faulty and must be replaced.

Nine times out of ten, the leak will be coming in around old or faulty flashing. Check these trouble spots first when you are looking for a leak: flashing around a chimney, vent stack, dormer, porch, or

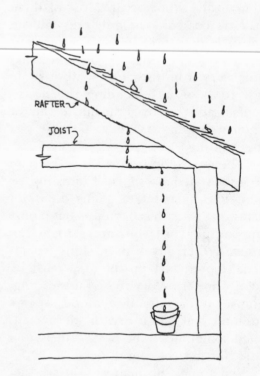

FIG. 10-5. TRACING THE PATH OF A LEAK

skylight. Wet spots will be visible under these areas during a storm and water stains will remain after the storm has passed.

You have to think like a drop of water to determine if water is getting in through the flashing. Go up on the roof and examine the flashing you suspect may be leaking. Pretend you are a drop of water running down the roof. Are there any holes or incorrect laps where the flashing above is lapped under the course below, as in the wrong version in Fig. 10-1? Water loves both these situations. If you find any, there are two ways to correct the inevitable leak. The quickest is to tar the gap heavily so that no water can get in.

This will last a year or two, until the tar weathers and cracks. The best solution is to reflash. Insert a new piece of flashing under the siding course above and make sure it laps over the first course of shingles, as in the right version in Fig. 10-1. You will have to pull out the nails attaching the piece of siding. Once the new flashing has been slipped under the siding, renail it so that the nails just barely catch the top edge of the flashing. This solution will last for fifteen or twenty years and, therefore, is the cheapest in the long run.

A trick to putting flashing in easily is bending it at an angle larger than the one formed by the roof and wall or roof and chimney (Fig. 10-6). This way when the flashing is installed the bend will keep the flashing tight against the roofing so that no rain can get blown under it. The point is not to nail into the part of the flashing that lies on top of the roofing. Nail holes only invite water in. If there are still gaps between the flashing and the roof, smear roofing cement underneath the flashing and push the flashing down into it. Roofing cement is a tarlike substance that comes in cans and caulk tubes. If this still doesn't eliminate the gaps, nail the flashing down in several places with roofing nails and dab the top of each nail with roofing cement.

Repairs for Damage Done by Water

ICE DAMS

An ice dam is formed when escaping heat from the house melts snow on the roof. The snow melt runs down the roof until it comes to the eave. The eave is colder than the rest of the roof because it

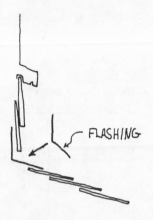

FIG. 10-6. A LARGER BEND IN FLASHING ASSURES A TIGHT SEAL AGAINST ROOFING

doesn't have a warm house under it. The water freezes when it hits the eave and begins to build up. Eventually, it forms a dam and the melted water running down the roof collects in a small lake (Fig. 10-7). The water in the lake backs up under the roof shingles and leaks into the house.

In many parts of the country people go to all sorts of lengths to avoid ice dams. In New England, it is common to see many houses with metal flashing as roofing over the eaves and asphalt shingles above them. The idea is that ice can't stick to metal and it will slide off. This works most of the time. Other people run electric wires over the eave to melt the snow. This makes their utility bill enormous, but it does help the problem.

But the most economical and sure solution to the problem of ice dams is a well-ventilated roof (Fig. 10-8). When cool air travels along the underside of the roof from eave to ridge, the temperature of various parts of the roof becomes uni-

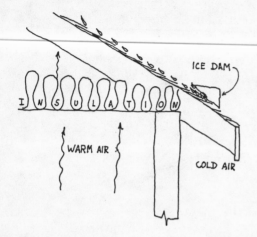

FIG. 10-7. AN ICE DAM

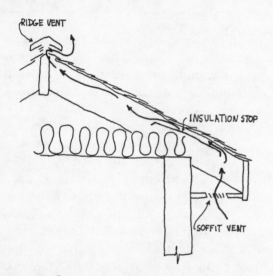

FIG. 10-8. PROPER VENTILATION
PREVENTS ICE DAMS

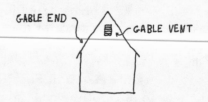

FIG. 10-9. GABLE-END VENT

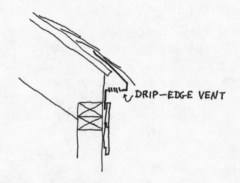

FIG. 10-10. RETROFIT EAVE VENTING

The best configuration for vents in a roof is soffit vents under the eave and a ridge vent at the top, as is shown in Fig. 10-8. Next best is soffit vents coupled with gable-end vents (Fig. 10-9). Having only a gable-end vent at either end of the house is better than no vents at all, but they are not sufficient to stop ice dams.

There are several ways of adding eave vents, if your house is not equipped with them (Fig. 10-10). A company named Air Vent Inc. has recently started making retrofit eave ventilation in the form of drip-edge flashing. It can be special-ordered from any good lumberyard that deals with contractors. The flashing is fitted under the starter course of shingles. This requires pulling out a lot of nails

form. The snow can't melt if the sheathing and roofing under it are cool, and the melted snow that runs down a roof on sunny days can't form an ice dam at the eave if the temperature of the eave is the same as the rest of the roof.

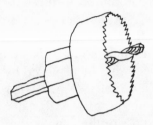

FIG. 10-11. A HOLE-SAW BIT

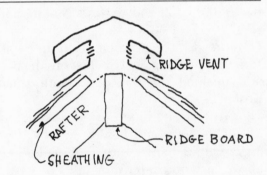

FIG. 10-12. RIDGE VENT

from a large number of shingles so that the vent can slip up unimpeded under the starter course.

Another method of adding vents is to install the round soffit vents under the eave. The 2-inch-diameter soffit vents can be purchased in any hardware or lumber store. A rather large hole of a diameter slightly larger than that of the vent must be drilled for them. A hole-saw bit is the right tool for the job, and that too can be purchased at the hardware store (Fig. 10-11). After the hole is drilled in the underside of the eave, the soffit vents are inserted. There should be two for each rafter space.

Soffit venting alone will do little to vent your roof unless it is coupled with a

ridge vent. A preformed ridge vent can be purchased at any lumberyard. Remove the cap shingles. This is the course of shingles at the peak of a roof that overlaps the last course of shingles on both sides. Cut the sheathing back 1 inch on either side of the ridge. The ridge vent is then installed in place of the ridge-cap shingles (Fig. 10-12). A new, very durable ridge vent (made by Core-a-Vent) consists of layers of corrugated polyethylene sheets.

LEAKS IN ROOFS

The shingles on the south face of a roof wear out faster than the ones facing other directions. These shingles are subject to extreme temperature differences because the sun can warm them up even in the dead of winter. A well-ventilated roof (see above) increases the life of the roof covering because it modifies the very high temperatures that occur on roofs in the summer.

To repair a roof leak, one first must be able to get up on the roof. This usually requires two ladders: one to get you up as high as the eave and the other hooked over the ridge to allow you to work on the roof. For more on ladder use and safety see pages 43–45.

Two methods of keeping oneself from sliding off steep roofs are shown in Fig. 10-13. People can sit unaided on roofs with angles lower than 27 degrees. In carpenter lingo, that's a 6/12 pitch. Carpenters don't use angles to describe roofs; they use pitch. Pitch is a ratio of the distance a rafter rises as it travels 1 foot horizontally (Fig. 10-14). Pitch is expressed in numbers. Roofs with a 4/12 pitch (18 degrees) are common in suburban houses. Roofs with a 12/12 pitch (45

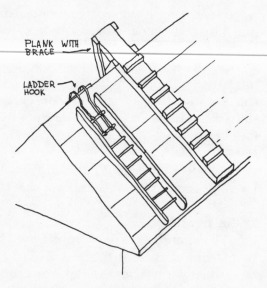

FIG. 10-13. LADDER ARRANGEMENTS
ON A ROOF

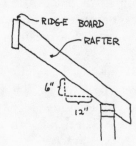

FIG. 10-14. ROOF PITCH

degrees) are common in turn-of-the-century houses. The steeper pitches of older houses require scaffolding.

If an asphalt shingle is cracked or damaged, it should be repaired by placing a tin shingle under it (Fig. 10-15). Pry up the damaged shingle. A flat bar, sometimes called a wonder bar, is the tool for the job (Fig. 10-16). Slip it up under the damaged shingle and aim it so that the notch in the flat end circles a roofing nail (Fig. 10-17). Roofing nails are short with large heads. They can be pried up by alternately pushing the bar closer to the nail and pushing the bar down with small pushes.

An asphalt shingle is approximately 36 inches long and has three tabs (Fig. 10-18). It is nailed with four nails, one above each notch. Jet shingles, a new type of shingle, have no notches and last a few

FIG. 10-16. FLAT BAR

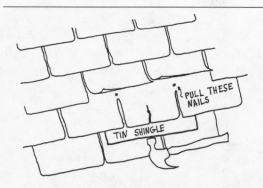

FIG. 10-15. REPAIRING A LEAK WITH A
TIN SHINGLE

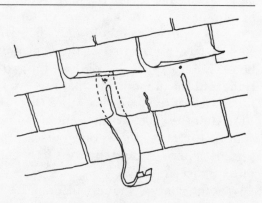

FIG. 10-17. PRYING UP A SHINGLE NAIL

years longer than traditional tab shingles. If you want to replace the damaged shingle, don't just replace the one tab; replace the whole shingle. Remove the four nails as described above. Insert the replacement shingle and renail.

A less common roof covering is wooden cedar shingles. When one of these cracks, a small tin shingle should be placed under the crack. It should be 8 inches long and wide enough to extend 2 inches beyond the crack on either side. If the tin shingle is being held tightly by the wooden shingles, don't nail it. If it's loose, put in two nails—one on either side of the crack. Tar the tops of the nails. When wooden shingles are badly cracked, they should be replaced. The procedure is the same for cedar shingles used on a roof or as siding (see pages 179–80).

Roll roofing is made of the same material as asphalt shingles, but it comes in 36-inch-wide rolls. Bubbles in the material should be slit down the middle with a utility knife—see (1) in Fig. 10-19. With a putty knife push some roofing cement into the slit (2). Nail the two flaps down (3) and dab roofing cement onto the nail heads. If there is a hole in the roof, an actual patch should be installed (4). Always dab exposed nail heads with roofing cement.

Slate roofs, which were popular before the turn of the century, can last fifty to a hundred years, but slate shingles can crack and break and should be replaced. Nail a strip of 2-inch-wide flashing material over the joint between the two shingles below the one to be replaced (Fig. 10-20). The strip should be long enough to be crimped over the replacement slate. Slip the new slate under the course above it, and fold the flashing strip up to hold it

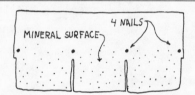

FIG. 10-18. AN ASPHALT SHINGLE

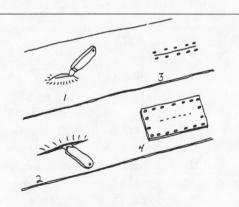

FIG. 10-19. PATCHING ROLL ROOFING

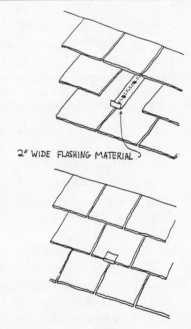

FIG. 10-20. PATCHING A SLATE ROOF

in place. Be especially careful while up on a slate roof; the old slates are slippery and can give way.

LEAKS AROUND FLASHING

Flashing forms the watertight joint between intersecting planes or around protrusions in the roof. Fig. 10-21 shows how flashing works around a chimney. The flashing consists of two parts: the base piece and the cap piece. The bottom edge of the cap flashing laps over the top edge of the base flashing to prevent leaks, and the top edge is grouted into the mortar joints of the chimney so no rain can gain entrance here. A chimney is a vertical plane intersecting a slanted roof. The flashing around a dormer is similar except that the siding serves the function of the cap flashing, and the base flashing is tucked under it.

The base flashing is made up of many pieces of step flashing, one piece under each course of shingles as in Fig. 10-22. Imagine a drop of water rolling down the outside of the chimney and trying to get in between the step flashing and the shingles. Even if a drop gets into the crack between shingles and flashing, it gets routed onto the topside of the shingle course below it.

There are two places where flashing tends to leak: the spot where the cap flashing tucks into the mortar joint and the joints between separate pieces of step flashing. Gaps may appear at either of these places. Resecure the cap flashing by driving small metal wedges into the mortar joint; this will hold the cap flashing in place. The metal wedges are made of folded sheet metal or lead. After the cap has been secured, caulk the mortar joint

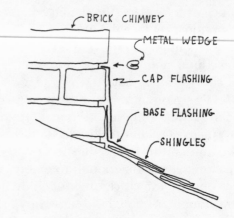

FIG. 10-21. CHIMNEY FLASHING

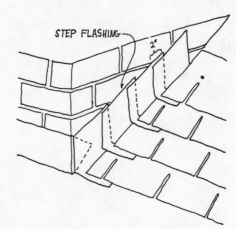

FIG. 10-22. FLASHING THE JOINTS IN A ROOF

so that no water can get in. A more permanent solution would be to repoint the joint. (See "Repointing," pages 185–86.) Vertical gaps between pieces of step flashing should be caulked with roofing cement.

If the flashing has been put in incorrectly, tarring the gaps will keep the weather out for a while. A common flashing mistake is installing the base flashing in one piece instead of in steps. The only way to prevent this configuration from leaking is to tar the joint between the shingles and the flashing. It is best, however, to replace it with step flashing.

Be mindful of the compatibility of various metals when working with flashing. Different metals touching each other will cause corrosion. When nailing flashing, use nails of the same material: aluminum nails with aluminum flashing and copper nails with copper flashing.

REPLACING SIDING SHINGLES AND CLAPBOARDS

The waterproof covering of the sides of your house is the siding. The degree to which the paint helps keep water out depends on the condition of the wood siding. If the wood is split and cracked, water can get behind it. Paint and caulking are stop-gap measures until you can replace the damaged piece of siding.

Each shingle is held on to the house by two small galvanized nails. The nails are covered by the shingle above to prevent leaks through the nail holes. To remove a damaged shingle, the nails must be sawed off with a hacksaw blade. The nail heads can be sawed off or the blade can be inserted under the damaged shingle and the nails sawed off closer to their base (as shown in Fig. 10-23). This is preferable. If the hacksaw blade is hard to move between the cedar shingles, pry up the damaged shingle a little with a flat bar. After the nails have been shorn, split the shingle into smaller pieces with a chisel and remove it (Fig. 10-24).

The new shingle should be approximately the same size as the old one. You

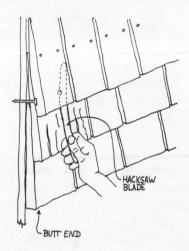

FIG. 10-23. SAWING OFF THE SHINGLE NAILS

FIG. 10-24. REMOVING A DAMAGED SHINGLE

can cut a large one down to size by scoring the shingle along the grain several times with a utility knife and breaking it along the score line. Smooth the edge with a block plane, if necessary (see Fig. 9-14). Slip the new shingle up under the course above. If it is too long, measure the distance from its butt end to the butt end of an adjacent shingle. Remove the replacement shingle and shorten it by this much by cutting the same amount off the thin end of the shingle. Replace the shingle and nail it 1 inch above the bottom edge. It will be impossible to nail the shingle so that the nail heads are covered, but the wood should swell around the nail so that no water can penetrate.

Clapboards are installed in courses as shingles are, but one clapboard can be anywhere from 3 to 18 feet long. If the whole board is damaged, then remove it. If only part of the clapboard is bad, that part can be cut out. Tape a scrap piece of wood over the clapboard below so that the saw won't damage it (Fig. 10-25). Inserting wedges under the damaged portion helps hold it away from the clapboard beneath it, making sawing easier.

When the board has been cut, insert your flat bar under the butt (thick) edge of the piece and pry it up. When the nail heads pop out, remove them. You may be able to remove the board at this point, but most likely the nails holding the course above will just catch the top of the piece you want to remove. Pull these nails also.

Tap the new piece up under the course above, using a scrap block to protect the butt edge from hammer marks (Fig. 10-26). Nail the new piece with galvanized siding nails (they have small heads), approximately 1 inch up from the bottom and in line with the nails above and below this course.

Sometimes clapboards crack horizontally. Gluing the board together prevents water from seeping into the crack (Fig. 10-27). First, pry the two pieces apart with a putty knife or screwdriver (A). The nails along the butt edge may have to be removed. Next, spread a waterproof glue

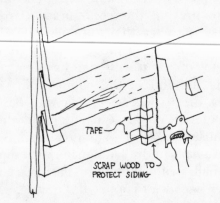

FIG. 10-25. REMOVING A CLAPBOARD

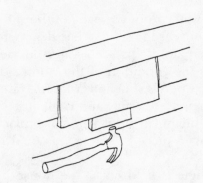

FIG. 10-26. REPLACING A CLAPBOARD

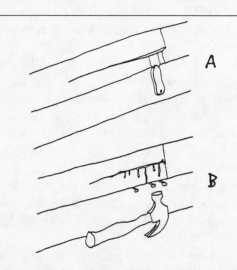

FIG. 10-27. GLUING A CLAPBOARD

like epoxy on both sides of the split. Finally, tap in a few nails along the bottom edge of the clapboard (B). When they are partially in, bend them up so that the pressure closes the crack. The nails will act as clamps. When the glue is dry, remove the clamp nails and renail the butt edge.

BASEMENT LEAKS

It is very difficult to keep basements dry. They have been described as "concrete boats in the water." In fact, they can be just that when the water table is high. Concrete itself is not impervious to water. To prevent leaking, basements are usually treated with a waterproof coating on the outside. If you have any friends who have wooden boats, you know that they are continually painting them to keep them from leaking. With basements this is far less practical. Once they are built and the dirt filled in around them, they can't be rewaterproofed without a lot of expensive excavation.

A good drainage system is essential. The ground around the foundation should slope away from the house. Gutters and downspouts should be in good working order so that they can carry the water that falls on the roof some distance from the house. Extending downspouts farther into the yard can reduce the amount of water in the soil near the basement wall. If the house is located on a hillside, a swale may be helpful in diverting runoff away from the house. (see Fig. 10-3).

The secret to a dry basement is to do it right the first time. Coat the outside foundation walls with a generous amount of waterproofing. This can either be a tar-like or cementitious coating. This alone

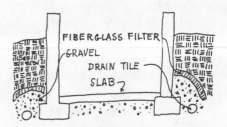

FIG. 10-28. BASEMENT DRAINAGE

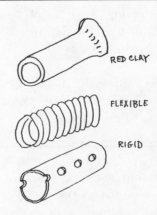

FIG. 10-29. PLASTIC DRAINAGE TILE

will not keep a basement dry year after year. For that you must ensure that no water is even near the basement. This requires good drainage and a lot of gravel (Fig. 10-28).

The idea is to replace the soil around the basement with gravel and sand, because these materials cannot hold water—water drains out of them. If there is gravel under the basement slab and gravel around the outside of the foundation walls, then water will never come in contact with the basement unless the water table is extremely high. Drainage tile should be put around the perimeter of the basement footing to carry away from the house water that drains down through the gravel (Fig. 10-29). Modern drainage tile is plastic pipe with holes in it so that water can get in anywhere. Drainage tile in older houses consists of 2-foot sections of red clay pipe placed end to end.

Of course, not all basements are constructed this way and many leak. There are three methods used to stop basement leaks:

1. Applying waterproof coatings to the inside of the foundation wall.
2. Patching cracks and holes in the wall.
3. Excavating the dirt around the exterior of the house and installing proper drainage, as described above.

It is possible for a homeowner to attempt the third method, but usually a contractor should be called. Installing proper drainage along with the installation of a waterproof coating on the exterior of the foundation wall is the only sure way of maintaining a dry basement.

Installing a waterproof membrane or coating works best if it can be applied to the side of the concrete exposed to water. Usually this means digging up the yard. Waterproof coatings don't work as well when applied to the inside of the basement wall. The moisture that wicks through the wall tends to push the coating off the wall. A coating with good bonding properties like epoxy resin is needed. There are several other coatings: bituminous compounds, fluosilicate compounds, and silicone preparations.

Water also can come in through the cracks in a foundation wall. If they are hairline cracks, the best material to use is epoxy resin. Epoxy paint may work if the cracks are quite narrow. If application of a coating doesn't stop the leakage, the cracks should be widened and filled with an epoxy mortar (a two-part epoxy system with sand filler).

When a basement has a water problem that coatings and patching don't seem to solve, there is one solution that involves digging inside the house (Fig. 10-30). You may want to hire a contractor to do this because it requires some special tools for cutting concrete, but these tools can also be rented. Cut out a 2-foot-wide band of the basement floor, starting at the foundation wall. Remove the concrete by using a jackhammer on this 2-foot-wide area. Dig down to the bottom of the footing and lay a 6-inch drainage tile around the inside perimeter of the footing. This pipe should be sloped from a designated high point at the rate of ⅛ inch per foot of run. The pipe can either run under the footing and out to a low spot in the yard (if there is one) or run into a sump pit. A sump pump is installed in the pit and pumps the water out and into the sewer pipe as the pit fills.

Another trouble spot for leaks is where the floor meets the wall. With a masonry chisel, cut a 2-inch-deep-×-1-inch-wide groove around the perimeter of

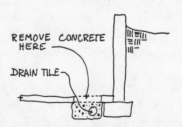

FIG. 10-30. INTERIOR DRAINAGE FOR
A BASEMENT

the basement where the wall and floor meet. Fill this groove with hot tar or a mixture of tar and sand. This will create a waterproof joint.

If you have a moist spot on the basement floor, it is important to determine what is causing it. Is water coming from the air or through the concrete slab? Taste the surface moisture to see if it's salty. If it is, the cause of the problem is probably that calcium chloride (a salt) was sprinkled over the floor before the surface was smoothed to speed the rate at which the concrete set in cold weather. Spread wet, thick newspapers over the spot and aim a fan there. The salt solution will migrate to the top of the newspapers and deposit the salt there. Remove the newspapers and repeat as necessary.

Another diagnostic test is to lay a 3- ×-5-foot piece of polyethylene plastic over the moist spot and tape the edges to the floor with duct tape. If water is coming up through the slab, it will collect under the plastic. The solution is to provide proper drainage, as described above.

Gutters

The purpose of gutters is to catch all the rain that falls on your roof and then drain it away from the house. Without gutters the rain would drip off the eaves onto the ground near the house where it can cause all sorts of problems: mud spattering on the siding, rot in the siding, and water in the basement.

Gutters should be cleaned out periodically to remove leaves and pine needles that can clog up the works and prevent drainage. A leaf strainer, which looks like an upside-down wire basket, can be

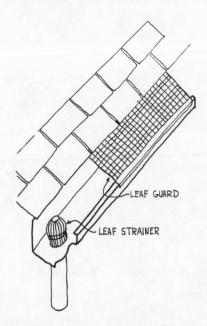

FIG. 10-31. LEAF GUARDS FOR GUTTERS

inserted into the downspout hole to keep debris from clogging it (Fig. 10-31). Leaf guards, which are made of wire mesh and fit over the gutters, also can prevent leaf buildup.

Occasionally gutters will leak. As in roof leaks, the actual leak may not be where the drips are observed. Use the techniques described earlier in this chapter to locate the origin of the leak. The best way to fix leaks in gutters is to fashion a patch out of sheet metal or fiberglass fabric. The sheet-metal patch is sealed to the gutter with asphalt roofing cement (Fig. 10-32). Coat the hole (A) and surrounding area with a generous amount of roofing cement (B). Apply a light-sheet-metal patch that overlaps the sides of the hole by at least 1 inch (C). Set it firmly into the cement and apply another coat

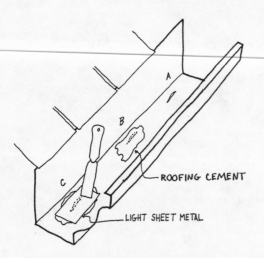

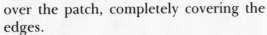
ROOFING CEMENT

LIGHT SHEET METAL

FIG. 10-32. PATCHING A GUTTER

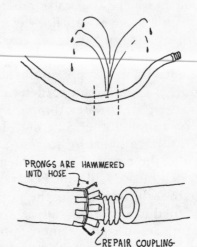
PRONGS ARE HAMMERED
INTO HOSE

REPAIR COUPLING

FIG. 10-33. REPAIRING A GARDEN HOSE

over the patch, completely covering the edges.

Fiberglass fabric is used in conjunction with a two-part epoxy mix. Clean the area around the hole and coat it with a portion of the mixture. Apply the fabric, and paint the remaining mixture over the cloth.

Garden-Hose Repair

A garden hose receives a lot of wear and tear from being yanked around corners and left outside to freeze and thaw with the seasons. Don't throw it away when it springs a leak—especially if it's a good-quality hose.

There are several products on the market that allow you to repair your hose. There are replacements for the repair of either the male or female end, as well as repair couplings to fix a leak in the middle of the hose (Figs. 10-33 and 10-34). Cut out the leaking part of the hose by making

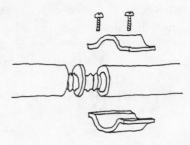

FIG. 10-34. HOSE-CLAMP REPAIR COUPLING

a cut on either side of the leak with a sharp serrated knife or hacksaw. Insert the coupling into both ends of the hose. Wetting the inside of the hose may make this easier. Fig. 10-33 shows the prong type of coupling. Once the coupling has been inserted into the hose, lay it across a hard surface and tap the prongs into the hose with a hammer.

Fig. 10-34 shows a clamp-type coupling. Of the two, the latter is easier to use and lasts longer. After the coupling has been inserted into the hose, a plastic clamp is tightened to hold it there. An automotive hose clamp would work also, but it wouldn't look as nice.

Masonry and Concrete

Contrary to what the little pig who built his house out of brick thought, houses made of brick and mortar don't last forever. Some old mortars have no portland cement in them and use animal hairs as a binder instead. Portland cement is made by burning a mixture of limestone and clay in a kiln; it helps hold the bricks in place. Old mortars eventually break down and lose their ability to adhere to brick. Water can get behind the brick as a result of poor flashing installation or structural damage to the roof. The brick and mortar absorb the water, and as the wall dries out the brick chips and the mortar pops out. Before beginning repairs to masonry or concrete, locate the cause of the damage and eliminate it.

REPOINTING

Repointing, or tuck-pointing as it is sometimes called, consists of chipping out old, damaged mortar and replacing it with new mortar. If you have a choice, schedule the work for spring or fall because 70 degrees is the ideal temperature for curing mortar. If you have to tuck-point when the temperature may dip below 40 degrees, enclose the area in plastic and maintain a temperature of 50 to 60 degrees. Mortar that freezes before it cures is brittle.

Repointing usually makes a mess, so lay a piece of plastic down on the ground under where you are working. When it's time to clean up, all you have to do is roll up the drop cloth and go to the dump with the rubble.

You will need two tools: a masonry chisel and a small trowel. Any masonry chisel that will fit into the mortar joint will do, but there is one chisel made especially for the job—a plugging chisel (Fig. 10-35). The mortar joint should be chiseled out to a depth of ½ to ¾ inch (Fig. 10-36). Wear safety goggles when chiseling. Hold the chisel at a sharp angle and strike the end firmly with a hammer. Work on removing inch-long pieces of mortar. Try to chisel so that there is a rectangular groove in the mortar joint.

Brush loose all particles and dust them out of the joint with a wallpaper-paste or whitewash brush. Next, wet the joint so that it's *damp* (if the joint is

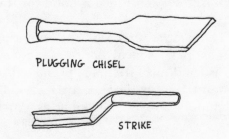

PLUGGING CHISEL

STRIKE

FIG. 10-35. MASONRY TOOLS

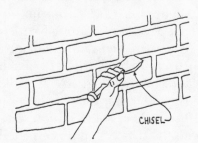

CHISEL

FIG. 10-36. CHISELING OUT A
MORTAR JOINT

FIG. 10-37. A HAWK

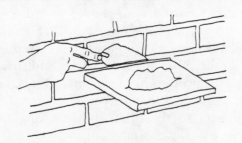

FIG. 10-38. TUCK-POINTING WITH A
TRIANGULAR TROWEL

soaked, the mortar will not adhere to the brick). An old paintbrush is good for this job.

The mortar used for tuck-pointing and most repairs involving cracks in concrete is sand mix. It comes premixed in 80-pound bags at lumberyards or concrete-supply houses. Mix only as much mortar as you can use in an hour. Add water slowly, until the mortar is the consistency of cottage cheese.

Put a trowelful on a small board. The board will be your hawk or mortar holder. If you have a lot of repointing to do, it will behoove you to nail a handle onto the bottom of your hawk, thereby making a professional model (Fig. 10-37). Hold the hawk just under the joint to be pointed (Fig. 10-38). Push some mortar into the joint with the trowel and make sure there are no empty spaces. Another tool that can be used in place of a trowel is a strike

(see Fig. 10-35). It has the advantage of actually being able to fit into the joint.

The last step is to finish off the joint. Let the mortar dry until your thumb leaves a clear impression in it. Then run the strike along each joint you've done to smooth the mortar. When the mortar has set enough to prevent smearing, brush off any loose particles.

When the mortar has had two weeks to cure, scrape off all the little particles with a masonry chisel or a wooden paddle. Scrub the wall with water and a stiff brush. If you've been messy, you may need to use a solution of 1 part muriatic acid to 20 parts water to remove the mortar stains. Muriatic acid is a weak sulfuric acid that is available at drugstores and building-supply stores. Wear rubber gloves, old clothes, and goggles when you use it. Cover the plants near the house and hose off the wall afterward.

REPLACING A LOOSE OR DAMAGED BRICK

If the brick is loose, remove it and chip off all the mortar. Most bricks will have to be chiseled out. Use a masonry chisel as in Fig. 10-36. Chip away at the brick and mortar and brush the dust and particles out of the joint. Dampen the replacement brick and the pocket into which it will go.

Now for the part that requires finesse. With a trowel "butter" the brick with mortar (Fig. 10-39). This is the term masons use when they deftly slap mortar on all sides of a brick. Also lay mortar against all sides of the pocket. Push the brick into place and use a strike to pack the mortar into the joint. Finish as described above.

PATCHING CONCRETE

It is common for exterior concrete to crack or chip. This usually happens when it gets a lot of wear, the way concrete steps do. The joint between new and old concrete is a cold joint. This means that there is no natural bonding between the two surfaces. A bonding agent like epoxy or latex must be used. Building-supply stores carry various patching mortars. Not all latexes and epoxies are suitable for exterior conditions; make sure you ask before purchasing one.

For patches that will be under a lot of stress, a reinforcement is necessary. Drive case-hardened nails into the old concrete (Fig. 10-40). If the concrete just chips and doesn't take the nail, drill holes for the nails with a small masonry bit and a hammer drill.

Fabricate a form from scrap lumber and brace it against the ground (Fig. 10-41). The braces won't have to hold much weight since the patch is small.

Paint the old concrete surface with the bonding agent, usually either latex or epoxy, and pack the mortar into the form. Two layers may have to be used for deep patches; the directions will specify. Fill the form to the level of the old concrete and smooth the surface with a trowel or board. Don't remove the form for a couple of days and don't let anyone walk on the patch until it is fully cured (about two weeks).

PATCHING BLACKTOP

Blacktop is considerably easier to patch than concrete. Various size bags of cold-mix asphalt-patching compound are available at building-supply stores. First, dig all loose material out of the hole. If

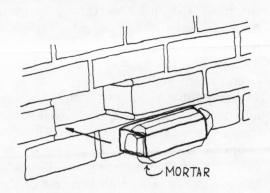

FIG. 10-39. REPLACING A BRICK

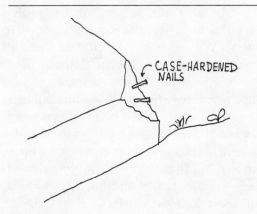

FIG. 10-40

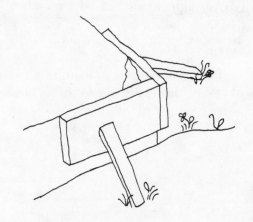

FIG. 10-41. PATCHING CONCRETE

the hole is deep (more than 4 inches), pour gravel into the hole to within 4 inches of the top. Tamp it down with a 2×4 to remove air spaces that could settle later, making your patch concave. Pour in some cold-mix to within 1 inch of the top and tamp it in the same way. Finish filling the hole until the patching compound is about ½ inch above the surface of the blacktop. The final tamping or rolling will bring it down flush with the rest of the surface. Driving a car over it will do the trick.

Blacktop surfaces must be sealed periodically to keep them impervious to water. When water penetrates through cracks that may develop, it can cause damage like heaving. Blacktop sealer can be purchased anywhere in 5-gallon buckets. Sweep the surface so it is clean. Scrape up any oil or grease spots and wash with detergent. Wet the area evenly with a hose, but make sure no water is standing in puddles. Stir the sealer and pour it onto the surface while the surface is still damp. Spread the blacktop sealer evenly over the entire surface with a push broom. Let it dry overnight before you drive over it.

Securing a Handrail

The moorings of handrails must withstand the daily force of a lot of weight. Handrails can be attached either to the house or to the concrete stoop.

If a handrail attached to the house keeps loosening and pulling out even after you tighten the screws, the location of the handrail brackets should be changed so that the screws can grip fresh wood. Another method of attachment is the one used for grab bars described on page 101.

When a handrail attached to concrete comes loose, the problem is usually that the screws that hold the base flange to the stoop have come loose (Fig. 10-42). If retightening them does no good, the concrete fastener (screw anchor or lag screw shield) is probably worn out. If screw anchors were the method of attachment, change to lag screw shields, because they are capable of withstanding more force. Installing a lag screw shield is depicted in Fig. A-5.

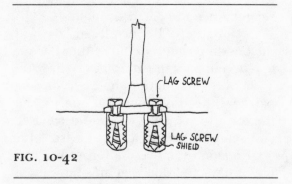

FIG. 10-42

11

FLOORS, STAIRS, AND RAMPS

The repairs of floors and stairs revolve around sags and squeaks. Squeaks prevent you from sneaking up the stairs late at night. Sags in a floor make baking a level cake almost an impossibility. One thinks of these as signalling major repairs, but that isn't necessarily so. Not all floor sags mean major repairs.

Floors

Floors are made up of crisscrossing layers (Fig. 11-1). The uppermost one is what we walk on. It is called the finish floor and can be carpet, vinyl, tile, or wood. Under that is the sub-floor, which is usually made of wider boards either diagonal or perpendicular to the joists. The joists support the dead load of both layers of flooring and the live load of furniture and occupants. Houses are usually too wide for one joist to span across, so most houses have a carrying beam in the basement that supports the ends of joists coming from opposite foundation walls (see Fig. 6-1).

The National Building Code says that floors should have bridging every 8 feet. Most old houses fall far short of this. The result is floors that are too springy. Bridging stiffens the floor, helping it act as a unit by connecting each joist to the one next to it. Houses built before 1940 have cross-bridging made of two 1×2s that crisscross between each joist (Fig. 11-1). More modern houses have solid blocking. They both serve the same purpose.

SAGGING FLOORS

Rarely does a sagging floor signal serious settling of the foundation (see Fig.

189

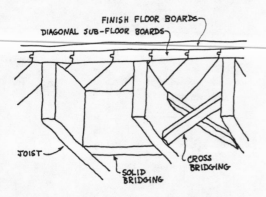

FIG. 11-1. COMPONENTS OF A FLOOR

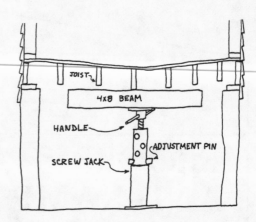

FIG. 11-2. JACKING UP A SAGGING FLOOR

6-24). Usually it means that a beam supporting the floor has cracked or sagged, and over the years the floor has molded itself to the sag. A sag can also be caused by inadequately sized joists. If a joist is too puny for the span, it will curve down in the middle. Generally, a slanting floor means the foundation has settled unevenly and a sagging floor signals problems with the joists or girder.

Convolutions in the floor caused by foundation settling should be corrected by a professional. However, a cracked beam or sagging undersized joists can be jacked up without too much trouble (Fig. 11-2).

The trick to jacking up a sag in a floor is to do it *slowly*. We're talking $\frac{1}{32}$ inch every four days. If it's done any quicker, the house will not have a chance to settle between each jacking and the plaster will crack.

At the lumberyard, purchase a screw jack and a 4×8 long enough to span the sag in the floor. If a 4×8 is unavailable, build one by nailing two 2×8s together.

A screw jack is a metal post with one threaded end that can be screwed up or down. Place the bottom of the screw jack directly under the middle of the sag in the floor above. The jack will be permanent, so make sure it's not blocking door swings or traffic. If the sag is in the second floor, requiring that the jack be in the living room, place it so that a partition or bookcase can be built around it. Also see that another jack is located in the basement directly under it, or all that you will accomplish is pushing down the living-room floor.

Remove the adjustment pin and slide the jack up until the beam, which is resting on the upper plate, almost contacts the joists above. Replace the pin in the slot that allows the jack to be nearest to this position and screw the handle clockwise, until the beam makes firm contact with the joists. Check to see that the jack is plumb. Now give the handle one-half turn and *stop*. That is enough pressure for a while. In four days you can give the handle a quarter turn. Continue jacking up

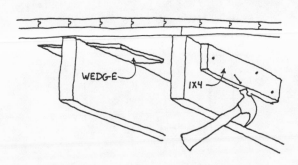

FIG. 11-3. SILENCING SQUEAKS IN THE
SUB-FLOOR

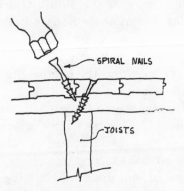

FIG. 11-4. STOPPING SQUEAKS IN THE
SUB-FLOOR

the sag one-quarter turn at a time, until the floor is even. The house needs time to settle between jackings. If you go faster, plaster may crack or pipes may burst.

SQUEAKS

Floors squeak because the wood has shrunk and left a space between the joist and sub-floor or between the two layers of flooring. When a person walks across the floor and steps over this gap, the wood flooring depresses, causing a squeak as wood rubs against wood. There are two causes of squeaking: movement of the finish flooring and movement of the sub-flooring. They have different solutions.

Movement of the sub-flooring is the main cause of squeaks. They are easy to fix if the joists beneath are exposed, as in a basement or crawlspace (Fig. 11-3). To locate a squeak, have someone walk on the floor above while you watch for movement between joists and sub-flooring. If just one board is moving, a cedar shingle wedge can be driven between the joist and board to fill the gap. If several boards

have separated from the joist, push a 1×4 up tightly against the sub-flooring and nail it to the joist.

If the ceiling below is not exposed, the repair must be made from above by nailing down through both the finish flooring and the sub-flooring into the joist. The trick here is to locate a joist in the squeaking area. Tap the handle of a hammer against the floor or ceiling. Listen for the different sounds the hammer makes as it moves across the surface. When it is tapping over a joist the sound will be more solid. Nail two 10d spiral nails into the joist from above (Fig. 11-4). Toe them in a little so that they form a V. This will help them grip. Countersink the nails with a nailset (see Fig. 3-6) and fill the holes with a putty that matches the color of the floor.

When the squeak occurs in an area covered by vinyl, tile, or carpet, these materials should be taken up before nailing. If, when you have removed any of these, you find that the floor below is plywood, you can forget the nails and use

drywall screws. If the floor is only plywood, as it is in some houses built since
1960, then you are not ruining its aesthetic beauty by driving a screw into it.
Just make sure that the head is flush with
or below the surface.

The easy way to drive a drywall screw
is to buy a Phillips bit from the hardware
store, insert it into the end of your variable-speed drill as if it were a bit, and drive
the screw in with the drill. Hold the screw
against the floor and place the Phillips bit
into the slot in the head of the screw. As
you press the drill into the screw with your
strong hand and squeeze the trigger, your
other hand holds the screw vertical until a
few threads have bitten into the wood and
it can stand up on its own. It takes a little
practice. After you've gotten it you'll love
putting in screws this way.

A less frequent cause of squeaks is
loose finish floor boards. The movement
of these boards can often be seen or felt
as you walk over the squeaky spot. There
are a couple of things you can do to
squeaks in the finish floor (Fig. 11-5). If
the joists are exposed below, the loose
boards can be pulled down tight against
the sub-floor by wood screws. Drill a pilot
hole through the sub-floor that is larger in
diameter than the shank of the screw.
Change bits and drill a smaller hole into
the underside of the finish floor board.
This hole should be small enough to allow
the tip of the wood screw to bite into the
wood fibers. For the method for choosing
the size of this bit, see pages 12–13 and
Fig. 2-8. When the screw is driven, it will
slip through the sub-floor and bite only
into the finish floor. This ensures the
drawing-down action.

If the joists below are not exposed,

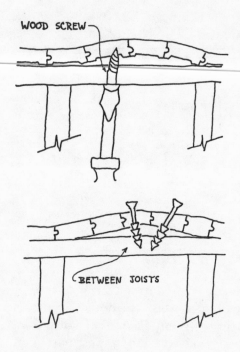

FIG. 11-5. SILENCING SQUEAKS IN
FINISH FLOOR

the repair must be done from above.
Drive two 6d nails down into the sub-floor
so that they are toed or slanted in a V. Use
spiral shank nails if they are available.
First, try driving the nails in along the
crack between boards. Place them 6
inches apart and countersink the nail
heads with a nail set. Driving them into
the crack will help conceal them. If the
squeak persists, drive pairs of nails into
the face of the board and conceal the
heads with putty.

When the cracks between boards are
wide enough, glue can be pushed between boards with a putty knife. Modern
glues are very strong and can stop
squeaks by bonding the boards together.
For fine cracks use a thin, watery glue.

Some lumberyards sell construction adhesives that can be mixed with water. Pour it into the cracks and wipe the glue off the surface. Also drive two 6d nails into the crack to hold the boards in place while the glue is drying. Do not walk over the area until the glue has thoroughly dried.

PATCHING VINYL

Patching vinyl is easy; matching the pattern is the tricky part. It helps if you have saved a piece of the vinyl from the scrap pile when it was laid. The scrap has not been exposed to the same traffic, but it is the same vintage as your floor. If you have no scraps, peruse the vinyl stores for pieces of the same pattern. The patch will stand out at first, but after it has been walked over for a month it will begin to blend in.

Place the vinyl scrap over the hole in the vinyl floor and secure it with masking tape, so that the pattern of the patch is in sync with the rest of the floor (Fig. 11-6). Be sure to remember where the hole is. Lay a ruler down over the vinyl and, while holding it firmly in place, cut down through both layers of vinyl with a utility knife. The object is to cut two identically shaped pieces out of both layers. Remove the tape and discard the remainder of the vinyl scrap. Set the patch aside.

The next step is to remove the vinyl within the cut lines. A putty knife should scrape it up. If the adhesive is not letting go, lay a damp cloth over the area and heat it with an iron (see Fig. 11-7). Scrape all loose adhesive off the underlayment over which the patch will go. The underlayment is the masonite.

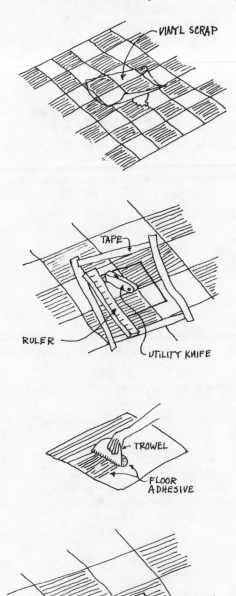

FIG. 11-6. PATCHING VINYL FLOORING

Floor adhesive can be purchased at lumber and hardware stores. Also buy an inexpensive spreader. Spread the adhesive on the back of the vinyl patch and press it into place. Roll a jar or rolling pin over the spot to assure bonding. Place some heavy books over the area until the adhesive sets.

REPLACING A TILE

Tile floors are not as common since the advent of vinyl. This doesn't stop the tiles from cracking or coming loose. Once again, it helps to have a few extra tiles stashed away so that the pattern of the floor can be matched exactly. If you don't, buy a couple from a floor-covering store.

To remove the cracked tile, lay a moist piece of cloth over the tile and go over it with an iron set at its highest setting. When the tile has been softened, scrape it up with the aid of a putty knife (Fig. 11-7). Clean the surface below the tile of excess adhesive. Spread floor adhesive on the back of the tile and press it into place. Roll the area with a rolling pin or jar and place weight over the spot until the adhesive has set.

REFINISHING FLOORS

Nowadays, most floor refinishing is done mechanically. The process requires three tools: drum sander, floor edger, and a scraper (Fig. 11-8). The two sanders can be rented at any tool-rental agency. They will also supply the sandpaper you need.

Some preparations must be made before you rent the sanders. Remove all the furniture you can and cover the rest with drop cloths. Make sure you can close off the room from the rest of the house. Closing doors will do, but rig up a curtain if there are no doors. The sanding will throw fine paint dust everywhere, even

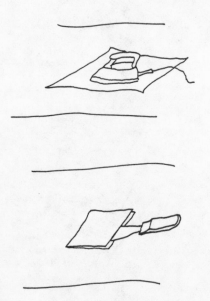

FIG. 11-7. REPLACING A FLOOR TILE

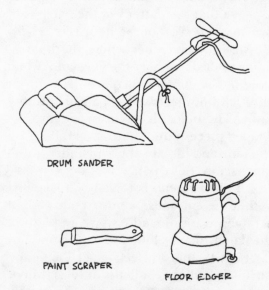

DRUM SANDER

PAINT SCRAPER

FLOOR EDGER

FIG. 11-8. TOOLS FOR REFINISHING
A FLOOR

into the workings of the toaster, so be forewarned.

Examine the floors carefully for any protruding nails. Pull or set below the surface any that you find. Such nails will shred the sandpaper. If you encounter any loose boards, secure them to the sub-floor or joists as described above.

When you go to rent the sanders, be sure that you leave the store with an understanding of how both tools work and how to change the sandpaper on each. Remember that the drum sander weighs 150 pounds. I forgot this the first time I sanded a floor and I had to flag down two guys in a utility truck to help me lift the sander up to the second floor of my house. Embarrassing—better to have friends at the other end to help you.

The drum sander is used to sand the greater part of the floor. The edger sands near the baseboard, where the drum sander can't reach. Begin sanding with the drum sander. Fig. 11-9 shows the sanding pattern for a room. Start against the right wall one-third of the way into the room. Push down on the handle so that the drum is not in contact with the floor. Turn the sander on, walk forward as if you were pushing a lawn mower, and slowly lower the sanding drum onto the wood. It's important to do this gradually or ridges will result. As you reach the end of the first pass, slowly raise the sander. Gradually lower it again as you pull it back over the area you just did. The sander cuts best when you're pulling it. Proceed across the room in passes that are approximately 2 to 4 inches apart. Gradually raise and lower the sander at either end of each pass.

When you reach the other wall, turn

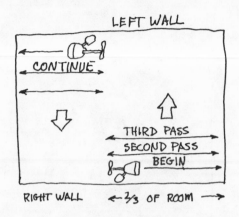

FIG. 11-9. SANDING CHOREOGRAPHY

around and, with the wall on your right, begin to sand the remaining third of the room. There will probably be a ridge where the first section meets the second, which you will need to feather as you go.

The above procedure should be repeated with three different grits of paper, starting with coarse and ending with fine. If the floor is covered with paint, a very coarse paper should be used first. Be sure to wear a mask and ear protection when you're sanding. If the floor has ridges or boards that are curled along the edge, one pass at a 45-degree angle to the floor boards will reduce the unevenness. Do this as a first pass.

The floor edger is a powerful sander that is equipped with two handles and wheels. Like the drum sander, it is a tricky tool to get used to, so start in a closet or an out-of-the-way spot. Move this sander from left to right in a semicircular pattern (Fig. 11-10). Sand the perimeter that was not sanded by the drum sander. Use the same or finer-grit paper. Use a very sharp paint scraper to get into the corners.

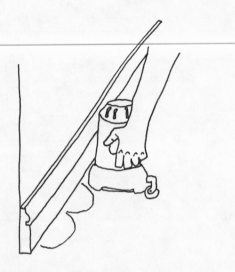

FIG. 11-10. USING AN EDGER

Clean up thoroughly when you're finished. Sweep the floors, walls, and the tops of door and window trim. Dampen a medium-size towel with paint thinner and swab it around the floor with a broom. This will pick up the finest dust. Vacuum the corners and you're ready to put on the finish of your choice.

Floor finishes fall into two categories: those that soak down into the pores of the wood and those that create a surface film, such as varnishes, shellacs, and polyurethanes. The one you choose depends upon the use of the room. Kitchen floors, for instance, where many spills take place, should be sealed with a surface film. Follow the manufacturer's directions strictly. Whatever you do, don't pick this time to rid the house of mice. After putting out poison we found a mouse belly up in the middle of the room, stuck in the polyurethane.

Stairs

Stairs are both a structural and aesthetic part of a house. They are the vehicle on which we travel from floor to floor and are, therefore, built to hold heavy loads. In many houses they are the first thing we see upon entering, and they are carefully fashioned to catch the eye. Because of the constant traffic over them, most repairs to stairs deal with squeaky treads or loose handrails.

A flight of stairs consists of three components: stringers, risers, and treads (Fig. 11-11). The stringer is usually a 2×12 set at an angle of about 35 degrees. Its bottom rests on one floor and its top on the floor above. A stringer is basically a slanted joist that carries the load on the stair. A stair that is 3 feet wide will have three stringers: two on either side and one in the middle. The 2×12 stringers are either cutout or full (Fig. 11-12). One type of stair common in older houses is a full stringer, which is dadoed (notched) to accept the treads and risers. The tread is the horizontal part of the stair that we usually call the step. The riser is the vertical board between treads. On basement stairs the riser is usually omitted.

A squeak is often caused by the movement of the tread as you step on it. It is rubbing on the top of the riser directly below or at its edge against the stringer. How one goes about eliminating the squeak depends on whether or not the stair is open from the back. If the back of the stair is covered with plaster or Sheetrock, the repairs must be made from the front (Fig. 11-13).

Have someone stand on the tread that is squeaking. This will hold it down

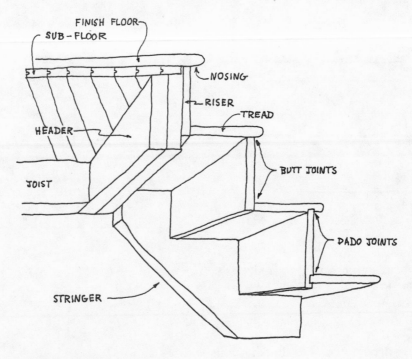

FIG. 11-11. THE PARTS OF A STAIR

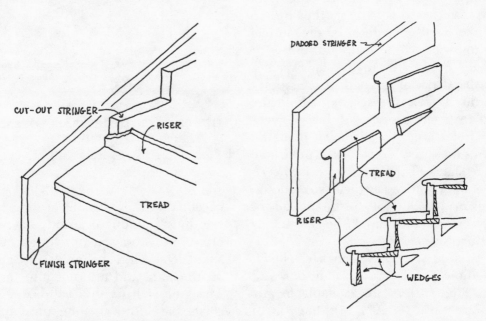

FIG. 11-12. TWO TYPES OF STRINGER

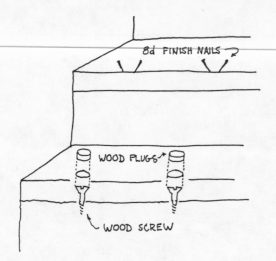

FIG. 11-13. STOPPING STAIR SQUEAKS
FROM THE FRONT

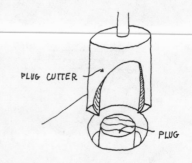

FIG. 11-14. PLUG CUTTER CUTTING
A WOODEN PLUG

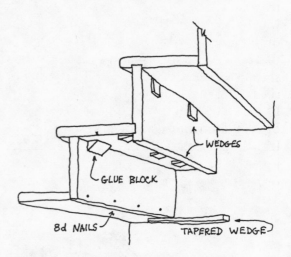

FIG. 11-15. STOPPING STAIR SQUEAKS
FROM BEHIND

while you drive two 8d finish nails through the tread and into the upper edge of the riser. Nail them in pairs and at an angle with each other so that they form a **V**. If the tread is made of hardwood like oak, you will have to drill pilot holes for the nails. Select a bit that's a hair smaller than the shank of the nail. If nails don't stop the squeak, use screws to hold the tread to the riser. First, drill a ⅜-inch-deep hole larger in diameter than the head of the screw. Next, drill a pilot hole for the shank of the screw (see Fig. 2-7). It should be as deep as the shank is long. Finally drill a pilot hole for the threads of the screw. This bit should be selected as described on pages 12–13.

After the screw has been driven in, fill in the hole with a wooden plug or wood putty. Plug cutters are available in any hardware store (Fig. 11-14). They fit in ¼- or ⅜-inch drills and work like a bit,

except that they dig out around a short standing column of wood that can be pried out with a screwdriver and used as a plug. Dab a little yellow carpenter's glue on the plug and insert it into the hole. The glue will dry in a half-hour. With a chisel, pare down the plug until it is flush with the surface. Chisel with the grain and take off $\frac{1}{16}$ inch of the plug at a time. Sand the plug until it's flush with the top of the tread.

If the stairs are open from the back, the squeak should be silenced from behind (Fig. 11-15). The risers and treads will be either butted or notched into each other. To determine if the joint is a dado joint, slip a knife blade up into the joint. Short wedges can be driven alongside riser and tread and into the dado to tighten up the joint. Pin the wedge in place with a small nail or brad.

Where the joint between riser and tread is a butt joint, reinforce the joint with 8d nails driven through the bottom of the riser and into the back edge of the tread. Triangular-shaped glue blocks should be mounted at the intersection of riser and tread. Spread yellow glue on the block and install it by moving the block back and forth with your fingers until you feel the glue grab. This is a rubbed glue joint. Drive two finish nails into the block to hold it in place while the glue is drying. The glue block increases the surface area and strength in the riser-tread joint. Install four blocks across a typical 3-foot-wide stair. These blocks can also be used to stop movement and squeaking where the tread and riser meet the stringer. Place one glue block per riser and one per tread.

RAILINGS

Handrails often become loose because of the rough and constant use that we inflict upon them. Handrails are held to the wall by brackets screwed into studs (Fig. 11-16). A wobbly rail is caused by enlarged screw holes. The remedy is to remove the rail and brackets and drive

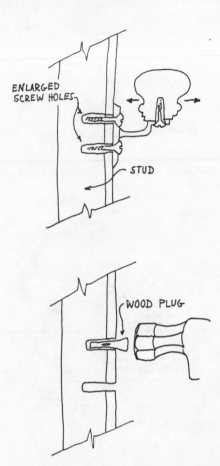

FIG. 11-16. FIRMING UP A LOOSE RAILING

whittled wooden pegs into the holes. Stick matches will also work. Reinsert the screws and the rail should be secure once again. If you find that a handrail bracket has not been fastened to a stud, move it so that the screws can be driven into a stud.

Bannisters also become loose over time. Some terminology is important here. What we call a bannister has two parts: the handrail and the balusters. It is the balusters that tend to come loose (Fig.

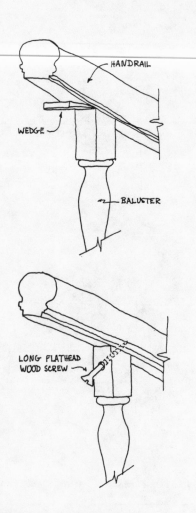

FIG. 11-17. TIGHTENING LOOSE
BALUSTERS

the handrail. Follow the directions given on pages 12–13 for drilling the pilot holes for the screw.

Ramps

Wheelchairs are designed to be remarkably mobile. However, there is one obstacle even the most athletic wheelchair user cannot negotiate—a stair or curb. This is why we have ramps. Many of us have had a disabled friend or relative come to visit only to find that the house is inaccessible to a wheelchair. Why not build a ramp?

Here are the design specifications for a ramp. The maximum slope of a ramp is 1 inch of rise for every 1 foot of run. Where a ramp changes direction, there should be a landing that is at least 5 feet × 5 feet. This allows the wheelchair user room to turn the chair around and a place to rest. There should also be a landing in front of each door. Where the door swings out, the landing should measure at least 5 feet × 6½ feet. The width of the ramp (36-inch minimum) should accommodate the wheels of the chair and the arms of the user. There should be a curb on either side and around the perimeter of each landing to keep the wheels from rolling off accidentally. There should be a handrail on either side of the ramp from 30 to 32 inches off the floor. The diameter of the handrail itself should be 1½ inches to allow it to be easily gripped.

A ramp can be built with 2×4s and 2×6s as the structural support, ¾-inch plywood or 1×3 boards as the surface, 2×2 curbs, and 2×4 handrails. Fig. 11-18 shows a typical structure. The landing outside the door is supported by

11-17). The joint between the top of the baluster and the handrail can be tightened in several ways. Drive a small wedge into the joint as far as it will go and chisel off the remainder of the wedge. This will keep the baluster from wobbling. Another method is to drive a long thin wood screw at an angle through the baluster and into

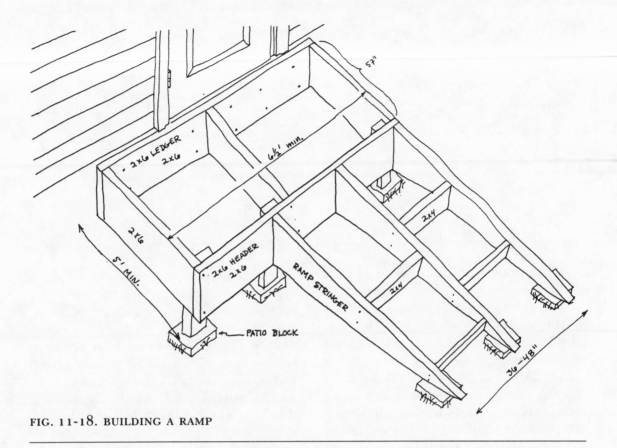

FIG. 11-18. BUILDING A RAMP

2×6s. For higher doors the landing can be raised by attaching two legs to the two corners not touching the house. An additional leg should go at the inside corner where the ramp meets the platform. The 2×6 against the house is nailed through the siding and into the header joist with 16d or 20d galvanized common nails, so no legs are needed here.

Build the landing first. Cut two 2×6s, 6½ feet long. These are the headers and ledger. Cut three 2×6 joists, 57 inches long. Nail the two long pieces and two of the shorter pieces together into a rectangle as shown in Fig. 11-18. Use two

16d common nails at each corner. When the rectangle is complete, add the middle 2×6 by nailing through the long pieces into this piece.

With a level, draw a level line on the siding under the door. The line should be at least 1 inch below the underside of the threshold of the door. Have a friend help nail the rectangular platform to the house. The top of one long 2×6 should be nailed along the line you've just drawn. Your friend should hold up the other side of the platform as you nail. So that your friend can eventually go home, nail three 2×4 legs along the 2×6 header farthest

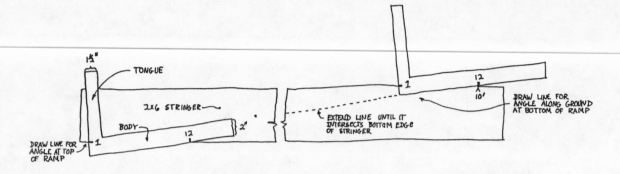

FIG. 11-19. USING THE FRAMING SQUARE TO LAY OUT THE ANGLE CUTS
ON A RAMP STRINGER

from the house. It looks nicer if the legs are inside the rectangle. Estimate the length of the legs by laying a level on one of the short 2×6 joists and ask your friend to raise the platform until it's level with the 2×6 nailed into the house. When the platform is level, measure down from the top of it to the ground at each leg location. Cut the 2×4 legs 1 inch shorter than this measurement. This will allow some last-minute adjustments when you nail the leg into the inside corner of the platform.

Place the level on one of the 2×6 joists. Have your friend lift the header until the level reads level. While the friend holds the header in that position, attach one leg by nailing two 16d galvanized common nails through the header and into the 2×4 leg.

Cutting the ramp stringers requires a few calculations. Measure the height of the platform again. Let's say it is 10 inches off the ground. According to the specification that a ramp rise 1 inch for every foot it travels horizontally, the ramp stringers must be 10 feet long. The tricky part

about these stringers is the top and bottom cuts. The framing square is the right tool for determining the angle of these cuts. It is made of thin metal in the shape of an L. The two legs of the L are different widths and lengths. The wider, longer one is called the body and is 2 inches wide and 24 inches long. The other leg is called the tongue and is 1½ inches wide and 16 inches long (Fig. 11-19). To measure the angle for the top cut, lay the framing square on the 2×6 as shown in the illustration. Align the 1 on the tongue and the 12 on the body with the bottom edge of the 2×6. Holding the square in this position, draw a line along the outside of the tongue. Cut along this line for the top cut angle.

Measure from the top of the 2×6 down its length and make a mark at 10 feet, right along the top edge of the 2×6. Lay the square on the 2×6 with the tongue toward the top of the ramp. Align the 12 on the body with the mark you just made on the 2×6, as shown in the illustration. Align the 1 on the tongue with the top edge of the 2×6. Draw a line along the body and extend it to the other edge of the 2×6. Cut along this line. When the stringer is held in place, the bottom cut should be parallel to the ground. Use this stringer as a pattern for the other two stringers.

To attach the stringers to the platform, first mark where each stringer should go. The ramp can come off the platform wherever you desire. The two outside stringers should be no less than 36 inches apart and the third should be located halfway between. Nail the top of a stringer to each mark by standing inside the platform and driving a 16d galvanized common nail through the 2×6 header into the wide end of the stringer.

Cut pieces of 2×4 to go between the stringers and attach them by nailing through the stringers and into the 2×4 support piece. Stagger these supports so that they all can be end-nailed. Place the ends of each ramp stringer and each post on a flat piece of stone set into the ground. This will help water drain away from the wood and prevent rot.

The surface of the ramp can be made of ¾-inch plywood or 1×3 slats. Plywood comes in 4×8 sheets. If the ramp is exactly 4 feet wide, no cutting to width is necessary. If the ramp is 36 inches wide, cut a 3-foot-×-8-foot piece out of the sheet of plywood. Measuring is the key (Fig. 11-20). At one end of the sheet, measure from one of the 8-foot edges in toward the center of the plywood and make a crow's foot mark at 36 inches. Do the same thing at the other end. For more information on transferring measurements, see pages 106–107 and Fig. 6-23.

Now you get to use one of the most fun tools there is: the chalk line (see Fig.

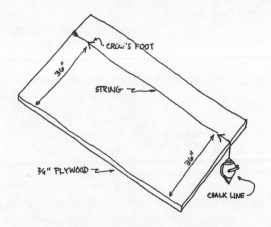

FIG. 11-20. MEASURING AND CHALKING
A LINE ON PLYWOOD

11-20). It is a tool for marking straight lines. A chalk line or chalk box is a teardrop-shaped container with a reel in it. String is pulled out and reeled in much like one does when using a fishing rod. The container is filled with colored chalk (usually red or blue), which coats the string as it is pulled out. The string is tightly stretched between two points like the two crow's feet on the sheet of plywood. While it is being held on the marks, someone "snaps" the string by lifting it off the surface an inch or two and letting it snap back. The result is a straight chalk-colored line on the board between the two points.

Cut the plywood along this line with a circular saw. If the ramp is 10 feet long, as it is in our example, you will need to cut another piece of plywood for the end of the ramp. Nail the plywood of the platform on first. Use 8d galvanized common nails. (They won't rust.) Then nail the longest ramp piece in place. With this piece in place, you can measure exactly the size of the remaining piece. The plywood on the ramp should be covered with a high-friction material that will ensure that the wheels don't slip. Rubber matting or mineral-surface roll roofing will do nicely.

Covering the ramp with a rubber mat is an invitation to rot. Water will be trapped under the mat for long periods. A better surface than plywood is 1×3 or 1×4 boards placed horizontally across the stringers and spaced ¼ inch apart. Any water that gets under the mat will drain down through the space between each board. This surface may take more time to lay down, but the material cost should be almost the same and it will last longer.

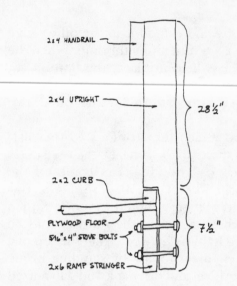

FIG. 11-21. HANDRAIL DETAIL FOR A RAMP

HANDRAILS AND CURBS

The curb will keep a wheelchair from accidentally rolling off the platform or ramp. It can be made of 2×2s or 2×4s. In Fig. 11-21 I've used 2×2s. Nail the 2×2s along the two edges of the ramp and around the perimeter of the landing, except where the ramp is located. Use 16d galvanized common nails.

The handrails must be installed securely because they will take a lot of stress. Wheelchair users sometimes pull themselves up ramps by using the handrails. The strongest way to secure the uprights is with stove bolts (Fig. 11-21). The uprights are installed with their 1½-inch edge toward the ramp. Each upright is 36 inches long and has a 7½-×-1½-inch notch cut out of the bottom. The notch fits over the curb and hangs down over the 2×6 stringer or joist, whichever the case may be. Two stove bolts are used to hold each upright to the platform or ramp (see Fig. A-2). The stove bolts should be ⅜ or 5/16 inch in diameter and 4 inches

long. Place the upright in place, plumb it with a level, and tack it with two 10d galvanized common nails. Drill two holes for the stove bolts with a bit the size of the bolt diameter. Tap the bolts through from the outside with a hammer and tighten the washer and nut from the other side with a crescent wrench. When you go to the hardware store to buy the nails and bolts for the ramp, be sure you know how many bolts to buy—two for each upright times the number of uprights. Space the uprights no less than 4 feet apart.

The handrail itself can be a 2×4 nailed to the tops of the uprights so that its 1½-inch edge is up. Fasten the handrail to the uprights with 16d galvanized common nails or bolt it in place with 5/16-×-3-inch lag screws. Use two nails or screws per upright. If a round handrail is desired, a standard handrail and brackets can be purchased from the lumberyard and mounted to the 3½-inch face of the 2×4 nailed to the top of the uprights.

12

DEALING WITH
HOUSEHOLD EMERGENCIES

Emergencies always happen suddenly. So now while everything is going smoothly, go down to the basement and locate all the main plumbing and electrical shutoffs and switches. Knowing where they are will allow you to respond to emergencies effectively.

A Broken Pipe

Run for the main shutoff valve near the water meter and turn it clockwise to turn off all the water to the house (Fig. 12-1). If the house does not have a shutoff valve just inside the basement wall, it will be outside in the ground in an accessible box. If you have a well instead, there should be a main shutoff on the house side of the pump. If there is no main shutoff in your house, then locate the shutoff valve nearest the pipe that has burst. It must be between the pipe and the water-main entrance into the house. Once the water has stopped spurting you can put a temporary patch on the pipe and then turn the water back on. This repair is explained in chapter 4.

A Blown Fuse

There is nothing more annoying than having the lights in part of the house go out. This means that the fuse or breaker for one electrical circuit in the house has blown and no electricity is going to the receptacles. The receptacles are commonly called outlets and are located on the walls near the floor. Several things are helpful in this situation. First, have a flashlight in the junk drawer. Second,

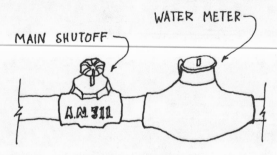

FIG. 12-1. MAIN WATER SHUTOFF

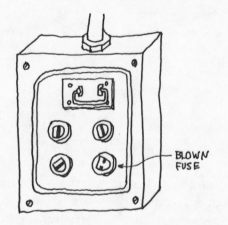

FIG. 12-2. PANEL BOX WITH FUSES

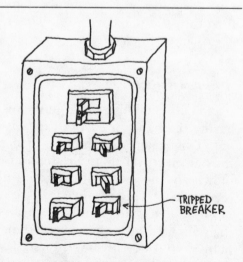

FIG. 12-3. PANEL BOX WITH CIRCUIT BREAKERS

know where the fuse or breaker box is. You should look for it on some bright, sunny afternoon so that you are ready for the dark, gloomy night when the lights go off.

An inspection of the fuse box should tell you which fuse is blown. It is the one whose metal tab is melted through (Fig. 12-2). Replace it with a good fuse of the same amperage. Each fuse is marked clearly on the face of the fuse. The two most common sizes are 15A and 20A. The "A" stands for amperes (amps), which is a measure of how much electricity is allowed to flow through the wires. This is discussed in greater detail in chapter 5. If you are fortunate enough to have a house that has a breaker box, all you have to do is carefully peruse the box until you see one switch that is in a different position from all the others (Fig. 12-3). This is the circuit breaker for the circuit that blew. Turn it all the way to off and then turn it on. (The blown position of the switch is between off and on.) Presto, the lights should come back on.

A Leaking Roof

The only way we know if our roofs leak is if water drips onto our living-room rug or somewhere else that is highly visible. After first putting a bucket in the living room (or wherever you see the leak) to catch the dripping water, you should then go up to the attic to search for the leak's origin. The only way to know exactly where the roof is leaking is to actually observe the water coming in. Once you know where the leak is, you can fix it on the next nice day (see chapter 10). Meanwhile, try to place another pan in the attic, so that

FIG. 12-4. TRACING A LEAK

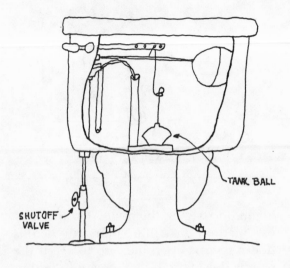

FIG. 12-5. TOILET PARTS

it catches the water as it drips from the rafter to the ceiling (Fig. 12-4).

A Toilet Overflows

This household crisis demands nerves of steel. Before you reach for the plunger, stop the flow of water to the toilet. If there is a shutoff valve on the supply line to the toilet, turn it clockwise and the water will be turned off. If there isn't such a valve, reach in the tank (the water is clean in the tank) and make sure the tank ball is tightly sealed over the outlet valve (Fig. 12-5). Once the water has stopped flowing into the toilet, the crisis is manageable. Now get the plumber's friend, the plunger, and plunge away at the clog. The best plungers for toilets are the molded type shown in Fig. 12-6. For more information, see chapter 4.

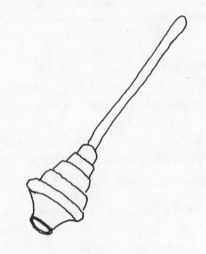

FIG. 12-6. PLUNGER—
A PLUMBER'S FRIEND

A Sink Stops Up

First, shut off any faucet or appliance (like a dishwasher) that is flowing into the sink. Once the flow is stopped, you can

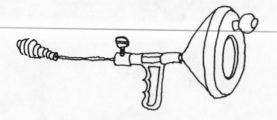

FIG. 12-7. A PLUMBER'S SNAKE

begin unclogging the drain. Try the easiest method first: the plunger. If this doesn't work, open the trap to see if the clog is there. If not, it is beyond the trap and a snake will have to be used to get at it (Fig. 12-7). All this is explained in chapter 4.

A Faucet That Won't Shut Off

Reach into the sink cabinet to find the shutoff valve and turn it clockwise. If there isn't one there, turn off the shutoff nearest the leaky faucet. This kind of emergency will make you wish you had a shutoff valve on each supply line. Someday when you have nothing else to do around the house you can install some. Repairing leaky faucets and installing shutoff valves are explained in chapter 4.

A Gas Leak

There is real danger here. Do the following in order:

1. Get all people out of the house.
2. Open the windows to let out the gas.
3. Turn off any burner that is on but unlit.
4. If the house still smells of gas, turn the main gas valve off. For a supply valve like that shown in Fig. 12-8, turn the handle so it is perpendicular to the pipe—this is off. Then call a repair person.

When a gas pilot light blows out, there will be a faint smell of gas. In this case open the windows and, after the room is aired out, relight the pilot.

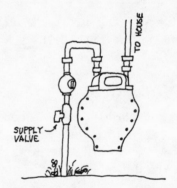

FIG. 12-8. GAS METER

APPENDIX

NAILS, SCREWS, AND GLUES

The Right Fastener for the Job

A fastener is any object or substance that joins two pieces of material together. It can be a nail, a screw, glue, or a specialized fastener like a screw anchor that anchors screws into Sheetrock walls. The carpenter's union I belong to is called the Brotherhood of Carpenters and Joiners, because joining requires skill.

If you know which fastener to use, any job will be a hundred times easier. Take plumbing, for example. If you think about running twenty continuous feet of copper pipe as compared with putting in that same length of pipe interrupted by fittings, shutoff valves, bends, and what have you, the latter seems (and, in fact, is) much more difficult. Or think about siding a 70-foot barn compared with siding a house with windows and doors. The second will take longer because every time a clapboard intersects a window there is a joint. And joints are what takes time and knowhow.

A joint is the point of connection of any number of pieces. The word "joint" also refers to the method of fastening used, be it metal fasteners or glues. Some joints are easier than others. The simplest joints are those between like substances. Two pieces of wood can be joined by a wide variety of screws and nails and almost any glue. Joining together dissimilar materials like wood and metal, concrete and wood, and glass and wood is the most difficult kind of joint. There are a few fasten s (machine screws, lag screws) and glues (poxy) that are made to do this.

Figures A-1, A-2, and A-5 and Table 3 will help you select the right fastener for the job. Try not to be intimidated by the plethora of fasteners. It is because joining is at the heart of the matter that there are so many.

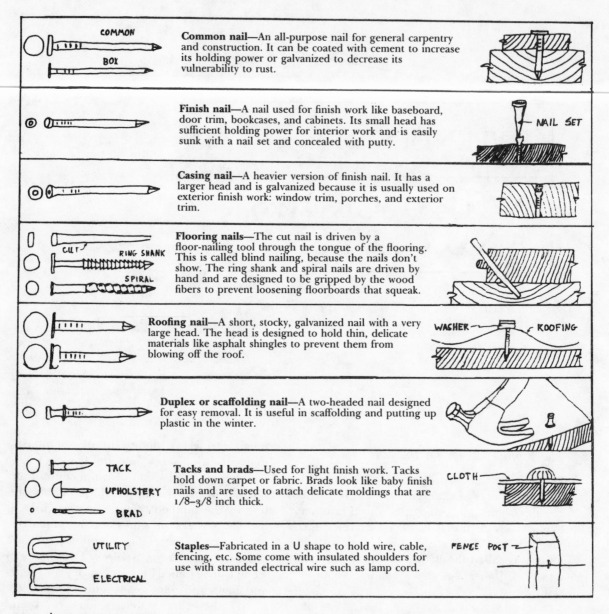

Common nail—An all-purpose nail for general carpentry and construction. It can be coated with cement to increase its holding power or galvanized to decrease its vulnerability to rust.

Finish nail—A nail used for finish work like baseboard, door trim, bookcases, and cabinets. Its small head has sufficient holding power for interior work and is easily sunk with a nail set and concealed with putty.

Casing nail—A heavier version of finish nail. It has a larger head and is galvanized because it is usually used on exterior finish work: window trim, porches, and exterior trim.

Flooring nails—The cut nail is driven by a floor-nailing tool through the tongue of the flooring. This is called blind nailing, because the nails don't show. The ring shank and spiral nails are driven by hand and are designed to be gripped by the wood fibers to prevent loosening floorboards that squeak.

Roofing nail—A short, stocky, galvanized nail with a very large head. The head is designed to hold thin, delicate materials like asphalt shingles to prevent them from blowing off the roof.

Duplex or scaffolding nail—A two-headed nail designed for easy removal. It is useful in scaffolding and putting up plastic in the winter.

Tacks and brads—Used for light finish work. Tacks hold down carpet or fabric. Brads look like baby finish nails and are used to attach delicate moldings that are 1/8–3/8 inch thick.

Staples—Fabricated in a U shape to hold wire, cable, fencing, etc. Some come with insulated shoulders for use with stranded electrical wire such as lamp cord.

FIG. A-1. NAIL TABLE

Nails

Nails come in all shapes and sizes: ½ inch to 12 inches long. The size of a nail is designated in inches and denoted by the letter "d." A nail bin in a hardware store might be labeled either "2½ inch common" or "8d common."

"8d" is spoken "eight penny." Penny originally referred to the price per 100 nails, but now it's related to size. The "d" refers to the English pence, which derives from *denarius*, a Roman coin that was the equivalent of a penny during the years of the Roman Empire. A 2d nail is 1 inch long. As nails get larger they

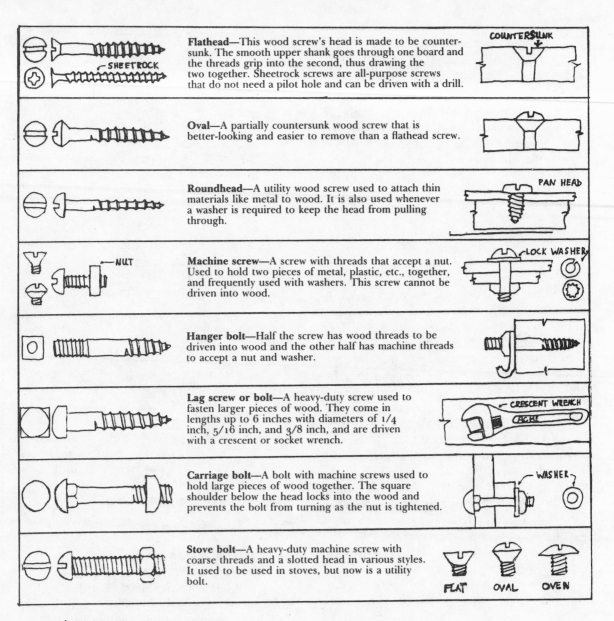

Flathead—This wood screw's head is made to be counter-sunk. The smooth upper shank goes through one board and the threads grip into the second, thus drawing the two together. Sheetrock screws are all-purpose screws that do not need a pilot hole and can be driven with a drill.

Oval—A partially countersunk wood screw that is better-looking and easier to remove than a flathead screw.

Roundhead—A utility wood screw used to attach thin materials like metal to wood. It is also used whenever a washer is required to keep the head from pulling through.

Machine screw—A screw with threads that accept a nut. Used to hold two pieces of metal, plastic, etc., together, and frequently used with washers. This screw cannot be driven into wood.

Hanger bolt—Half the screw has wood threads to be driven into wood and the other half has machine threads to accept a nut and washer.

Lag screw or bolt—A heavy-duty screw used to fasten larger pieces of wood. They come in lengths up to 6 inches with diameters of 1/4 inch, 5/16 inch, and 3/8 inch, and are driven with a crescent or socket wrench.

Carriage bolt—A bolt with machine screws used to hold large pieces of wood together. The square shoulder below the head locks into the wood and prevents the bolt from turning as the nut is tightened.

Stove bolt—A heavy-duty machine screw with coarse threads and a slotted head in various styles. It used to be used in stoves, but now is a utility bolt.

FIG. A-2. SCREW TABLE

increase in length at the rate of 1d equals ¼ inch, up to 10d (3 inches). From then on it's arbitrary. A 16d nail, one used for framing houses, is 3½ inches long.

Nails are made of various metals. Nails that are to be used inside are made of steel. When a nail is to be exposed to the weather, it is coated with zinc in a process called gal-vanizing. Lumberyards carry each nail size in galvanized and bright (uncoated steel). Roofing and siding nails are always galva-nized. Cement-coated nails are nails that have been coated with a substance that melts as the nail is driven in. This makes driving the nail easier. The cement then bonds with the wood fibers, making the nail difficult to pull out.

Nails can also be made of aluminum. They are very expensive. Aluminum nails are used underground in wooden foundations and as siding nails. Case-hardened nails are steel nails whose outer layer has been hardened. This keeps them from bending and allows them to be driven into concrete, as when furring strips are attached to a basement wall so that Sheetrock can be nailed into the strips.

Screws

There are basically two kinds of screws: those that are driven into wood and those that are driven into or through metal. The difference is in the threads. A wood screw has larger threads that taper at the tip of the screw. A metal screw or bolt has very regular threads and a blunt tip that is designed to accept a nut. Frequently machine screws require a washer. There are many types, including several varieties of lock washer designed to keep the nut from loosening with vibration.

Screws are driven with either a standard or Phillips screwdriver (Fig. A-3). I've heard that the Phillips screwdriver was invented by a frustrated automechanic named Phillips who was driving a slotted screw into the side of a newly painted Porsche. His screwdriver slipped out of the slot and put a long gash in the new finish. That very day he developed the Phillips head, which grips the screw better.

Screws are named by giving their length and shank diameter (gauge) and by stringing all words that would possibly describe them together in one sentence. If I were at a hardware store getting screws for a bookcase, I would say, "I want twenty, inch-and-one-half, number-eight, flathead, chrome screws." If I wrote that out, it would look like Fig. A-4. The last part of that long string of characteristics is the finish. Not all screws have a chrome finish. There are also brass and aluminum

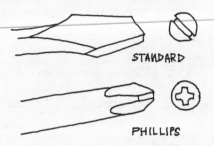

FIG. A-3. TWO TYPES OF SCREWDRIVERS

FIG. A-4. NAMING SCREWS

screws. Steel screws with a chrome finish are stronger than screws made of brass or aluminum, which are soft metals. When strength is needed, use steel screws.

Special Fasteners

FOR HOLLOW WALLS

The interior walls of houses used to be plaster and lath (1 inch thick); now they are Sheetrock (½ inch thick). Both materials cover hollow walls. If you're going to hang something heavy on the wall, like a bookshelf, it should be screwed into the studs. Lighter things like mirrors, toilet-paper dispensers, and pictures can be attached to the Sheetrock over the hollow part of the wall by using hollow wall anchors (see Fig. A-5). There are several different kinds, but they all work the same way: a movable part within the wall expands to clamp against the Sheetrock or plaster and lath.

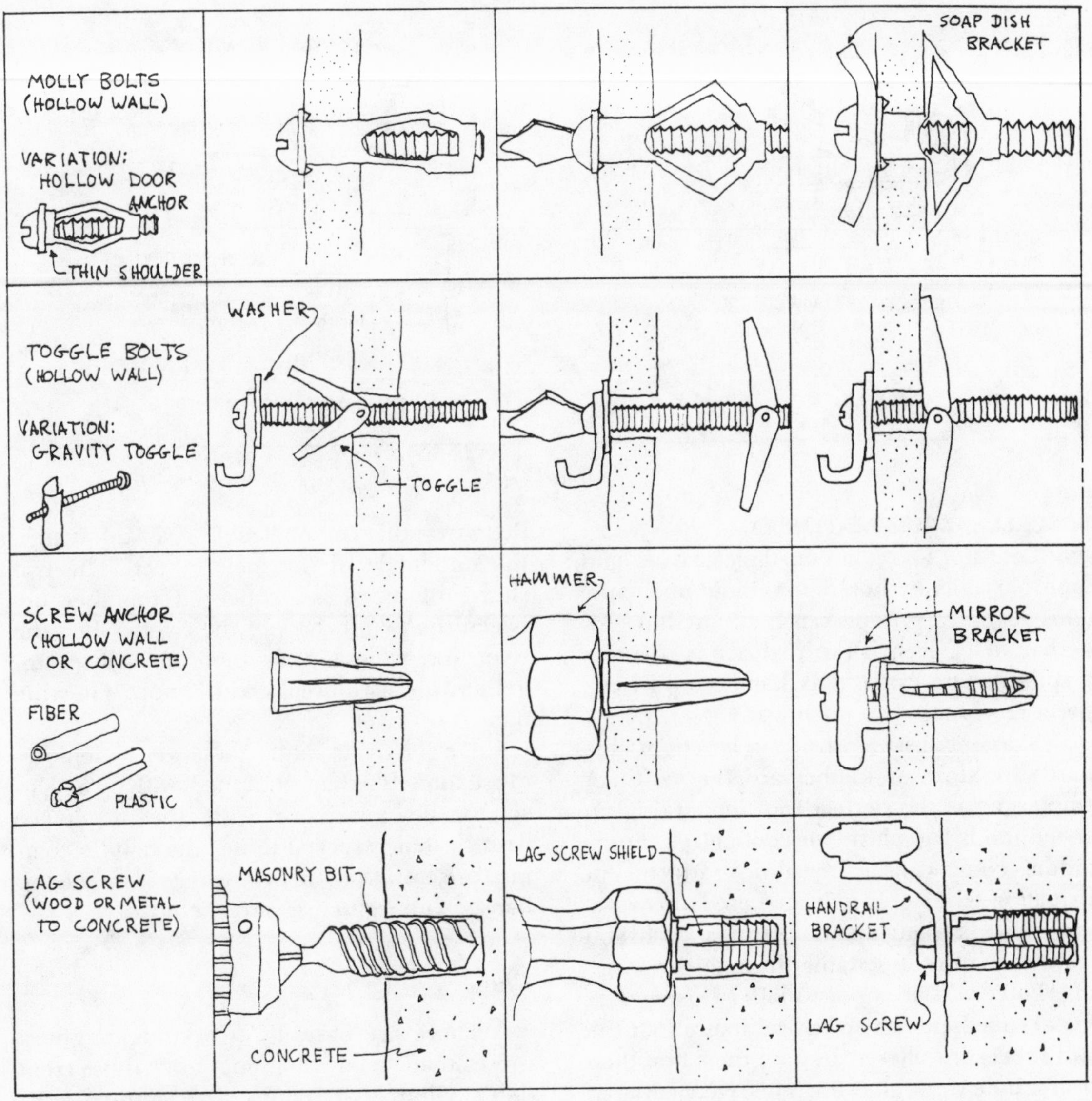

FIG. A-5. SPECIAL FASTENERS

CONCRETE FASTENERS

Joining dissimilar materials together is the most difficult fastening job of all. It calls for a special fastener. Lag screw shields and screw anchors (see Fig. A-5) each attach wood or metal to concrete. After a hole is drilled in the concrete to the size specified on the anchor, the anchor is dropped in. As the screw is inserted, the plastic or fiber of the screw anchor or the lips of the lag screw shield expand and grip the sides of the hole.

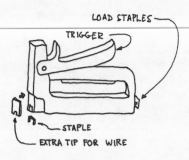

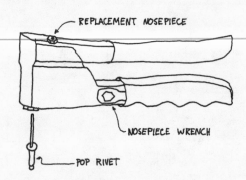

FIG. A-6. STAPLE GUN

FIG. A-7. POP RIVET GUN

MISCELLANEOUS FASTENERS

Let's not forget about staples, rivets, and tape. No toolbox should be without duct tape. This silvery gray tape can hold anything together. Why, even as I write this, it is acting as a splint on my cracked ax handle until I can get a new one.

Staple guns can be purchased at any hardware store or lumberyard (Fig. A-6). A staple gun is the perfect tool for tacking up sheet goods like plastic or roofing felt. Some models come with a grooved-nose attachment that allows the staple to be centered over wire. This makes tacking up phone wire a cinch; you can never miss and staple through the wire.

Pop rivets are used to join two sheets of metal together (Fig. A-7). Make sure that the two sheets are where you want them and then drill a hole through both. The rivets come in small packages and look a little like double-headed nails. The double-headed part is the rivet. It is on a wire that is inserted into the rivet gun. There are different-size rivets and each requires a certain size hole. Next, insert the pop rivet into the rivet gun and push the rivet through the hole. Squeeze the handle several times until you hear a pop. When you squeeze the handle, a gripping mechanism within the gun pulls the wire up. The head of

the wire pulls the malleable rivet up against the underside of the metal sheet. The two sheets of metal are squeezed together between the two flanges of the rivet. When the rivet gun cannot draw them any closer together, the wire breaks with a pop. Thus the name pop rivet.

Larger rivets require a larger nosepiece. Most models come equipped with two. Unscrew the nosepiece with the nosepiece wrench that is tucked under the handle coating. Unscrew the other nosepiece from the top handle and tighten it into the nose.

Glues

There are basically two kinds of glues: those that need clamping and those that don't. Glues that require no clamping have good gap-filling capabilities. Epoxy, the third type in Table 3, would be good for repairing the broken stem of a wineglass where several shards were never recovered. These kinds of glues are especially good for general repairs.

Other glues like white and yellow glues require clamping in order to form a secure bond. The glue must be compressed into a thin glue line one or two molecules thick for the optimal bond between the two surfaces.

Table 3.
THE RIGHT GLUE FOR THE JOB

FOR USE ON	TYPE	CHARACTERISTICS	COMPONENTS	APPLICATION	CLEANUP/ SOLVENT	BRAND
Furniture repairs, furniture building, and cabinet-work	Aliphatic (yellow glue)	Similar to white glue but stronger. Often called carpenter's glue. Dries clear; bond is affected by water and swings in temperature. A good indoor glue.	One part in a squeeze bottle. Ready to use.	Requires clamping for 30 minutes. Sets up overnight.	Warm water	Titebond, Elmer's Carpenter's Wood Glue
Model work, china, glass, fabric, and furniture repairs	Cellulose	Water resistant, strong, quick-drying. Dries clear or amber.	One part. Ready to use.	Hold parts firmly in place while glue sets. Reaches 60% strength in 2 hours.	Acetone (nail polish remover)	Duco Cement, Ambroid
Wood, metal, china, glass, and plastics	Epoxy	Waterproof, very strong, quick-drying. Good for bonding dissimilar materials like metal to wood or glass to metal. Excellent on dishes; it's waterproof. Dries clear.	Two parts— mix amounts needed.	No clamping. Sets in up to 1 hour. Apply with throwaway brush.	Acetone (this glue is hard to clean up).	Weldwood Epoxy, Duco Epoxy
Wood, ceramic tiles, and plastic	Mastic	All-purpose construction adhesive. Bonds ceiling tiles to ceiling, paneling to walls, or tiles or plastic to walls. Dries brown.	One part. Thick paste. Comes in tubes or cans.	Caulking gun or trowel. No clamping required.	Mineral spirits, turpentine, gasoline	PL 400, Max Bond, Wall Bond, Liquid Nails
Furniture, paper, and ceramic tiles	PVA (Polyvinyl acetate)	A good all-around household adhesive. Recommended for use on metal or when excessive heat or moisture might occur. Dries clear.	One part liquid. Ready to use.	No clamping necessary.	Warm soapy water	Scotch Wood and Paper Glue, Fast'n-It

Table 3. (*Continued*)

FOR USE ON	TYPE	CHARACTERISTICS	COMPONENTS	APPLICATION	CLEANUP/ SOLVENT	BRAND
Crafts, china, glass, marble, porcelain, and wood	PVC (Polyvinyl chloride)	Highly water resistant, dries fast and clear.	One part liquid. Ready to use.	No clamping necessary.	Acetone	Sheer Magic
Clothing, carpets, tents, and boat sails	Acrylo-nitrile	Waterproof, stronger than stitching, yet flexible. Can be used on metal and glass. Dries brown.	One part. Ready to use.	No clamping necessary.	Acetone	Pliobond, Duvo Darn
Masonry, glass, metal, tiles, many plastics	Styrene butadiene	Excellent for replacing ceramic tiles. Water resistant. Has good gap-filling properties that provide bonds to irregular surfaces. Dries brown or white.	One part, thick glop. Ready to use.	No clamping necessary.	Mineral spirits, turpentine	Black Magic, White Magic
Plastic laminates, cement veneers	Contact cement	Usually used to glue sheets of materials like plastic laminates to countertops or veneer to wood.	One part. Must coat both surfaces. Let dry and assemble.	Brush, no clamping.	Warm water or mineral spirits, depending on type	Duco or Weldwood Contact Cement

Most of these glues are used in furniture making, but I have included one of the most common, yellow carpenter's glue, in the table (the first type). It is appropriate for some wood and furniture repairs around the home.

Clamping often has to be creative (Fig. A-8). It is rare that a C-clamp will fit. I use rubber bands, string, and wire a lot. A few glues like cellulose (second in the table) just require pressure—i.e., you hold the parts together for a minute.

Assembly time is the time you have in which to get the pieces where you want them after you've spread the glue on them. It varies from three to fifteen minutes, but no matter how long it is, it still always seems like it's not enough. I always warn friends that I'm a different person when I'm dealing with glue. To

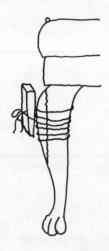

FIG. A-8. CLAMPING IRREGULAR PIECES

minimize interpersonal strife, try to have everything ready and near at hand when you glue.

The hardest part of gluing is to get glue completely down into a crack. When a piece of wood is cracked but not broken, or the edge of the countertop is coming unglued, glue just won't ooze in there on its own. If the surfaces are smooth and regular and if a playing card will fit between the pieces, spread glue on the card and drag it between the surfaces, thereby spreading glue on each piece. For jagged cracks, I've had luck using a vacuum cleaner. Spread a bead of glue on top of the crack and hold the vacuum cleaner hose, equipped with the attachment with the smallest opening, against the bottom side of the crack. The glue gets pulled through as neat as you please.

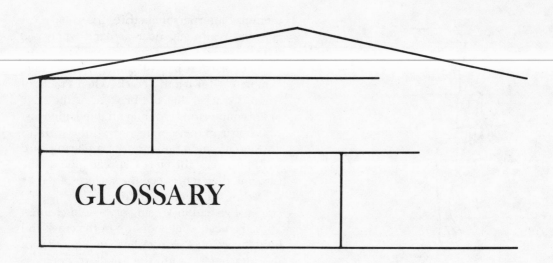

GLOSSARY

Alkyd paint: A recent hybrid of oil-base and latex paint.

Apron: A horizontal piece of narrow wood just below the stool in interior window trim.

Awning window: A window with a sash that's hinged at its top and opens like an awning.

Ballast: A little transformer in a fluorescent light fixture that creates the power surge needed to illuminate the lamp.

Bearing: Resting upon; supported by.

Bevel: To cut at an angle. The angle cut on the edge of a board or door.

Bifold door: A door that runs on a track hidden in the ceiling and folds over itself. Commonly used on closets.

B-I-N: A brand name of pigmented shellac used to seal knots, nails, and stains before painting.

Binding: Friction against the blade of a saw that makes sawing difficult.

Bottom plate: The horizontal framing member that is nailed to the bottom of the studs in a wall.

Butt joint: The simplest joint—the square edge of one board meets the square edge of another and they are held together with nails and/or glue.

Cap shingles: The specially cut shingles that lap over two sides of a roof as the topmost course.

Capillary action: The movement of water uphill between two surfaces that are close together.

Casement window: A window with a sash hinged on one side. Currently the most common window used in houses.

Casing: Another word for window or door trim.

Caulk: A thick, puttylike substance that is applied to joints to prevent water leakage. It is usually applied with a caulk gun.

Cement-coated nails: Nails coated with an adhesive that increases the holding power of the nail three- or fourfold.

Chalking: A condition of paint in which the paint gradually turns to powder.

Chuck: The part of a drill that holds the bit.

Chuck key: A small metal tool that tightens the teeth of the chuck around a bit.

Clinched: Bent over; usually said of a nail that protrudes through a board.

Coal chisel: A heavy metal chisel with an extraordinarily hard tip that is used on masonry and metal.

Cold joint: A joint between two slabs of concrete where there is no bonding between the two.

Contact cement: A type of glue for fastening sheet goods to a surface.

Cornice: An eave that has been enclosed.

Countersink: The tool that cuts a conical or cylindrical indentation into wood so that the head of a screw will be flush with the surface or covered with a peg.

Counterweight: A weight that slides up and down within a wall pocket and counterbalances the weight of the sash of a double-hung window, enabling it to stay open.

Course: A row of shingles or horizontal siding.

Crow's foot: A V-shaped mark used to make a measurement on wood.

Curtailed stud (cripple stud): A stud that doesn't extend all the way from bottom plate to top plate, but is interrupted by a header or sill.

Curved-claw hammer: A hammer with a curved (as opposed to a straight) claw, which pulls nails more easily.

Cut in: To carefully paint around the perimeter of a surface or window without getting paint on adjacent surfaces.

D-penny: The unit of measurement used to denote different sizes of nails.

Dado: A three-sided recess cut in wood.

Dead load: The weight of the stationary construction materials in a building—walls, plaster, shingles.

Door closer: The bicycle-pump-like mechanism that closes doors slowly and prevents slamming.

Door shoe: A type of weatherstripping for the bottom of a door.

Door stop: The thin molding that is nailed to the face of the door jamb to prevent the door from swinging through.

Double-hung window: A window with two sashes that move vertically.

Drip cap: A molding placed above the exteriors of doors and windows that diverts water away from the house and makes it drip instead of seeping in.

Dry rot: A term applied to wood that has been subjected to rot in the past.

Drywall: Sheets of white chalky gypsum covered with thick fire-resistant paper, which is used as an interior skin for walls. Also called gypsum board, plasterboard, and Sheetrock.

Eave: The part of the rafters that overhangs the sides of a house.

End grain: The open, porous grain on the sawed-off ends of boards.

End-nail: To drive nails through the face of one board and into the end of another.

Face frame: The front of a cabinet into which the drawers and doors fit.

Face-nail: To nail together the faces of two boards when the nail is fairly perpendicular to the surface of the wood.

Factory edge: The perfectly straight edge that is cut into the long dimension of plywood at the factory.

Fascia: A flat, horizontal board nailed to the ends of rafters to form a finished eave.

Female end: A plumbing part whose inside is threaded and/or accepts a male part, which in turn has threads around its outside.

Ferrule: A metal band that, when crimped, secures something in place.

Finish: A term used to denote methods, nails, or tools used in the final stages of working wood.

Finish floor: The top surface of a floor—i.e., hardwood flooring, parquet, or carpet.

Fixture: In plumbing, a sink, tub, washer, et cetera. In electrical work, lamps.

Flange: A flap or widening of a base or foundation.

Flashing: Sheetmetal used in roof and wall construction, especially around chimneys, windows, and vents, to prevent water from entering.

Flush: Adjacent surfaces even with each other.

Flush door: A door used widely in modern construction consisting of thin plywood veneer covering a 2×2 frame.

Footing: The base of support below a foundation wall or column.

Form: The structure into which concrete is poured.

Foundation: That portion of a structure located below the first floor, which carries the weight of the building.

Framing: The process of erecting the structure of a house.

Framing member: The structural parts of a house that give it shape and strength: studs, joists, and rafters.

Furring: Narrow strips of wood that are evenly spaced and attached to a surface to form a nailing base for another surface.

Gable end: The triangular-shaped end of a gable-roofed house.

Glue block: A triangular block used to strengthen the joints of fine furniture.

Glue film: The thin (.005 inches), even layer of glue between two pieces that bonds them together.

Green concrete: Concrete that has not completely hardened. It may be green for up to two weeks.

Grounding: The connection of any part of an electrical system to the earth.

Gutter: A pipe at the eave that catches rainwater and shunts it away from the house.

Gypsum board: See drywall.

Hardwood: Wood that comes from deciduous trees, those that shed their leaves at the end of the growing season.

Hawk: A board for holding mortar. Can be flat or V-shaped.

Header: The horizontal structural member that supports the load over or around an opening for a window, door, or stairwell.

Hinge: A device used on a door whose leaves are mortised (cut) into the door and jamb.

Hinge pocket: The chiseled-out rectangles in a door or door jamb into which a hinge leaf fits.

Hopper window: A window with a sash that is hinged at the bottom; it resembles a hopper when open.

Ice dam: Melted runoff from a roof which has frozen at the eave. Causes water to back up and leak into a house.

Infiltration: Uncontrolled ventilation of a house through cracks.

Inside dimension: The distance between two things.

Jamb: The top and two sides of the window or door frame that are grazed by the window or door.

Joint compound: A white plasterlike substance used to cover the joints between sheets of drywall. It is sometimes called "pipe dope."

Joist: One of many parallel framing members

that support the floor and ceiling of a house.

Kerf: The groove cut out by the blade of a saw.

King stud: The second stud in on either side of window and door openings. It is full length, and along with the trimmer supports the header.

Latex paint: A type of paint made by suspending pigments in water by the addition of emulsifiers.

Lath: Thin strips of wood fastened to the frame of a house to form a base for plaster.

Layout: The pencil marks on a board that indicate what cutting and nailing are to be done.

Ledger: A board or strip that is attached to the framing and supports a load like the joists for a floor.

Level: Parallel to the horizon.

Lineal foot: Having length only—pertaining to a line 1 foot long.

Live load: The weight that movable objects such as people, furniture, snow, et cetera, add to a house.

Load: The weight that a structure, board, or surface carries.

Load-bearing: Carrying part of the load of a house, such as a wall that supports the ceiling joists and rafters.

Lockset: The knob and internal mechanism that allows doors to be opened and locked.

Lug: The small protrusions of the side jambs above the dado in a door frame.

Machine screw: A metal screw with threads that are designed to screw into a nut or a prethreaded hole in metal.

Male end: A plumbing part the outside of which is threaded and/or fits into a female end.

Mastic: A heavy-bodied adhesive that is usually waterproof and is used to adhere tile, vinyl, wood, and metal. It comes in cans or caulk tubes.

Meeting rail: The horizontal pieces of the sashes of a double-hung window, which touch in the middle when it's closed.

Mineral spirits: A petroleum distillate used as a solvent for paints and varnishes.

Miter: An angle cut at the end of both members of a joint that is one-half the angle formed by both pieces.

Mudsill: A 2×8 that rests on the top of the foundation walls and on which the joists rest. Wood that has been treated against rot makes the best mudsill.

Muntin: The small piece of wood that separates panes of glass in a window sash.

Nail set: A small punchlike tool, which, when struck with a hammer, pushes a nail below the surface of wood.

Nailing base: Boards used as backing or support behind a wall or ceiling so that another board can be nailed to the backing board.

Nominal size: The dimensions of a board as described by its name (e.g., 2×4). Not to be confused with its actual dimensions.

Non-load-bearing partition: A wall that supports nothing other than its own weight.

Oil-base paint: A type of paint made by dissolving pigments in oil that is thinned with a solvent.

On center (o.c.): A way of describing the spacing of framing members or nails by indicating the distance from the center of one to the center of the next.

Outside dimension: The distance between two things *plus* the thickness of the two things.

Panel door: A door containing four or five panels surrounded by stiles and rails.

Parting stop: The molding that separates the sashes in a double-hung window.

Partition wall: A wall that separates a building into rooms.

Penny: See D-penny.

Penta: The shortened name for pentachlorophenol, a highly toxic chemical used as a wood preservative. (Also the name of a specific brand.)

Pigment: Solid coloring agents used in paint.

Pilot hole: A small hole drilled in a material to make the driving of a screw possible.

Plasterboard: See Drywall.

Plumb: Vertical—at right angles to the horizon.

Portland cement: A type of cement used in mortar to form the bond between bricks.

Primer: A paint that seals the surface and binds subsequent coats to itself.

Pry: To use a lever like a crowbar in moving an object.

R-value: The resistance to heat loss of any substance, but particularly insulating materials.

Rabbet: A two-sided recess running along the edge of a piece of wood.

Racking: The tendency of square objects to become parallelograms (i.e., not square) over time.

Rafter: One of the sloping beams that supports a roof.

Rail: Any horizontal member of a sash or face frame.

Rasp: A coarse file used to shape wood.

Ratchet: A mechanism that allows forceful turning in one direction only.

Receptacle: An electrical outlet into which small appliances are plugged.

Repointing: The process of replacing the mortar between bricks. Also called tuckpointing.

Resin: The substance that forms the film in paints, varnishes, and lacquers. Resins can be natural or synthetic.

Rip: To saw a board parallel to the grain.

Riser: The vertical face of a step between two treads.

Roll roofing: Heavy asphalt-impregnated felt that has been sprinkled with mineral bits. It is available in 36-inch-wide rolls and makes a relatively inexpensive roof.

Roofing: The materials (shingles, tile, roll roofing) applied to the roof to make it waterproof.

Roofing cement: A thick tarlike substance used in waterproofing roofs.

Rottenstone: A powdered limestone that is used in polishing varnished surfaces to produce a satin finish.

Rough opening (r.o.): The opening in the framing of a house for a door or window.

R.p.m: The abbreviation for revolutions per minute.

Sash: The frame that holds glass in a window. It may be movable or fixed.

Sash balance: A spring-loaded device for keeping the sash of a double-hung window open.

Saw table: The flat part of a circular saw on which the saw rides.

Sealer: A pigmented shellac that prevents knots, nail heads, and stains from bleeding through paint.

Set screw: A machine screw that is screwed through the side of a sleeve to hold an object in the middle of the sleeve in place.

Sheathing: The boards or sheets that are attached to the exterior of studs and rafters to form the nail base for the roof shingles or siding of a house.

Sheetrock: A brand name for a kind of plasterboard. See Drywall.

Shim: A small thin wedge.

Siding: The exterior skin of a house.

Sill: The lowest member of the exterior of a window or door frame.

Sliding door: A door that slides back and forth in one plane and is not hinged.

Soffit: A small false ceiling, like the underside of a cornice.

Softwood: Wood that comes from evergreen trees.

Spackle: A plasterlike putty used for patching holes and cracks in wall surfaces.

Spall: To chip or break off.

Square: Possessing right (90-degree) angles.

Starter: A device that generates a surge of electricity to illuminate a fluorescent lamp.

Stile: Any vertical piece of a cabinet or a window sash.

Stool: The horizontal member of interior window trim that fits over the sill and extends inside.

Stringer: The part of a stair that carries the weight—usually a 2×12.

Stud: One of a series of vertical structural members of a wall.

Sub-floor: Boards or plywood laid directly on floor joists. Boards for the finish floor will be laid over them.

Surform plane: A plane with a rasplike bottom used in shaping wood.

Swale: A ditch used to divert water away from a house.

Taping: The application of tape and joint compound to the cracks between pieces of Sheetrock to hide the joint.

Tenon: The tonguelike part of a mortise-and-tenon joint that fits into a cavity (mortise) in the other piece.

Tensile strength: The resistance of a material to forces tending to tear it apart.

Texture paint: Paint containing a substance like sand, which produces a textured surface when applied.

Threshold: A piece of wood or metal at the bottom of the door between the two door jambs.

Toenail: To drive a nail at a slant to the initial surface.

Toespace: The recess at the floor line of base kitchen cabinets that allows one to work comfortably.

Tread: The horizontal part of a step.

Trimmer: The stud or joist that frames the rough opening and supports the header.

Vapor-barrier: A waterproof material, such as 6 mil polyethylene or special paint, applied to the interior surface of exterior walls in cold climates, or to the outside walls in hot climates, to prevent the movement of water vapor from inside the house through the wall to the outside.

Vehicle: The liquid part of paint that carries the color. It can be either water or oil.

Veneer: A thin layer of wood that is glued to the surface of lesser grades of wood, in order to upgrade them.

Waste side: The part of the board that is on the opposite side of the cut line from the measured piece.

Water table: The level of the groundwater.

Weathering: The mechanical and chemical disintegration of the surface of wood.

Weatherstrip: Narrow strips of metal, vinyl, foam, or clay that, when installed around doors and windows, prevent infiltration.

Window bar: A specialized tool used on windows—part delicate crowbar and part putty knife.

Window stop: Interior molding that holds the sashes of a double-hung window in place.

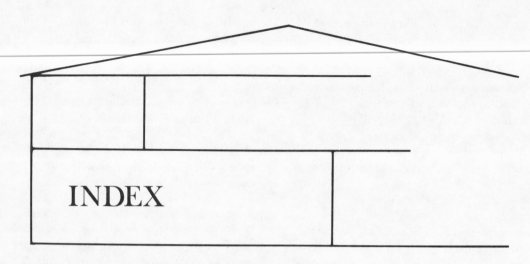

INDEX

NOTE: *Page numbers in italics refer to illustrations.*